Decision Analysis with Supertree

Peter McNamee
John Celona
Strategic Decisions Group

SECOND EDITION

STRATEGIC DECISIONS GROUP

2440 Sand Hill Road, Menlo Park, California 94025-6900

Decision Analysis with Supertree
Peter McNamee
John Celona

Printed in the United States of America

10 9 8 7 6 5 4 3 2

Publisher: Strategic Decisions Group
Editors: Mimi Campbell, Bill Roehl, Mary Story
Typography and Layout: Don Creswell and T/D Associates
Cover Design: Rogodino & Associates

Dedication

We would like to dedicate this book to our wives and families—Tereza, Patrick, Christina, and Andrew McNamee, and Karen Schwartz, who endured Macintosh widowhood and orphanhood during the long weeks, weekends, and months while this book was being written. Without their constant support and indulgence, this project would have never come to fruition.

Preface

In the three years since the first edition of this book, the authors have seen a dramatic evolution in the practice of decision analysis. The number of companies using decision analysis as an approach to problem solving has grown rapidly. Our experience during this period has shown that practical as well as analytical skills are needed for successful implementation of a decision analysis program.

As a problem-solving approach, decision analysis involves far more than the use of decision trees as a calculational tool. It is a process of framing a problem correctly, of dealing effectively with uncertainty, of involving all the relevant people, and, above all, of communicating clearly. Accordingly, in addition to the analytical techniques used in decision analysis, this book presents material that the authors hope will assist the reader in integrating these techniques into a practical and satisfying problem-solving process.

The influence diagram has emerged as a powerful tool in this decision analysis process. In the initial stages of defining a decision problem, it is a natural and simple way to represent the problem, to communicate about decisions and uncertainties, and to allow everyone to contribute insights and expertise. During later stages of the process, it is an efficient way to organize tasks, store data, and even perform the analysis.

The influence diagram and the decision tree form a natural pair of tools, each with its own strength and source of insight. This second edition of *Decision Analysis with Supertree* introduces influence diagrams at the beginning and uses them throughout. We have added an appendix (Appendix B, "Influence Diagram Theory") that gathers in one place the information on influence diagrams presented in the body of the book.

Chapter 2 ("Uncertainty and Probability") has been split in two in this edition, with material dealing with dependent probabilities and Bayes' Rule presented in a new chapter, "Probabilistic Dependence," that follows the chapter "Decisions Under Uncertainty." This rearrangement presents the reader with the elements of decision tree analysis before delving into the complexities of probabilistic dependence.

We have also improved the student version of Supertree included with this book. Supertree is a flexible and powerful computer program for calculations involving decision trees. The student version contains all the features of the professional version but is limited to evaluating trees with fewer than 200 endpoints. Larger trees that have been evaluated by the teacher's professional version can also be examined using the student version.

Similarly, included with this edition is a student version of Sensitivity, a computer program that automates the necessary but tedious process of performing sensitivity analysis to find the most critical variables in a decision problem. The student version contains all the features of the professional version but is limited to sensitivities for fewer than 12 variables.

In several examples and problems, we use hand calculations to teach readers what the computer programs do. In principle, this text could be read (and many of the problems done) without using computer software. However, the software enables the student to experiment with trees, link them with such modeling packages as Lotus 1-2-3 or Microsoft® Excel, and obtain a richer understanding of the material. In addition, when the student uses decision analysis in a real problem, being familiar with decision analysis software is essential.

We hope this book will lead the student to develop an appreciation of the power, practicality, and satisfying completeness of decision analysis. More and more, decision analysis is becoming accepted as the best way to address decision problems. Being a decision analyst is an exciting and satisfying occupation. This text is designed to emphasize this. Furthermore, since texts tend to remain on students' shelves, we hope this book will be of assistance long after the course is done.

The text is intended for a short (about one-month) course in decision analysis in business schools. It could also be part of an analytical methods course. The general philosophy of the book, however, is more consonant with extending the course by having the student apply decision analysis to more complex cases, perhaps based on real data or problems supplied by local businesses.

Decision analysis is both young enough that its founders are alive and active in the field and old enough that the literature on the field has grown large. We have chosen not to write a book bristling with footnotes. Rather, we have chosen to list in the bibliography several books in different areas for readers interested in those topics. We ask our colleagues not to take offense if their names or works are not explicitly referred to in this book. We gratefully acknowledge their contribution of accumulated wisdom and knowledge, which has made decision analysis a useful and powerful management tool.

We especially thank all the people who contributed their useful comments and constructive suggestions, including Charles Bonini, Max Henrion, and Myron Tribus. Dr. Bonini kindly allowed us to use the IJK Products and Hony Pharmaceutics problems that appear in Chapters 4 and 7, respectively. We also thank Yong Tao, who assisted in constructing problems for the book. We are particularly indebted to Ronald A. Howard and James E. Matheson for contributions and insights, which appear throughout this book.

Peter McNamee
John Celona
Menlo Park, California

Contents

Appendix A – Probability Theory 231

Appendix B – Influence Diagram Theory 263

CONTENTS

1

Introduction

Origins of Decision Analysis

Decision-making is one of the hard things in life. True decision-making occurs *not* when you already know exactly what to do, but when you do not know what to do. When you have to balance conflicting values, sort through complex situations, and deal with real uncertainty, you have reached the point of true decision-making. And to make things more difficult, the most important decisions in corporate or personal life are often those that put you in situations where you least know what to do.

Decision science evolved to cope with this problem of what to do. While its roots go back to the time of Bernoulli in the early 1700s, it remained an almost purely academic subject until recently, apparently because there was no satisfactory way to deal with the complexity of real life. However, just after World War II, the fields of systems analysis and operations research began to develop. With the help of computers, it became possible to analyze problems of great complexity.

Out of these two disciplines grew decision analysis: the application of decision science to real-world problems through the use of systems analysis and operations research. Decision analysis is a normative discipline, which means it describes how people should logically make decisions. Specifically, it corresponds to how (most) people make decisions in simple situations and shows how this behavior should logically be extended to more complex situations.

Four Levels of Decision Analysis

Decision analysis functions at four different levels—as a philosophy, as a decision framework, as a decision-making process, and as a decision-making methodology—and each level focuses on different aspects of the problem of making decisions.

A Philosophy

As a philosophy, decision analysis describes a rational, consistent way to make decisions. As such, it provides decision-makers with two basic, invaluable insights.

The first insight is that uncertainty is a consequence of our incomplete knowledge of the world. In some cases, uncertainty can be partially or completely resolved before decisions are made and resources committed. However, in many important cases, complete information is simply not available or is too expensive (in time, money, or other resources) to obtain.

Although this insight may appear obvious, we are all familiar with instances in the business world and in personal life in which people seem to deny the existence of uncertainty—except perhaps as something to be eliminated before action is taken. For example, decision-makers demand certainty in proposals brought before them. Twenty-year projections are used to justify investments without any consideration of uncertainty. Time and effort are spent to resolve uncertainties irrelevant to the decision at hand. And this list could, of course, be greatly extended.

The second basic insight is that there is a distinction between good decisions and good outcomes. Good outcomes are what we desire, whereas good decisions are what we can do to maximize the likelihood of having good outcomes. Given the unavoidable uncertainty in the world, a good decision must sometimes have a bad outcome. It is no more logical to punish the maker of a good decision for a bad outcome than it is to reward the maker of a bad decision for a good outcome. (Many types of routine decisions have little uncertainty about outcomes; thus, in these cases, it is not unreasonable to associate bad outcomes with bad decisions.)

This insight, too, may seem obvious. Yet how often have we seen corporate "witch hunts" for someone to blame or punish for unfortunate corporate outcomes?

A Decision Framework

As a framework for decision-making, decision analysis provides concepts and language to help the decision-maker. By using decision analysis, the decision-maker is aware of the adequacy or inadequacy of the decision basis: the set of knowledge (including uncertainty), alternatives, and values brought to the decision. There is also a clear distinction between decision factors (factors completely under the decision-maker's control) and chance factors (uncertain factors completely outside the decision-maker's control). Moreover, the decision-maker is aware of the biases that exist in even the most qualitative treatments of uncertainty. He or she knows these biases exist because people are not well trained in dealing with uncertainty and because they are generally overconfident in describing how well they know things.

A Decision-Making Process

As a decision-making process, decision analysis provides a step-by-step procedure that has proved practical in tackling even the most complex problems in an efficient and orderly way. The decision analysis cycle provides an iterative approach that keeps the focus on the decision and that enables the analyst to efficiently compare the decision alternatives. Modeling, both deterministic and probabilistic, reduces the problem to manageably sized pieces and allows intuition to function most effective-ly. Knowledge of the biases in probability estimation enables the decision-maker or analyst to take corrective action.

A Methodology

As a methodology, decision analysis provides a number of specific tools that are sometimes indispensable in analyzing a decision problem. These tools include procedures for eliciting and constructing influence diagrams, probability trees, and decision trees; procedures for encoding probability functions and utility curves; and a methodology for evaluating these trees and obtaining information useful to further refine the analysis.

It is a common mistake to confuse decision analysis with constructing and manipulating influence diagrams and decision trees. The real contribution and challenge of decision analysis occur at the much more general level of defining the problem and identifying the true decision points and alternatives. Many decision analyses never reach the point of requiring a decision tree. Nonetheless, obtaining a full understanding of the philosophy and framework of decision analysis requires some familiarity with the methodology, including trees.

Focus of This Text

Since its birth in the 1960s, decision analysis has developed into several different schools, though differences in schools are mostly differences of emphasis and technique. One school focuses on directly assessing probabilities and the different dimensions of value and spends much effort exploring the trade-offs between the uncertain outcomes. Another school focuses more on the art of bringing an assembled group of people to choose a course of action.

This text concentrates on the approach that grew out of the Engineering-Economic Systems Department at Stanford University and that was pioneered as a practical methodology at SRI International. This approach is characterized by models that take the burden of estimating values and outcomes in complex situa-tions off the individual's shoulders. A computer model is constructed to reduce a complex problem into manageable components. An influence diagram or decision tree is used to divide uncertainty into subfactors until the level has been reached at which intuition functions most effectively. This modeling approach is especially appropriate in business decisions, where the expertise of many individuals and groups must be combined in evaluating a decision problem.

The type of problem considered in this book is the archetypal decision problem: a single decision-maker using the knowledge of a number of "experts" to make a business decision based on a single principal value (money). The single decision-maker requirement can be relaxed somewhat to take group or societal decision-making into account. True multiple decision-maker problems, however, go beyond the scope of decision analysis and bring in elements of game theory.

There are a number of other types of problems to which decision analysis has been applied with some success. These applications tend to fall into three areas—personal, scientific, and societal.

Personal decision-making frequently involves difficult and sometimes complex value considerations, such as the life-death-pain-resources trade-offs found in medical decisions; these important areas are, unfortunately, also beyond the scope of this book.

Scientific decision-making (e.g., the choice of experiments to be funded) also involves special value considerations, since it involves making a controversial comparison of the worth of different scientific results and of the resources required to obtain these results.

Societal decision-making, finally, provides one of the most frustrating and fascinating applications of decision analysis. Not only is there no single decision-maker (but rather a decision-making process), but there is also no single set of values that characterizes society. Rather, conflicting sets of values characterize groups within society. There are even values attached to the process used to make the decision.

In these problems, as in all decision analysis applications, the analysis aims at providing insight into the problem, at opening channels of communication, at showing where differences in values or information do or do not affect decisions, and at directing future efforts in ways that will most improve decision-making.

Chapters 2, 3, 4, and 5 develop the methodology of decision analysis. The problems at the end of each chapter are an essential element in the process of learning the new concepts introduced in these chapters. Chapters 6, 7, 8, and 9 address the process of decision analysis in the business environment (and in other environments as well). The only real means for internalizing all the contents of these chapters is to take part in several decision analyses. As a result, we suggest several projects to simulate parts of real-life analyses.

Appendix A reviews the aspects of probability theory important for decision analysis. Readers desiring a review of probability theory may wish to read this appendix before proceeding to Chapter 2. Appendix B gathers into one place the elements of influence diagram theory that are used in the book. The remaining appendixes will help the reader use the Supertree and Sensitivity software.

Problems and Discussion Topics

1.1   Describe the difference between good decisions and good outcomes.

1.2   Describe your own approach to making important decisions. Do you use a systematic approach in making them? Do you try to make decisions in a consistent manner? Have you been satisfied with the major decisions you've made so far (or just happy or unhappy with the outcomes)?

1.3   How did you make your decision on which college to attend? Does hindsight reveal any shortcomings in the decision process?

1.4   What concerns would you like a decision-making methodology to address?

1.5   Describe a decision you currently face in which uncertainty is an important factor. Will you find out the outcome of the uncertainty before or after you make your decision?

2

Uncertainty and Probability

Probability: A Language of Uncertainty

Uncertainty is a fact of life in the modern world. Both in business and in personal life, there is an almost universal realization that few things can be counted on as certain, at least in the long run. In the business world, recessions come and go, competition comes up with new and unexpected challenges, consumer preferences change (sometimes seemingly at random), accidents or labor problems unexpectedly interrupt business, lawsuits threaten the existence of the company, and so on. And this is true in personal life as well. How will a new job or personal relationship work out? What are suitable investments against the future? In both areas, the list of uncertainties can be expanded indefinitely.

Thinking clearly about these uncertainties—whether to plan better, to make better decisions, or to communicate better about plans and decisions—is important. The key to thinking and communicating clearly about uncertainty is the use of probabilities to describe uncertainty. Fortunately, probability language reflects intuitive concepts of uncertainty. A review of the aspects of probability theory that we will use can be found in Appendix A. Most readers, however, will find that reading this appendix is not a prerequisite to following the development of ideas in this book.

In this chapter, we concentrate on describing and communicating about uncertainty. In Chapter 3, we deal with how to make decisions under uncertainty.

Along with precise language about uncertainty, we will use two equivalent graphic representations that make it easier to express and to communicate about complex uncertainties. The first of these is the influence diagram. Influence diagrams are an efficient, compact, and intuitive way of representing the uncertainties in a problem and the relationships between the probabilities that describe these uncertainties. In this section, we use influence diagrams to describe uncertainty.

Later in this chapter, we introduce another representation for uncertainty—the probability tree. These two representations serve complementary purposes. Influence diagrams are a natural way to develop and understand the overall picture; probability trees provide a framework that facilitates calculations with probabilities and the development of insight into the solution of a problem.

The example we will use throughout this chapter and the following three chapters is the semifictional one of Positronics, a manufacturer of sophisticated scientific instruments. This example contains elements from many different cases the authors and their colleagues have worked on. It would be rare for one case to exhibit all these elements. All Positronics discussions are set in italics.

Positronics had decided to bid on supplying MegaCorp with 100 instruments. Positronics estimated it could build them for $4,000 each; the president of Positronics decided to offer the 100 instruments for $500,000. Positronics' only real competitor was Anode Industries, a company with the same reputation for reliability and quality as Positronics. For this reason, the president of Positronics was sure the order would be given to the lower bidder.

Positronics had formed a team to discuss allocating resources to filling the order should its bid be accepted. At the team's first meeting, it became apparent that everyone was worried about the possibility of losing the bid. The head of marketing put himself on record as saying that it was quite likely that Anode would come in with a bid higher than Positronics'. During the discussion, someone noticed the head of production was looking a little uneasy. Some questioning revealed that he was by no means certain of the costs to produce the instruments and that a winning bid of $500,000 might well make Positronics lose money.

The team leader decided that there was a deeper problem here than had been expected. To focus the discussion, she elicited from the group an agreement on what they were worried about: everyone was worried about the uncertainty in the profit resulting from the venture. The team leader took a large sheet of paper and wrote the word "Profit" with an oval around it (Figure 2–1a); the oval indicates that profit is an uncertainty. This was the beginning of the "influence diagram" for the problem, a diagram that starts with and focuses on the ultimate, key uncertainty in the problem.

The team proceeded to look for other uncertainties relevant to (influencing) the uncertainty on profit. Most important in most people's minds was the uncertainty in Anode's bid: if Anode were to bid less than $500,000, Positronics would lose the bid. The team leader added an oval to represent Anode's bid and drew an arrow from the Anode Bid oval to the Profit oval to represent the fact that learning Anode's bid would help answer the question of what profit could turn out to be (Figure 2–1b).

The team then asked if there were other relevant uncertainties. The head of production reminded the team of the uncertainty on production cost. Accordingly, another oval was added to represent the uncertainty on Positronics' cost, and an arrow was drawn from the Cost oval to the Profit oval (Figure 2–1c). At this point, the oval representing Profit was doubled to indicate that, given Anode's bid and Positronics' cost, there would be no remaining uncertainty—it would be simple to calculate profit.

─────────────── **Figure 2–1** ───────────────

Development of the Influence Diagram of the Positronics Bid Venture

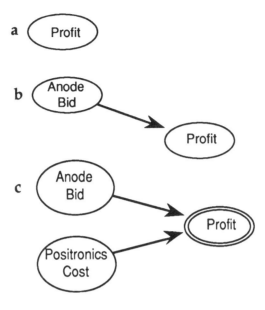

The meeting made it clear that there were two key areas of uncertainty to work on: the size of Anode's bid and the amount of Positronics' costs. It was also apparent that if preliminary analysis warranted, the team's task might be extended to finding the optimal level of Positronics' bid. All the other concerns (contingency plans, hiring policy, etc.) would fall into place after these three areas were better understood.*

The influence diagram is a very useful representation of problems involving uncertainty. Not only is it a concise statement of the problem, but it also gives the analyst a valuable tool for finding the structure of problems, for organizing the tasks of an analysis, and for eliciting the data and judgments necessary to analyze an uncertainty. Further, as we will see in Chapter 3, it is straightforward to extend the use of influence diagrams to problems that involve decisions as well as uncertainties.

Three elements of the influence diagram were introduced in the preceding example and are defined below.

- An oval represents an uncertainty. Inside the oval is written a descriptor (or variable name) to identify the set of events (or the quantity) about which we are uncertain or a question to which we would like an answer. Uncertainties are one of several types of "nodes" that we use in influence diagrams.

---

*The experienced reader might correctly object that things almost never happen this way. Meetings of this sort are often filled with worries and discussions that turn out to be irrelevant to the problem at hand, while the true uncertainties and decisions are often hidden and discovered only by the careful work of someone who listens, observes, and avoids common prejudices and preconceptions.

- An arrow represents an influence. The arrow between the Anode Bid oval and the Profit oval is read as "Anode Bid influences Profit." This simply means that if we knew what Anode's bid turned out to be, it would help us determine what our profit would be. The concept of "influence" is an important one and will be made more precise in succeeding chapters.

- A double oval represents an uncertainty that ceases to be uncertain once we know how all the uncertainties turn out in the nodes that have arrows pointing to it. This is a "deterministic" node since its value is determined by the nodes that influence it.

The remaining elements concern decisions and will be introduced in the next chapter. The steps for drawing an influence diagram are summarized below.

1. Determine the one key uncertainty you would like resolved—that is, that you would like an answer to. Write it down and put an oval around it.

2. Ask whether there is another uncertainty that—if you knew how it turned out—would help you resolve the uncertainty you identified in step 1. If there is another uncertainty, write it inside an oval and draw an arrow from this oval to the oval drawn in step 1.

3. Repeat step 2 until all *important* uncertainties influencing the key uncertainty (identified in step 1) are identified. An uncertainty is important in this context only if resolving its uncertainty helps resolve the uncertainty in the key variable. As you repeat step 2, check whether arrows should be added to or from all the uncertainties.

4. Ask whether there are uncertainties that would help resolve the uncertainties identified in step 2. If there are, add them to the diagram. Terminate the process when adding another oval does not help you understand the problem.

5. Check whether any of the uncertainties you have identified are completely resolved (determined) if you have all the information indicated by the arrows. Add another oval around these determined nodes to make a double oval.

Influence diagrams are used throughout this book, and their properties will be introduced as needed. The reader desiring a preview or review of influence diagram theory should consult Appendix B.

Why Bother with Probabilities?

People often claim that they deal adequately with uncertainty through the ordinary use of language and that the quantitative methods we propose are much too elaborate and unnecessary for any problems except very technical and complicated ones.

However, if we ask people to define just what they mean by such common describers of uncertainty as "probably" or "very likely," we usually find a great deal of ambiguity. The authors and their colleagues have demonstrated this ambiguity in seminars attended by high-ranking executives of many of the country's large companies. The executives are asked to define a number of terms, such as "likely," "very likely," or "probably," by assigning a range of probability to each term (e.g., "likely" means 60 percent to 80 percent probability). Although the exercise is not rigorously and scientifically conducted, two results occur so consistently that they warrant attention.

1. If we compare the probability ranges of the group for any one term, the ranges vary greatly. If we form some sort of composite group range spanning the individuals' ranges, there is very little difference between such terms as, for example, "likely" and "very likely."

2. In any moderate-size group, we find people who assign nonoverlapping probability ranges to the same word. For instance, one person might state that "unlikely" means 20 to 30 percent while another might put it at less than 5 percent. While these people may think they are effectively communicating about the likelihood of an uncertain event, they actually have quite different judgments about the likelihood and are unaware of the differences.

Positronics was just beginning to use decision analysis and had just discovered how differently participants at the meeting were using the same terms. It turned out that when the head of marketing said it was "quite likely" that Anode would bid higher than Positronics, he had meant that there was a 60 to 80 percent chance Anode would bid higher. When the president of Positronics heard this, he was more than a little disturbed, since he had assumed that "quite likely" meant something on the order of 90 to 95 percent. The lower probability argued either for more contingency planning by the production staff or for a lower bid. Of course, a lower bid would increase the likelihood of the newly perceived possibility that high production costs could lead to a loss for Positronics.

Verbal descriptions of uncertainty tend to be ambiguous or ill-defined, but numerical probability statements clearly and unambiguously describe uncertainty. Yet many people are overwhelmed with the idea of using probability. After all, probability is a rich and complicated area of study. However, conducting a decision analysis requires knowing only a few simple properties. While applying probabilities in decision analysis is at times subtle, common sense and careful reasoning are usually more useful than technical sophistication.

What Are Probabilities?

Before we proceed further, let us pose a somewhat philosophical question: what do probabilities represent and where do they come from?

Probabilities represent our state of knowledge. They are a statement of how likely we think an event is to occur.

This simple but profound concept can be illustrated by the example of three people considering an oil-drilling venture in a new area. One person is the president of the company. He has been around for a long time, and his experience tells him that there is a 20 percent chance that there is recoverable oil in the area. The second person is a technical expert who has just finished studying the most recent seismic and geological studies on the area. She assigns a 60 percent probability that there is oil there. The third person is someone out at the drilling site; they have just struck oil, and he would assign a 100 percent probability to finding oil.

Who is right? They *all* are right, assuming that they all are capable of processing the knowledge available to them. (Fortunately, decision-makers in business situations are rarely incompetent or incorrigibly optimistic or pessimistic.) The general acumen of the president, the technical and statistical data of the analyst, and the simple observation of the person at the site—these are different sets of knowledge.

This view of probability as an expression of a state of knowledge has profound consequences. We comment on it in one way or another in every chapter of this book. This perspective on probabilities is called the Bayesian point of view.

Frequently, the nervous decision-maker will ask, "What are the correct probabilities?" Unfortunately, there are no "correct" probabilities. Probabilities represent the decision-maker's state of knowledge or that of a designated expert source of knowledge. Probabilities thus represent a person's judgment and experience and are not a property of the event under consideration. We can worry about whether the expert has good information, whether the probabilities represent the information adequately, whether the state of information should be improved, or whether efforts should be made to elicit the probabilities better. These questions examine the quality of the probabilistic information, but they are not attempts to get the "correct" probabilities.

We do not, however, imply that data are irrelevant. One of course wants the best data and statistics available and to consider the advice of the most experienced people available (another form of data). Unfortunately, the hard decision problems usually involve uncertainties for which definitive data are either not available or not completely relevant. And, when the decision needs to be made, the decision-maker must consider how relevant even the best data are to predicting the future.

Using Intuition Effectively _____

The "Divide and Conquer" Approach

To help the individual think about uncertainty, decision analysis makes judicious use of the "divide and conquer" approach. To do this, the overall uncertainty is divided into a reasonable set of component uncertainties (and, as we will see in Chapter 3, decisions), which are then treated individually. We have seen an example of this approach in the development of the influence diagram for the Positronics case.

This approach reduces the complexity and scope of the problem to a level at which intuition can function effectively. This is important because, as discussed above, probabilities are statements derived from a person's state of knowledge. It is very difficult (if not impossible) for a person to give meaningful probabilities on an uncertainty that is complex or that includes factors beyond his or her immediate knowledge and experience.

Dividing the uncertainty is also useful in helping different people in a company communicate about the uncertainty and contribute to the analysis. Since different people bring different expertise and experience to the decision-maker or decision-making process, dividing the uncertainty into small pieces enables each individual to contribute precisely within his or her area of expertise.

In the case of Positronics, the problem already showed a natural division into two subcomponents: the uncertain size of Anode's competitive bid and the uncertain cost of production if Positronics won the contract. It seemed natural that the uncertainty in the production cost would be best estimated by someone from the manufacturing or production staff, while the uncertainty on the size of the competitive bid would best be estimated by someone from marketing or upper management. Assignments for further study were made accordingly.

Passing the Clairvoyance Test

One of the most common barriers to the use of intuition and to effective communication is lack of clarity in defining the event to which we are assigning probabilities.

To test the clarity of definition, we use the clairvoyance test. The clairvoyant is a hypothetical person who can accurately answer any question, even about the future, but who possesses no particular expertise or analytical capability. Thus, for instance, when asked about production costs in the year 2010, the clairvoyant might "look" at a company's annual report for the year 2010 and report the answer he sees there.

The clairvoyance test is a mental exercise to determine if the clairvoyant can immediately tell us the outcome of a chance node or if he needs to know other things first. An immediate prediction means that the uncertainty is clearly defined. If the clairvoyant would have to ask some questions first, then we have not clearly laid out exactly what the uncertain quantity is.

For instance, imagine we ask the clairvoyant what production costs will be in the year 2010. The clairvoyant would have to ask whether the costs are in today's dollars or 2010 dollars; whether they include or exclude depreciation, fixed costs, and allocated expenses; whether they are given in terms of an advance in technology or an evolution of the product; etc. Our response, of course, is to define better what we mean by production costs so they more nearly pass the clairvoyance test.

The clairvoyance test is surprisingly difficult to pass. Yet if it is not passed, we will find that uncertainty compounded with an ill-defined quantity yields results of dubious quality at best. The problem becomes even more acute when information obtained from different people is compared. The time spent in taking—and passing—this test is well rewarded by a lack of confusion and greater insight later on.

The Positronics staff agreed on definitions for the uncertainties that passed the clairvoyance test. Cost was a well-defined measure that excluded depreciation, allocated costs, and truly fixed costs. Anode's bid was interpreted strictly in terms of the deliverables called for in the request for bids.

Assigning the Numbers

Using Trees

To put explicit values on probabilities, we use drawings called "distribution trees" to represent the data in the nodes of the influence diagram—the information on how each uncertainty may turn out. It is called a distribution tree because it has a line (branch) for each possible outcome. In statistical terms, this is the distribution of possible outcome. The data in this form are then combined into a "probability tree" that both graphically describes and numerically analyzes the problem. Each uncertainty node we have identified in the influence diagram becomes an uncertainty or chance node of the probability tree.

What does a distribution tree look like? Shown in Figure 2–2 is the skeleton of a three-branch distribution tree. At the branching point on the left is a circle to indicate that this is an uncertainty or chance node. Associated with each branch is an outcome. The set of outcomes describes all the different events that could occur at that node—all the ways the uncertainty could be resolved.

─────────────── **Figure 2–2** ───────────────

Skeleton of a Three-Branch Distribution Tree

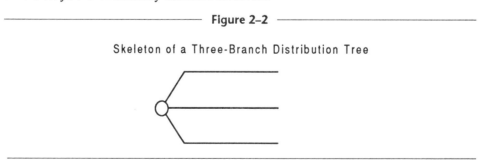

The set of outcomes at a chance node must be mutually exclusive and collectively exhaustive. That sounds more complicated than it really is. Mutually exclusive means that the way an uncertainty turns out must correspond to only one of the outcomes (i.e., there is no overlap in the list); collectively exhaustive means that the way the uncertainty turns out must correspond to one of the outcomes (i.e., all possible outcomes are included in the list).

The Data in the Nodes

After some work, the Positronics staff came up with the following probability assessments to represent their perception of the uncertain future. To keep things simple, the staff judged it sufficiently accurate to divide both quantities (Anode's bid and Positronics' cost) into three ranges, thus creating three discrete outcomes for each node.*

First, the three possible states representing Anode's bid were chosen. The Anode bid could be less than $500,000, between $500,000 and $700,000, or greater than $700,000. The marketing personnel used their judgment to assign the following probabilities: a 35 percent chance the Anode bid will be less than $500,000, a 50 percent chance it will be between $500,000 and $700,000, and a 15 percent chance the bid will be greater than $700,000. These definitions and probabilities can be thought of as being contained "inside" the Anode Bid oval in the influence diagram. Shown in tree form (Figure 2–3), the outcomes are on each branch, the probability of the branch occurring is at the left of each branch, and the circle at the branching point indicates that it is an uncertainty node. To keep notation compact, all values in the figures are shown in units of thousands of dollars—e.g., $500,000 is shown as 500.

--------------------------------- Figure 2–3 ---------------------------------

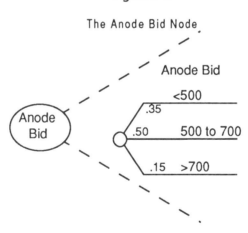

The Anode Bid Node

Similarly, Positronics' cost could turn out to be less than $300,000, between $300,000 and $500,000, or greater than $500,000. There is a 25 percent chance Positronics' cost will be less than $300,000, a 50 percent chance it will be between $300,000 and $500,000, and a 25 percent chance it will be greater than $500,000 (Figure 2–4).

---

*Chapter 8 gives much more careful procedures for eliciting probabilities. The informal process used here is appropriate only when an uncertainty is unusually well understood.

--------------- Figure 2–4 ---------------

The Positronics Cost Node

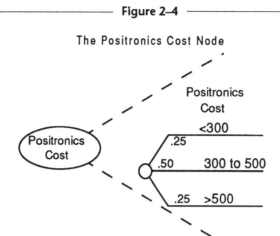

The range of values assigned to Positronics' cost is very large, with about a factor of two (<300 to >500) uncertainty. It is rare to find so great an uncertainty on costs, except in one-of-a-kind construction or in very large projects.

Drawing the Probability Tree

All these data now are put together to create a "probability" tree. This probability tree represents all the different combinations of events that can occur and their probabilities. How are the data joined together to create a probability tree?

Pick an order in which to display the two uncertainty nodes. The order is arbitrary for the present example. The rules applicable in more complicated cases are presented in the next chapter. In Figure 2–5, we choose Anode Bid to be the first node and Positronics Cost to be the second. The deterministic node, Profit, will be at the right-hand side of the diagram.

--------------- Figure 2–5 ---------------

Influence Diagram Prepared for Drawing the Tree

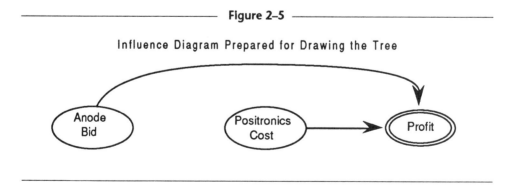

At the end of each of the branches of the first node (Anode Bid), attach the second node (Positronics Cost), as in Figure 2–6. We will deal with the deterministic node (Profit) shortly.

—————————————————————— Figure 2–6 ——————————————————————

Probability Tree Displaying the Probability of Each Path Through the Tree

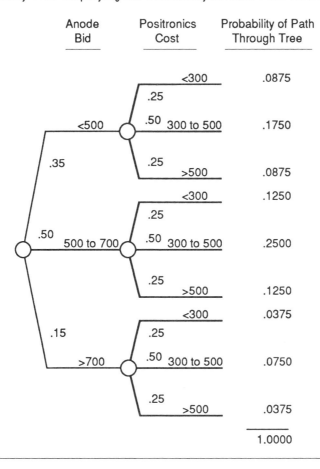

The final column in Figure 2–6 has been added to clarify the meaning of the tree. The probability of each of the nine scenarios (paths through the tree) has been calculated by multiplying the probabilities that occur at each branching. These products are referred to as joint probabilities. Thus, the scenario of Anode bidding less than $500,000 and Positronics' cost being less than $300,000 (the topmost path through the tree) is $.35 \times .25 = .0875$. The sum of all the joint probabilities is 1, as it must be.

We can see that however difficult it is to assign the probabilities for each chance node, it would be much more difficult (if not impossible) to directly assign the joint probabilities. The "divide and conquer" technique reduces scope and complexity so that judgment and intuition work effectively.

You can conserve space by drawing the tree in the more compact form shown in Figure 2–7. This form of the tree is often referred to as a "schematic tree." Drawing the tree with nodes following each other like this means that each branch of the left node leads to the next node on the right. Thus, the implication is that each node is duplicated as many times as necessary to produce the full tree structure.

— **Figure 2–7** —

Schematic Tree for the Uncertainties

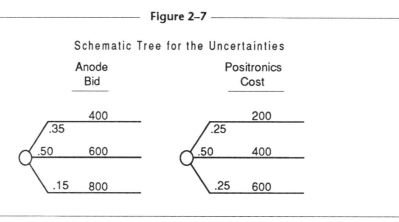

A refinement has been added in Figure 2–7. The outcomes on each branch are now single numbers that represent the ranges of the original outcome. For instance, the Anode bid can be $400,000, $600,000, or $800,000. We have approximated the original ranges by discrete values, resulting in the Anode bid having only three values. (The procedure for doing this is described at the end of this chapter.) Clearly, the more branches we have, the narrower we can make the ranges and the better a single number can represent the range. On the other hand, the more branches, the larger the tree.

A Value Function

We still have not dealt with the deterministic (double oval) node, Profit, which appears in the Positronics influence diagram (Figure 2–5). This is the node for which there is no remaining uncertainty, once we know the outcome of the nodes that influence it. Its value is determined by the outcomes of the influencing nodes. Thus, unlike the other two nodes, the profit node needs only a value function (a formula) that translates the uncertainties in the chance nodes into the uncertainty on the value of interest to the decision-maker. (We discuss value functions in detail in Chapter 3.)

Positronics had decided that profit was the prime value in this case. The deterministic node for profit can therefore be thought of as having an equation "inside" the node (Figure 2–8).

The completed probability tree is shown in Figure 2–9.

The values in the column on the right are needed to complete the probability tree and allow analysis. Sometimes the value model comes from a subjective assessment where the values for each scenario are assessed directly rather than calculated. Sometimes the value model is a simple relationship (as in the Positronics case) where the value can be calculated by a single equation. However, most often the value model is implemented as a computer program (or spreadsheet) that calculates how revenues and costs develop over time, figures tax effects, calculates a cash flow, and so forth.

—————————————— **Figure 2–8** ——————————————

Influence Diagram Showing Equation "Inside" the Profit Node

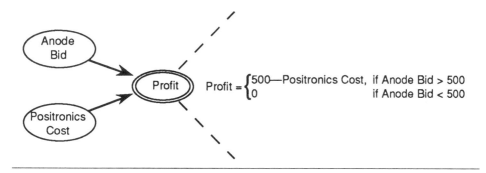

$$\text{Profit} = \begin{cases} 500 - \text{Positronics Cost,} & \text{if Anode Bid} > 500 \\ 0 & \text{if Anode Bid} < 500 \end{cases}$$

—————————————— **Figure 2–9** ——————————————

Completed Probability Tree

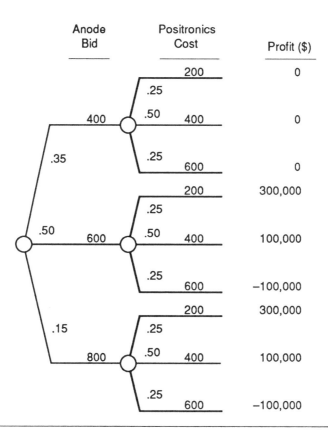

Computer Representation and Input _____

Figure 2–9 is a completed probability tree. Before analyzing the tree, we will enter it into the Supertree computer program. Analyzing large trees by hand is tedious and prohibitively time consuming. Thus, to use decision analysis successfully and routinely, a computer is essential.

To prepare the tree for entry into Supertree,* it is necessary to make some modifications, as shown in Figure 2–10.

_____ **Figure 2–10** _____

Probability Tree Modified for Entry into Supertree

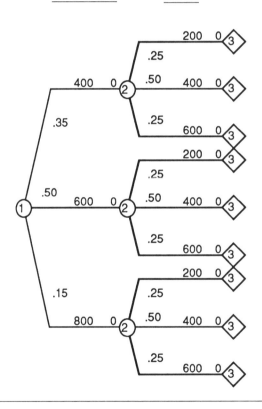

_____

*Refer to Appendix C for information on the PC-DOS/MS-DOS version of Supertree. Appendix D similarly describes the PC-DOS/MS-DOS version of Sensitivity (discussed in Chapter 6). These are the versions of Supertree and Sensitivity used on both the IBM Personal Computer and other compatible computers and the ones used in the illustrations in this book. Supertree input and output on the Macintosh or other systems is similar to what is shown in this book.

The following four elements have been added to the tree to make it suitable for entering into Supertree:

- A new type of node has been added—the endpoint node (shown as a ◊). This is the node Supertree uses to assign a value to a scenario or path through the tree. Usually this node corresponds to a deterministic node in the influence diagram—Profit, in the Positronics case. All paths through the tree must terminate on the right in an endpoint node.

- The nodes have been numbered. Here, Anode's bid is node number 1, Positronics' cost is node number 2, and the endpoint node is node number 3. Node numbers in Supertree must be positive integers. Making the numbers increase from left to right in the tree helps you remember the structure while analyzing the tree.

- Each chance node has been given a node name, ANODEBID and COST.* In Supertree, the node name not only describes the node, but is also a variable that takes on as a value the outcomes of the node. Thus, the node names are variables that can be used by the endpoint node (value model) to calculate a value for each path through the tree. For instance, Supertree will give the variable COST a value of 200, 400, or 600 depending on the path through the tree being evaluated.

- A reward of $0 has been assigned to each branch of the chance nodes and appears to the right of the outcomes on the branches. (In hand-drawn trees, they usually appear under the branches.) Rewards are quantities added to the values at the endpoints and are a quick way to represent the benefits (costs if negative) associated with a particular branch. By convention, rewards are normally not shown explicitly when they are zero.

Input data for the tree are entered by the Input option of the Structure menu of Supertree. The active response will be highlighted on the screen; we can go from entry to entry by using the Return key or the cursor (arrow) keys. Figure 2–11 shows the entries needed to enter nodes 1 and 2 into Supertree.

Before entering node 3 (the endpoint node), we need to decide how to use the endpoint to place values at the end of the tree. We could type in numbers directly, but this works only for very small trees. In this case, we will use Supertree's capability for evaluating an endpoint expression using Basic syntax. We can use numbers, operators, and node name variables in this expression. (See Appendix E for details.)

---

*Node names in Supertree must begin with a letter and be composed of letters and digits. Supertree distinguishes between upper and lower case. Therefore, the node name ANODEBID is not the same as the node name anodebid or Anodebid.

Figure 2–11

Entry of Chance Node Data into Supertree

NODE NUMBER:1

TYPE:CHANCE   OUTCOMES DEPEND ON NODES:
NUMBER OF BRANCHES:3   PROBABILITIES DEPEND ON NODES:
NODE NAME:ANODEBID

| | | | SUCCESSOR |
| PROBABILITY | OUTCOME | REWARD | NODE |

```
  __.35_____400_____0_____2_
  |
 C__.50_____600_____0_____2_
  |
 |__.15_____800_____0_____2_
```

NODE NUMBER:2

TYPE:CHANCE   OUTCOMES DEPEND ON NODES:
NUMBER OF BRANCHES:3   PROBABILITIES DEPEND ON NODES:
NODE NAME:COST

| | | | SUCCESSOR |
| PROBABILITY | OUTCOME | REWARD | NODE |

```
  __.25_____200_____0_____3_
  |
 C__.50_____400_____0_____3_
  |
 |__.25_____600_____0_____3_
```

The equation for profit was shown in the Profit node. The proposed bid is $500,000, and the value is 500 – COST if Positronics wins the bid. So, we could write the endpoint as follows:

$$(500 - COST) \qquad (2\text{-}1)$$

However, what happens when Anode bids less than Positronics? Positronics loses the bid and does not get the profit described above. To model this, we can use a programmer's trick. In Basic (and other programming languages), we can write a relational expression that compares two values with such operators as < (less than), = (equal to), <= (less than or equal to), etc. The result of this operation is either "true" (with a result of 1) or "false" (with a result of 0).[*]

---

[*] In almost every computing language, true is equal to 1. In Basic, true is equal to –1. Supertree violates this Basic rule by taking true equal to 1 in Basic syntax expressions.

We can describe whether or not Positronics wins the bid with the expression 500 < ANODEBID. This expression is true (equals 1) if ANODEBID is greater than 500 and false (equals 0) if ANODEBID is less than or equal to 500. If we multiply (500 – COST) by this expression, we will zero out profits in the cases where Positronics loses the bid. Putting these together in a single expression, we obtain:

$$(500 - COST) * (500 < ANODEBID) \qquad (2\text{-}2)$$

This expression will yield the profit values shown before. The last information needed for node 3 is that it depends on nodes 1 and 2, which means it needs the values of the variables ANODEBID (node 1) and COST (node 2) to calculate values. This information was already in the influence diagram (Figure 2–5) in which the Profit node was influenced by the Anode Bid node and by the Positronics Cost node. "Depends on" in Supertree is the same as "is influenced by" in influence diagram language.

We can now enter node 3 into Supertree, as shown in Figure 2–12. Supertree will request the name of the program to be used—the entry BASIC indicates that an expression will be entered in Basic syntax. At the bottom of the screen, Supertree will display its summary of the endpoint expression—the B$ in Figure 2–12 records the fact that Basic syntax is used.

Figure 2–12

Entry of Endpoint Node Data into Supertree

NODE NUMBER:3

TYPE: ENDPOINT

Name of program: BASIC

Expression:
  (500-COST)*(500<ANODEBID)

Nodes upon which endpoint depends:
  1 2

RESULTING ENDPOINT EXPRESSION:
B$(500-COST)*(500<ANODEBID)

Once we have entered the structure of the tree, it must be evaluated (as shown in Figure 2–13). The Evaluate option uses the endpoint node(s) to find the values associated with each path through the tree. While this task is trivial in this case, for trees with hundreds of paths and for models that take many seconds to run, evaluation is a major, time-consuming task.

--- **Figure 2–13** ---

Evaluate Screen

```
Supertree will check input compatibility and will then evaluate endpoints;
    this may take some time.
Do you wish to continue with this evaluation? YES
>> TOTAL OF 9 MODELS RUN
>> ENDPOINT VALUES ASSIGNED                6/1/90  12:00  BIDDING TREE
```

Before evaluating the tree, Supertree checks that the structure and input are consistent and sensible (from a computer's point of view). However, Supertree gives the user considerable latitude in describing the tree and using endpoints; as a result, we could enter a tree and model that cause Supertree to encounter an error during the evaluation, resulting in an error message.

Analyzing the Tree

Now that the tree has been evaluated, we will determine what information can be drawn from it. First, we will examine how the component uncertainties have translated into uncertainty on the value of ultimate interest to the decision-maker. If we go to the Analyze menu of Supertree and choose the Plot option, Supertree will display a number of questions (shown in Figure 2–14).

We will leave the order of nodes the same for now by pressing Return (we will see the usefulness of node reordering later) and then select a plot at the first node to see the overall probability distribution for the entire tree. Select a cumulative plot and a single distribution. (Multiple distributions show the individual distributions at each branch of the selected node.)

When we are through we press the F1 key to process the information; the word WAIT appears in the upper right corner of the screen while Supertree is processing. Supertree then displays the smallest and largest values in the distribution as suggested limits for the plot. We can use these by entering a Return or we can enter other limits. The resulting plot appears in Figure 2–15.

--- **Figure 2–14** ---

Screen Display for Plotting a Cumulative Distribution

```
Present Order of Nodes:
  1 2
New Order of Nodes:
  1 2
Node at which to plot the probability distribution or distributions? 1
Cumulative or histogram plot? CUMULATIVE
Single or multiple distributions? SINGLE
Label for axis? Profit ($000)
Smallest and largest values in distributions are: -100.0 300.0
Enter lower and upper limits for display: -150 350

>> Distribution Plotted      6/1/90  12:00  BIDDING TREE
>> EXPECTED VALUE = 65.0
```

———————————————————— **Figure 2–15** ————————————————————

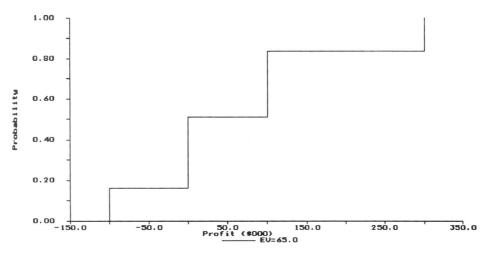

Cumulative Plot of Probability Distribution on Profit in the Positronics Venture

Because a cumulative probability plot (like the one shown above*) is the most efficient means of presenting information for decision analysis, we use it throughout this book. The plot is worth studying closely, since it answers most of the questions the decision-maker will ask.

The plot gives the probability (the vertical axis) that the venture's value will turn out to be less than or equal to the value shown on the horizontal axis. Thus, the plot above indicates that there is:

- No probability of the venture being worth less than –$100,000

- A .1625 probability of its being worth less than or equal to –$100,000 (.1625 that it is equal to –$100,000)

- A .5125 chance of its being worth less than or equal to $0 (.1625 that it is equal to –$100,000 and .35 that it is equal to $0)

- A .8375 probability of its being worth less than or equal to $100,000

- A 1.0 probability of its being worth less than any value above $300,000.

---

*The Supertree graphics in this book were produced by the professional version of Supertree. The student version of Supertree uses simpler plotting methods.

You may object that it is impossible to read the graph with this much accuracy, and indeed it is. However, if you look back at the trees in Figures 2–6 and 2–9, you will find the exact probabilities and values combined in the plot above. We have transcribed these probabilities and values exactly to illustrate where the plot comes from. The cumulative plot is a convenient way to display the probabilities and values for each path so observations like those above can be made.

The staircase nature of the graph is, in this case, imposed partly by the discrete approximations used to turn an originally continuous range of bids and costs into nine (3 × 3) different cases. If the ranges had been broken into more segments, the distribution would have been smoother. But there would still have been a step at $0 corresponding to the probability that the bid was lost.

Using the Histogram option of the Plot command is another way to represent the probability distribution for the venture's value. In a histogram plot, the horizontal (value) axis is divided into a number of equal-sized ranges or bins. The height of the bar drawn for each bin is the probability (vertical axis) that the value falls in the bin. The input data for the histogram (Figure 2–16) are similar to those for the cumulative plot.

After processing the plot, Supertree requests the limits to use (just as in the cumulative plot), the number of bins, and the scale for the vertical axis. Supertree suggests a vertical scale that will create a plot that just fits on the screen.

─────────────────── **Figure 2–16** ───────────────────

Screen Display to Plot a Histogram

```
Present Order of Nodes:
  1 2
New Order of Nodes:
  1 2
Node at which to plot the probability distribution or distributions? 1
Cumulative or histogram plot? HISTOGRAM
Single or multiple distributions? SINGLE
Label for axis? Profit ($000)

Smallest and largest values in distributions are: -100.0 300.0
Enter lower and upper limits for display: -100 400
Number of bins for data on this range? 5
Maximum probability on vertical axis? 0.35


>> DISTRIBUTION PLOTTED      6/1/90  12:00  BIDDING TREE
>> EXPECTED VALUE = 65.0
```

───

The histogram reveals that there is:

- A .1625 probability of the bin ranging from –$100,000 to $0

- A .35 probability of the bin ranging from $0 to $100,000

- A .325 probability of the bin ranging from $100,000 to $200,000

- A .1625 probability of the bin ranging from $300,000 to $400,000.

_____ **Figure 2–17** _____

Histogram of Probability Distribution on Profit in the Positronics Venture

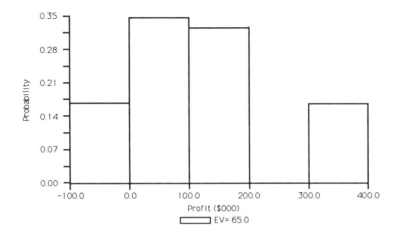

A value is in a bin if it is greater than or equal to the lower bound of the bin and less than the upper bound of the bin (less than or equal to the rightmost bin). Once again, these probabilities and values can be obtained from Figures 2–6 and 2–9.

How Much Detail Is Enough?_____

In an actual case, the value model might be more complex, and there might be more nodes in the tree or more branches on the nodes. While such complexity may be appropriate, more detail may not add insight. Hence, the results shown in the cumulative and histogram plots may be close to representing the essentials of the situation. Before succumbing to the temptation to make an analysis more complicated, we should pose the following questions:

- Will a more complicated value model really change the values that much?

- Will more nodes or more branches at a node really change the probability distribution that much?

- Will the added detail really add insight?

- Is the focus shifting from "a model adequate to make a choice" to a "good model of reality"?

Often, the essential insight into a decision problem is conveyed by results almost as simple as those shown here. That a decision has proved much simpler to grapple with than one would have supposed is an insight a decision-maker really appreciates.

With the initial analysis completed, the decision analysts were preparing to present their results to the president of Positronics. They decided to avoid puzzling him with the complications of understanding a cumulative probability graph and instead used the histogram. During the presentation, the president began asking questions like "What's the chance we will make a substantial profit?" and "What's the chance we will lose money?" which the analysts realized could be read directly off the cumulative probability graph. Being experienced presenters, they had a copy of the cumulative probability graph ready in the set of backup materials they had prepared for the presentation.

To everyone's astonishment, the president was genuinely surprised by the results. After some discussion, everyone agreed that he was surprised because the explicit judgments inherent in the probabilities had opened up new channels of clear communication. For one thing, the president had not appreciated just how worried production was that the cost of producing the instruments might be much higher than expected. The analysis also enabled the president to see how the uncertainties in cost and in Anode's bid combined into an overall uncertainty. Looking at the cumulative and histogram plots, he now had a good idea of the uncertainty and risk in his current bid strategy. He did, however, ask whether there was a single number that could be used to characterize the worth of the venture when he was comparing it with other ventures or speaking to members of the board (who were probably not interested in details of this rather minor facet of the business).

Certain Equivalent and Expected Value

One of the goals of decision analysis is to give a single number that characterizes a probability distribution. This number is called the certain equivalent and is the value that, if offered for certain, would represent to the decision-maker an even exchange for the uncertain venture described by the probability distribution. (This topic is discussed extensively in Chapter 5.) There is, however, a quantity closely related to the certain equivalent but easier to use and understand: the expected value. The uncertain venture is described by a probability distribution—a set of possible outcomes and the probability that each outcome occurs. Figures 2–15 and 2–17 show the probability distribution for profit in graphical form. The expected value of a probability distribution is obtained by multiplying each outcome by its probability of occurring and then by adding the products. The data plotted in figures 2–15 and 2–17 are shown in the trees in figures 2–6 and 2–9.

The data in these trees can be combined in what is called the "roll-forward" evaluation (Figure 2–18). The roll-forward evaluation rolls all the information forward—i.e., to the right-hand side of the tree. This means that for each path through the tree, there is a value (Figure 2–9) and a probability (Figure 2–6). Multiply the value by the probability at the end of each path and add the results to obtain the expected value.

The expected value can also be obtained through the "rollback" evaluation, a much more general technique that is easier to use. In the rollback, we start at the right-hand edge of the tree and replace each chance node with its expected value. (Multiply the value on each branch by its probability and sum the products.) We then move to the left and continue the process, except that what was the rightmost column of nodes

──────────────────── **Figure 2–18** ────────────────────

Expected Value Determined Through Roll-Forward Evaluation

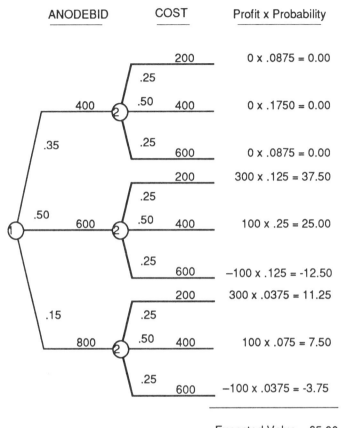

| ANODEBID | COST | Profit x Probability |

Expected Value = 65.00

has now been replaced by expected values. This procedure continues until all the nodes have been replaced and we are left with the expected value of the tree.

We can see the rollback process through the Display option of the Analyze menu. The data entry screen for the Display option appears in Figure 2–19. As in Plot, Supertree asks for the order of nodes and then requests the number of the first and last nodes to be drawn. For very large trees, drawing the whole tree takes a prohibitive amount of time and computer memory and would add little, if any, insight. Finally, Supertree asks whether we wish single or double spacing in the drawing. For large tree drawings, we can conserve space by single spacing.

In the output in Figure 2–19, we see how the COST node expected values are the branch values for ANODEBID, which lies to the left of COST. For instance, the branch with the ANODEBID equal to 800 replaces the COST node with its expected value, which is calculated below.

$$(300 \times .25) + (100 \times .50) + (-100 \times .25) = 100 \qquad (2\text{-}3)$$

————————————————————— **Figure 2–19** —————————————————————

Display of Tree Illustrating Rollback

```
Present Order of Nodes:
  1 2
New Order of Nodes:
  1 2
First Node: 1
Last Node: 2
Single or double spacing? SINGLE


   PROBS ANODEBID  EXP VAL   PROBS COST  EXP VAL

                              _0.250_200_____.0
   _0.350_400_____.0_C_0.500_400_____.0
   |                          |_0.250_600_____.0
   |                          _0.250_200_____300.0
   C_0.500_600_____100.0_C_0.500_400_____100.0
   |                          |_0.250_600____-100.0
   |                          _0.250_200_____300.0
   |_0.150_800_____100.0_C_0.500_400_____100.0
                              |_0.250_600____-100.0

   >> Tree Drawn     6/1/90  12:00   BIDDING TREE
   >> Expected Value: 65.0
```

The expected value of the ANODEBID node is then:

$$(0 \times .35) + (100 \times .50) + (100 \times .15) = 65 \qquad (2\text{-}4)$$

If we wish to see only the expected value of the tree, Supertree performs this operation in the Rollback option of the Analyze menu (Figure 2–20).

Given a large number of identical uncertain ventures, the average value would be the expected value. For instance, in a coin toss that yields a prize of $1, the expected value is:

$$(.5 \times \$1) + (.5 \times \$0) = \$0.50. \qquad (2\text{-}5)$$

We would expect to be about $50 richer after flipping the coin 100 times. Of course, the problem is that we are often presented with one-of-a-kind situations. For the coin toss example, if we are offered a single coin flip with a prize of $1, we will either walk away with $1 or with nothing. Still, it is not unreasonable to value the opportunity at the $0.50 expected value for decision-making purposes. For much larger values (e.g., a single coin flip with a prize of $1,000), the expected value may not adequately give us the value of the uncertain venture. If it does not, we should use the probability distribution. For most problems we will encounter in practice, the certain equivalent will not be very different from the expected value. In addition, the methods of tree evaluation are similar for both measures. Thus, it will prove simple to make the transition from one measure to the other.

Figure 2–20

Display Showing Use of the Rollback Option to Obtain the Expected Value

```
Present Order of Nodes:
  1 2
New Order of Nodes:
  1 2
>> Expected Value: 65.0
>> Tree Rollback    6/1/90  12:00  BIDDING TREE
```

Encoding Probabilities[*]

How does one obtain probabilities in practice? Obtaining probability distributions for use in decision analysis is no easy task. People are not trained in thinking about uncertainty, so the exercise of assessing probabilities can be uncomfortable and difficult. In this section, we briefly describe the encoding process and how to discretize the resulting continuous distributions. In Chapter 8, we further discuss the encoding process and give an actual procedure to follow. We also further discuss the commonly encountered biases that must be counteracted (as much as possible) to obtain accurate information.

To obtain probabilities, a tree can be set up and people can be directly asked to write probabilities on it. Another quick way to get a probability distribution is from existing "range data." Unfortunately, while both these procedures are easy and take relatively little time, they tend to yield "bad" probabilities because they do not allow the analyst to counteract common biases. Earlier, we emphasized that probabilities represent a person's state of knowledge and that there are no "correct" probabilities. Biased probabilities are those that do not adequately represent what a person really knows; something prevents him or her from using or expressing this knowledge correctly.

The most common types of bias cause people to think they know things better than they do. In other words, their probability distributions are usually much too narrow and understate the uncertainty. Another type of bias occurs because most people are unfamiliar with probability theory and make false analogies or draw false conclusions about probability.

---

[*] Reading this section may be postponed until after Chapter 5 has been read.

Obtaining the Data

In encoding continuous numerical variables, the analyst usually assesses the cumulative probability distribution directly. This process will allow the analyst to counteract the biases during the assessment. The cumulative probability graph is obtained by plotting responses to such questions as "What is the likelihood that costs will be less than $500,000?" or "Less than $650,000?" (Actually, it is best to ask these questions using a reference device such as a probability encoding wheel—see Chapter 8.) The result of such an assessment process will be a set of points and a smoothed curve such as the one in Figure 2–21 for Positronics' cost.

──────────── **Figure 2–21** ────────────

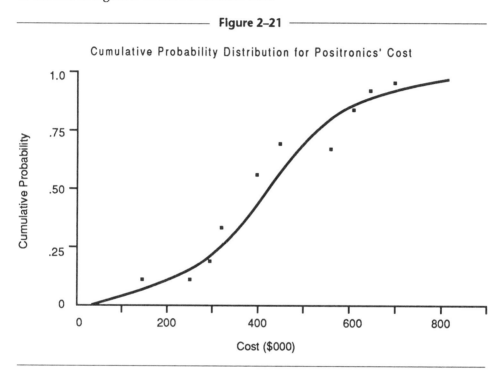

Cumulative Probability Distribution for Positronics' Cost

Discretizing the Data

In tree analysis, we usually make a discrete approximation by setting up nonoverlapping (mutually exclusive) ranges that encompass all possible values (collectively exhaustive), by finding the probabilities that the values fall in these ranges, and by then choosing a value to represent that range. (This is the approximation.) By doing this, we have converted a continuous variable to a discrete variable and a probability density function to a probability mass function.

Given a continuous probability distribution such as the one shown above, how does one perform this approximation? One widely used technique is to select the number of outcomes and the values of the probabilities you want and then draw a horizontal line at these probabilities. In Figure 2–22, we have chosen the number of outcomes to be three. We have also chosen the probabilities .25 for the lower range (line at .25), .5 for the middle range (line at .25 + .50 = .75), and .25 for the top range (line at .25 + .5 + .25 = 1).

Next, we draw a vertical line at A, choosing point A so that the shaded area to the left of the vertical line is equal to the shaded area to the right. (The eye is surprisingly good at doing this.) These two areas are marked by the letter "a." Then we pick a point, B, at which to draw a vertical line with the shaded area to the right being equal to the shaded area to the left. Finally, we pick the third point, C, at which to draw the vertical line balancing the two shaded areas.

Figure 2–22

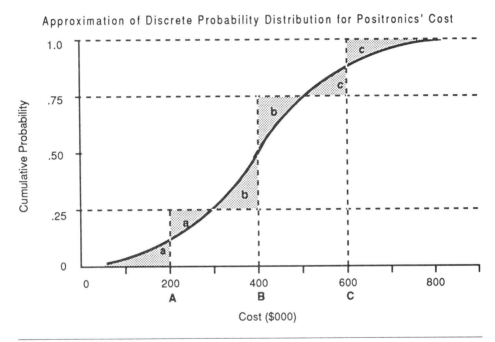

The procedure sounds much more complicated than it is in practice. The result is that we now have approximated the continuous probability distribution; the discrete probability distribution is shown in tree form in Figure 2–23. The actual values are A = 200, B = 400, and C = 600. These values are used for Positronics' cost in this chapter. In general, the values for A, B, and C will not come out evenly spaced.

The reason the procedure works is that we divided the continuous probability distribution into ranges with associated probability when we drew the horizontal lines. In Figure 2–24, we see that the first range was from negative infinity to x and had probability .25. The second range was from x to y and had a probability of .5. The third range was from y to infinity and had a probability of .25. (For this example, x = 300 and y = 500, corresponding to the ranges in Figure 2–4.) Picking point A in such a way that the shaded areas are equal is a visual way of finding the expected value, given that you are in the lowest range. (Proving that the expected value makes the shaded areas equal is a nice exercise in calculus.) Choosing the expected value to represent the range is a natural approximation and is commonly used. There are, however, other possible choices.

─────────────── **Figure 2–23** ───────────────

Discrete Probability Distribution in Tree Form

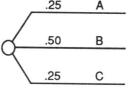

Using Range Data

We see that the final result was three numbers, with probabilities of .25, .50, and .25. There is a shortcut for assessing these values directly. This method is frequently used in the early stages of analyzing a problem when you have obtained ranges within which the values of variables are expected to fall. (See Chapter 6 for a discussion of Sensitivity Analysis.) The ranges are typically defined by best guess, low value (10 percent chance it could be less), and high value (90 percent chance it could be less or

─────────────── **Figure 2–24** ───────────────

Ranges Associated with Approximate Discrete Probability Distribution for Positronics' Cost

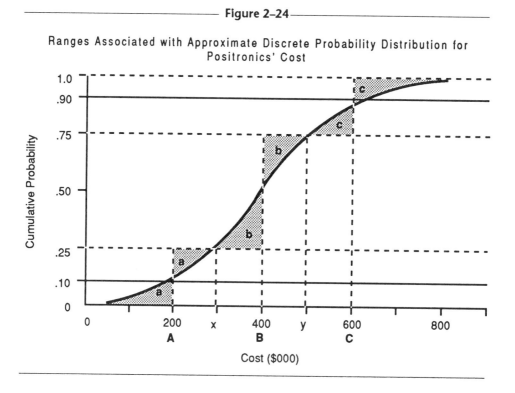

10 percent chance it could be greater). As a quick way of setting up a tree, these three values can be used for B, A, and C, respectively. But remember that you want to encode probabilities more carefully later on!

Figure 2–24 shows why this procedure works. There is about a 10 percent chance the value will be less than A and about a 10 percent chance that the value will be greater than C—and this is how we defined the ranges! (This property is almost exact for a Gaussian or normal distribution and is quite good for most of the distributions you find in practice.) Finally, the best guess can be used for B unless you know the distribution is very asymmetric. Thus, in summary, we can take the "10 percent, best guess, 90 percent" range numbers and use them in a tree with .25, .50, and .25 probability, respectively.

Beware, however, of "best guesses" that come from a business plan and are far from the median value. Also, be alert for ranges that are too narrow or are given without sufficient thought and reflection.

Summary

Probabilities are a precise way of expressing a person's information about an uncertain event. Judicious use of the clairvoyance test and the divide and conquer approach make the use of probabilities an intuitive as well as precise process.

Influence diagrams and probability trees constitute a framework to hold and process probability statements. The influence diagram is a powerful tool for structuring a problem. The probability tree is the tool used most often for calculating with probabilities.

The primary output of the analysis is the probability distribution on value. This information can be represented graphically by a cumulative probability plot or by a histogram. For the Positronics case, the graphs showed the uncertainty in profit.

A single measure to represent the value of an uncertain venture is the expected value of the probability distribution. For the president of Positronics, this number provided a starting point for putting a value on his uncertain venture.

Finally, care and skill are required in the assignment of probabilities. A simple example showed how information on Positronics' cost can be used for input to the probability tree.

Problems and Discussion Topics

2.1 Consider today's weather forecast. Are the chances of rain or sunshine expressed verbally or with probabilities? What is your probability of rain given that weather forecast? If your probability is different from the forecast, is the difference because you and the forecaster have different states of knowledge or because of some other reason?

2.2 In the section "What Are Probabilities?" (page 10) are statements like "Probabilities represent our state of knowledge." Such statements are sometimes misinterpreted to mean that probabilities are arbitrary numbers between 0 and 1. In fact, probability is a well-defined concept with very strong implications. For example, if two people have exactly the same information (knowledge) about an event, they should assign the same probability to this event. Furthermore, if new relevant information becomes available, the prior probability assignment will have to be changed (updated).

What else can you infer from the statement "Probabilities represent our state of knowledge"?

2.3   Why is an influence diagram (or similar method) necessary for understanding complex uncertainties? How do the procedure and graphical form of an influence diagram deal with the problem?

2.4   What is the relationship between each component of an influence diagram (arrows, ovals, and double ovals) and the components of a probability tree?

2.5   Can you draw a probability tree directly without first drawing an influence diagram? When would this be a bad or good idea? Does your answer depend on the level of expertise of the person doing the analysis?

2.6   In the section "Using Intuition Effectively" (page 11), we discussed how to define uncertainty clearly and the role of the clairvoyant in the clairvoyance test. How can the clairvoyant help you? Can the clairvoyant change your future?

2.7   What do you do when an uncertainty fails the clairvoyance test? How might this change your influence diagram? How might this change the structure of your probability tree?

2.8   The expected value is sometimes described as the mean value you would expect to achieve if you undertook the same venture many times. Unfortunately, since many decisions are one-of-a-kind decisions, there is no opportunity to repeat them and establish a historical mean. Suppose, though, that a venture had just been resolved (all the uncertain events had happened) and you were now faced with an identical one. Would your prospective expected value for the second venture be the same as it was for the first? Why or why not?

2.9   You are going to the movies tonight with a new date. You plan on treating, but your date may want to go Dutch treat (each person pays) or treat you. You figure the three outcomes are equally likely. The cost for the movie is $5 per person. You plan to at least buy popcorn if your date wants it (with a 4 out of 5 chance that he or she will). However, you have forgotten how much the large popcorn costs. You would give 5 out of 10 that it costs $2 and split the rest of the probability between $1.50 and $2.50.

You just discovered that you only have $10 cash right now. What is the expected cost of going to the movie tonight? What is the probability that it will cost you more than $10? What is the probability that it will not cost you anything?

2.10 Your prize Rapid Ripe tomato plant has flowered and is ready to start producing fruit. If all goes well, your plant will produce tomatoes by the end of the week. It will then produce a new set of flowers and blossoms next week. Unfortunately, your area is subject to blossom wilt, which causes the tomato flowers to fall off.

If the blossoms fall off, a new set of blossoms will not emerge until next week, and tomatoes will not be ready until the end of that week.

Luckily, each time blossoms fall off, the plant builds up its resistance; the probability of each succeeding blossom falling off is then only half as much. You estimate that the probability of this first set of blossoms falling off is .40.

a. Draw the influence diagram for this problem and then draw the probability tree.

b. What is the probability tomatoes will be ready in the third week?

c. What is the expected number of weeks you will have tomatoes over the next three weeks?

d. What is the probability you will lose the blossoms one or more weeks of the next five weeks?

2.11 You have discovered the lights on Van Ness Avenue in San Francisco are synchronized, so your chances of getting a green light at the next intersection are higher if you have not been stopped by a red light at the last intersection. You estimate that there is a 4/5 chance of getting a green light if the previous light was green. Similarly, there's only a 1/4 chance of getting a green light if the last light was red. Because Van Ness is a major throughway, you estimate there's a 2/3 chance of the first light being green.

a. Draw the influence diagram for this problem and then draw the probability tree.

b. What is the probability that the second light will be green?

c. Out of the first three lights, how many lights can you expect to be green?

d. What is the probability of the third light being green when the first one was red? (Hint: draw a tree with three nodes representing the first three lights.)

2.12 An excess probability distribution plots the probability that the value is greater than a given number. Plot the excess probability distribution for the initial Positronics tree (Figure 2–9). What is the probability the value is greater than $130,000?

2.13 Plot the probability mass function for the initial Positronics tree (Figure 2–9). What is the difference between the mass function and the histogram? (The probability mass function is defined in Appendix A.)

2.14 Suppose the closing trading price for platinum on the world markets today was $550 per ounce. (Does this pass the clairvoyant test?) Toward the end of the day, you put in an order to your broker to purchase one, two, or three contracts to sell 100 ounces of platinum one year from now, depending on how many contracts were available. Given the low volume in platinum contracts recently and given how late you called in, you figure there is about a .3 chance you got one contract, a .6 chance you got two, and a .1 chance that you got three

You decide to seek out further information on the future of platinum prices. A very nervous metals broker gave you the following distribution on the closing trading price one year from now.

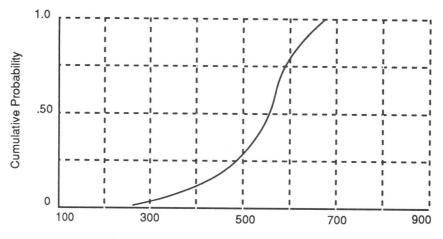

Trading Price of Platinum One Year from Today ($ per ounce)

a. Draw the influence diagram for this problem. Is there any information not reflected in the influence diagram, and, if so, how does the influence diagram relate to it?

b. Discretize the distribution above into a chance node whose branches have probabilities of .25, .50, and .25. What is the expected price of platinum one year from now?

c. Put together the complete probability tree describing your profit if you hold on to however many contracts you get until fulfillment. Assume you can buy the platinum you need to fulfill the contract(s) just before you need it. What is your expected profit from holding the contract(s)?

d. Discretize the distribution again, but this time into a two-branch node with probabilities of .5 and .5; then incorporate this node into the complete probability tree. Now, perform probability sensitivity analysis on the probabilities for platinum price by systematically changing the pair of probabilities—for instance, (1, 0), (.9, .1), (.8, .2), and so on. At what probability of the high level of platinum price does your

̄ ᵔ ⁿrofit from holding the contracts become negative? (The Ana - tivity Probability option described in Chapter 3 will
ᵢwer this question.)

ᴨt reflected in the influence diagram? Why or why not?

2.15 Show that balancing areas in the discretization process is equivalent to choosing the expected value given that you are in the range. The expected value, given you are in the range $a \leq x \leq b$, is:

$$\frac{\displaystyle\int_a^b x f(x)\, dx}{\displaystyle\int_a^b f(x)\, dx}$$

where f is the probability density, and the cumulative probability density is

$$P(x)_\leq = \int_{-\infty}^{x} f(x)\, dx$$

(Hint: you will probably need to do an integration by parts.)

3

Decisions Under Uncertainty

What Is a Good Decision?

One common way people distinguish good decisions from bad ones is by looking at the results of the decision. Most people, however, realize this criterion is not very satisfactory. For one thing, while the results may not be apparent until much later, we would like to immediately characterize the decision as good or bad. In addition, all we see are the results of the chosen alternative—there is usually no way to see the results that would have occurred if a rejected alternative had been chosen and, thus, no way to see whether we have really chosen the better alternative. Most troublesome, however, is evaluating the situation when someone "lucks out" with what seems to us undeservedly good results. Should you call the decision "good" in this case and reward the decision-maker accordingly?

One of the fundamental benefits of decision analysis is that it can distinguish good decisions from bad ones. Furthermore, it provides a criterion for establishing whether a decision is good or bad.

Decision analysis starts by defining exactly what a decision is—the commitment of resources that is revocable only at some cost. If we do not commit resources, it is almost meaningless to say we have made a decision. The alternative "Do nothing" is a commitment of resources in the sense that an opportunity has been rejected.

Decision analysis, then, clearly lays out the four elements of rational decision-making (Figure 3–1). The first element is information, or "What do I know about the world and the business or personal opportunity under consideration?" An important component of this knowledge is an assessment of uncertainty (or "What *don't* I know?") The second element is alternatives, or "What courses of action are open to me?" The third element is values, or "What do I want?" Finally, there's logic, or "How do I put knowledge, alternatives, and values together to arrive at a decision?"

───────────────────── **Figure 3–1** ─────────────────────

The Elements of a Good Decision Analysis Process

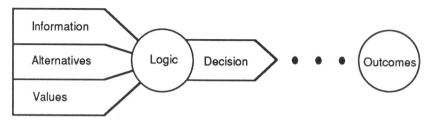

Given these elements, we can now characterize a good decision as one that is logically consistent with the information, alternatives, and values brought to the decision. In the decision analysis process, we can explicitly record the principal inputs to the decision-making process and establish that a good decision was made *before* the results of the decision are known. This minimizes the problem of "Monday-morning quarterbacking," which can have an insidious effect on the morale of a company. Furthermore, in decision analysis, you can disagree with the information or values the decision-maker brings to the problem to the extent that you would have chosen another alternative—and still say that the decision-maker made a good decision. In corporate practice, other sets of information (and values, if appropriate) can be substituted in the evaluation for the decision-maker's. By doing this, we can test not only whether the same alternative would be chosen, but also what the loss in value would be from choosing the other alternative. These results could then be filed as sort of a minority report to the record of the decision.

Why is it important to be able to determine whether a decision is good or bad? For one thing, the decision-maker will sleep better realizing that, given the time and resources available, he or she has done the best job possible. In addition, in corporate decisions (such as those made by electric utility companies), it may later be necessary to justify to stockholders, regulators, or other stakeholders that a good decision was made, even though a bad outcome ensued. Finally, we like to identify people who make good decisions so that they can be rewarded and promoted. Judging by results rather than by good decisions discourages people from taking a course of action with any risk in it—unless the results will not be known until the distant future!

One frequent objection to this definition of a good decision is, "That all sounds fine, but, in reality, it's results that count, and you can't tell me that in the real world a decision that leads to bad results is a good decision!" For operational decisions, there is much truth in that objection. However, there is seldom significant uncertainty in operational decisions. Consequently, if we correctly process the information available to us and follow up diligently, our decisions will usually lead to good results. It is in decisions involving significant uncertainty (typically strategic decisions) that the distinction between good decisions and good outcomes becomes important.

A second objection is that uncertainty represents inadequate knowledge and that a decision made with inadequate knowledge cannot be a good one: garbage in, garbage out. While the quality of the available information is certainly an important consideration, waiting for more information is frequently not advisable. Specifically, while the option of waiting and gathering more information to reduce the uncertainty should be included among the alternatives considered, information-gathering requires money (incurring information-gathering costs) and time (risking competitors' actions, opportunity lost, revenue lost). Furthermore, information-gathering will usually be incomplete and resolve only some of the uncertainty. Finally, some uncertainties cannot be resolved, either in principle or in practice, until the actual results occur. Decision analysis addresses these concerns explicitly with the value of information and value of control concepts and calculations, which are described in this chapter.

Recasting the Problem As a Decision Problem

Decision and Value Nodes

The president of Positronics was by now becoming uncomfortable with his decision to bid $500,000. Correction—He had not yet submitted the bid and committed himself, so he had not yet really made the decision! To ease his discomfort, he requested the analysis be redone for different bids. The analyst suggested rephrasing the problem in terms of a decision tree, which would not only automatically handle different potential bids, but would also allow further analysis to clarify the decision. The analyst first added the decision to the influence diagram, using a rectangle to denote it. Then she drew an arrow from the decision node to the profit node, since the level of bid affects the profit. Finally, she changed the double oval around the Profit node to a double octagon to denote the fact that profit is the criterion to be used when making the decision.

——————————— **Figure 3–2** ———————————

Influence Diagram of the Positronics Bid Decision

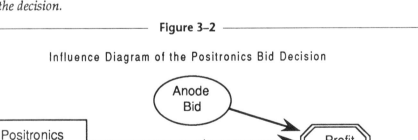

In Figure 3–2, we have introduced the remaining elements of influence diagrams. In Chapter 2, we saw the uncertainty node (represented by an oval), the deterministic node (represented by a double oval), and influences (represented by arrows.) Here, we introduce the decision and value nodes and extend the concept of influence.

A rectangle represents a decision. Inside the rectangle is a descriptor (or variable name) to identify the set of events (or the quantities) among which the decision-maker is choosing.

An octagon represents a value node, inside which is a descriptor of the value measure. The value measure is the quantity that the decision-maker uses in making decisions; as discussed later in this chapter, the decision-maker will choose the alternative that maximizes some function of the value measure. The value node is just a chance node drawn with a special symbol to represent its special role.

A double octagon represents a value node that has ceased to be an uncertainty because all the uncertainty has been expressed in the nodes that influence it. It is just a deterministic node with a special role with respect to decisions.

The arrow representing an influence now has added meaning. The basic concept of influence is flow of knowledge: the person providing the probability distribution for the node at the head of the arrow has information about what happened at the node at the base of the arrow. In addition, when decision nodes are involved, this information flow implies a chronology. The following are the four ways in which an arrow can be used:

- *Uncertainty Node to Uncertainty Node* —The outcome of the uncertainty at the base of the arrow is provided when probabilities are assigned for the node at the head of the arrow. This means that the probabilities at the node at the head of the arrow are conditional on the resolution of the uncertainty at the base of the arrow. (Conditional probabilities are treated extensively in Chapter 4.) For the special case of a deterministic node at the head of the arrow, the influence means that the resolution of the uncertainty at the base of the arrow provides a value to be used in the deterministic node.

- *Decision Node to Uncertainty Node* —The alternative chosen at the base of the arrow is provided when probabilities are assigned for the node at the head of the arrow. This means that the probabilities at the node at the head of the arrow are conditional on the alternative chosen at the base of the arrow. This means that the decision is made *before* the resolution of the uncertainty.

- *Uncertainty Node to Decision Node* —The outcome of the uncertainty at the base of the arrow is known when the decision is made. This means the uncertainty is resolved (and the results learned) *before* the decision is made.

- *Decision Node to Decision Node*—The alternative chosen at the base of the arrow is known and remembered when the decision is made at the head of the arrow. This implies that the decision at the base of the arrow is made *before* the decision at the head of the arrow.

"Information flow" means that information is available to the person providing the probabilities or making the decision. Thus, we could have a node "Sales, 1995" influencing "Sales, 1993." This would not imply backward causality in time! Rather, it would mean that the person providing probabilities for Sales, 1993 would be given information on the Sales, 1995 outcome: "If you knew Sales, 1995 were high, what would be the probability distribution for Sales, 1993?"

Rules for Constructing Influence Diagrams

To construct an influence diagram, follow the procedure outlined in Chapter 2. Two elements must be added to this procedure. First, decision nodes (drawn as rectangles) are to be identified in addition to the uncertainties as we work back from the one key uncertainty. Second, one uncertainty should be enclosed in an octagon to indicate its role as the value measure for decision-making.

Four rules must be obeyed if you wish to construct meaningful influence diagrams.

1. *No Loops*—If you follow the arrows from node to node, there must be no path that leads you back to where you started. This is most readily understood in terms of the information flow indicated by the arrows.

2. *Single Decision-Maker*—There should be just one value measure (octagon) and all decisions should be made to maximize the same function (expected value or certain equivalent) of this value.

3. *No Forgetting Previous Decisions*—Each decision should be connected to every other decision by an arrow. This will establish the order in which the decisions are made and indicate that the decision-maker remembers all his previous choices.

4. *No Forgetting Previously Known Information*—If there is an arrow from an uncertainty node to a decision node, there should be an arrow from that uncertainty node to all subsequent decision nodes.

Constructing the Decision Tree

After some discussion, the Positronics staff identified four different alternatives for analysis—three levels of bid ($300,000, $500,000, and $700,000) and the alternative not to bid. The square at the branching point in the tree in Figure 3–3 indicates a decision node, and each branch is an alternative. There are no probabilities associated with the branches because the node represents a decision, not an uncertainty. The value node now needs some modification because it is influenced by the decision node.

To join the pieces in a tree, we must be a little more careful than we were in the approach described in Chapter 2. The following procedure will transform an influence diagram into a decision tree.

1. Arrange the decision nodes such that all arrows with a decision node at their base or head point to the right-hand side of the page. Arrows pointing to or emanating from decision nodes imply a chronology that must be followed in decision trees. By convention, the chronology of decisions in a decision tree flows from left to right, and therefore, these arrows must point from left to right.

Figure 3–3

Data Describing Positronics' Decision

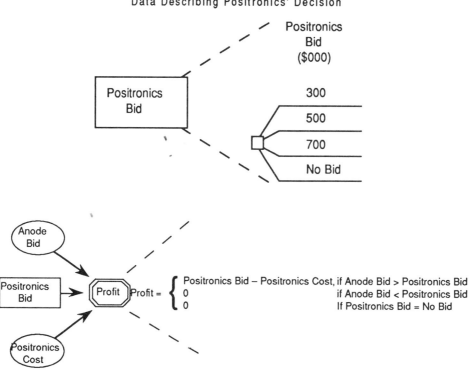

2. Arrange the uncertainty nodes so that no uncertainty node is to the left of a decision node unless there is an arrow from that node to the decision node. In a decision tree, the outcome of a node to the left of a decision node is known to the decision-maker when he or she makes the decision; in an influence diagram, this means there is an arrow from the uncertainty node to the decision node.

3. Arrange, insofar as possible, the uncertainty nodes so that all arrows point to the right. This will cause conditional probabilities to be displayed simply on the tree.

4. Make the deterministic value node a tree endpoint node. This will usually involve calculations to find the value associated with each combination of events at the nodes that influence the value node.

5. Now convert the diagram to a decision tree. Draw the content of the leftmost node in tree form. To obtain the complete tree, draw the content of the next node at the end of each branch of the preceding

node, and repeat this process until all the nodes are drawn. To obtain the schematic tree, draw the contents of the node in order, with the understanding that each branch of a node leads to the node to its right.

Figure 3–4 is the rearranged influence diagram for Positronics and the schematic tree. Some commonsense modification of this last step is needed in asymmetric situations. For instance, the No Bid branch of the decision need not be joined to the Anode Bid node or the Positronics Cost node, since both these nodes are irrelevant if no bid is made.

Figure 3–4

Translating the Influence Diagram into a Schematic Decision Tree

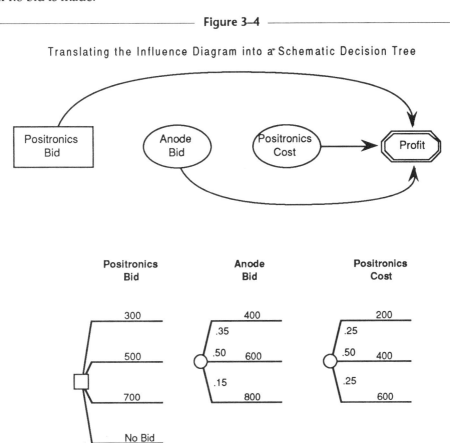

Decision or Uncertainty?

Graphic conventions are important in forming both influence diagrams and decision trees. As we have noted, a decision node is represented graphically by a square or rectangle, while chance nodes are represented by circles or ovals. This graphic convention helps to avoid confusion about what is a decision variable (completely under the decision-maker's control) and what is an uncertainty (or chance) variable (completely out of the decision-maker's control).

The distinction between decision and chance variables is occasionally not as clear cut as we might think. Sometimes the analyst can choose which variables are decision variables and which are chance variables. For instance, the price of a product and the volume of sales cannot normally *both* be decision variables. You can set the price and then let the market determine the quantity sold or you can set the volume sold and then let the market determine the effective price realized. If nothing in the structure of the problem dictates which is the decision variable, the analyst must decide. In making the choice, the analyst should consider the impact of the choice on modeling the problem and on assessing probabilities. What is the easy or natural way to model? How do people think about the problem? How will it be easiest to assess probabilities?

There are several important differences in handling decision nodes and probability nodes. A decision node does not have any probabilities associated with the branches. Consequently, for the rollback procedure for tree evaluation introduced in Chapter 2, instead of replacing the node with its expected value (as we do with a chance node), we replace a decision node with the value of the branch that has the maximum value to the decision-maker. In other words, at a decision node we choose the alternative (branch) that gives us the most of what we want.

The order of nodes in the probability tree was fairly arbitrary, dictated mainly by the requirements of how people think best about the uncertainties. In a decision tree, however, the ordering of nodes implies a sequence of events. Time proceeds from left to right in the tree. If two decisions occur in a tree, the decision to the right is made after the one to the left; and the decision-maker remembers the choice made in the first decision when making the second decision. In addition, the uncertainty of any chance nodes that occur to the left of a decision node is resolved before the decision is made. That is, the decision-maker knows what actually happened before having to make the decision. However, node ordering is important only relative to the decision nodes. The ordering of the chance nodes relative to one another is still arbitrary. Thus, in Figure 3–4, Positronics makes its bid decision before it knows Anode's bid and before it knows what its own costs will be.

The outcomes or branches of a decision node should be a list of significantly different alternatives. Unlike the outcomes at a chance node, the list of alternatives at a decision node need not be mutually exclusive and collectively exhaustive (mutually exclusive: you cannot choose more than one branch; collectively exhaustive: every possible alternative is represented by a branch). However, if the alternatives are not mutually exclusive, confusion may arise. It is very important to have a list of significantly different alternatives. (A collectively exhaustive list of alternatives is impossible for all but the simplest problems.)

Finding even a few truly different alternatives requires creative thinking before and during the decision analysis process. All too often, the decision process is hobbled by a lack of genuinely innovative possibilities. In the Positronics bidding case, we are looking only at different bid levels. Other alternatives might involve forming a joint venture to bid with another company more experienced in building this kind of instrument, performing some cost studies before bidding (we consider this later in the chapter), or exploring the possibility that MegaCorp would accept a bid of some fixed markup on cost (with appropriate safeguards against irresponsibility in cost overruns).

Tree Input

We have already done most of the work to prepare the Positronics data for input to Supertree. The schematic tree has been created (Figure 3–4). Now we need to number the nodes. We will stay with our practice of having node numbers increase from left to right in the tree (Figure 3–5).

—————————————— Figure 3–5 ——————————————

Decision Tree Modified for Entry into Supertree

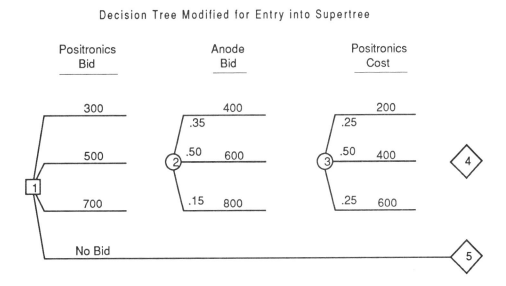

To modify our existing tree (Figure 2–10) in Supertree, we first need to renumber the existing nodes to make room for the new node 1; Anode's bid was originally node number 1. We could enter all the data for the tree. If we have saved the tree entered in Chapter 2, however, we can use the Recallfile option of the File menu to retrieve the data. We can then use the Renumber option (Figure 3–6).

Figure 3–6

Supertree Screen Display for Increasing Node Number

```
Increase all node numbers at and above node number: 1
Number by which to increase these node numbers: 1
```

We can then enter the decision node as node 1, as shown in Figure 3–7.

Figure 3–7

Supertree Screen for Entering the Decision Node

```
                         NODE NUMBER:1

TYPE:DECISION                    OUTCOMES DEPEND ON NODES:
NUMBER OF BRANCHES:4
NODE NAME:BID
                                         SUCCESSOR
            OUTCOME          REWARD      NODE

          __300_____0_____2__
          |
          |__500_____0_____2__
         D
          |__700_____0_____2__
          |
          |__NOBID_____0_____5__
```

The main differences from the entry screen for chance nodes is the lack of a column for probabilities and the lack of an entry for dependent probabilities. We have given the decision node the name BID and can use this variable in the endpoint model. The Show option (Figure 3–8) lists the endpoints, including node 4 (which we have modified with the Input option). Node 4 now uses the BID variable and depends on nodes 1, 2, and 3. Node 5 is a new numerical endpoint entered with the Input option (using Value for the name of the program) with a value of zero.

─────────────────────── **Figure 3–8** ───────────────────────

Display of Decision Tree Data in Supertree

Tree name: BIDDING TREE

STRUCTURE	NAMES	OUTCOMES	PROBABILITIES
1 D 2 2 2 5	BID	300 500 700 NOBID	
2 C 3 3 3	ANODEBID	400 600 800	.35 .50 .15
3 C 4 4 4	COST	200 400 600	.25 .50 .25
4 E	B$(BID-COST)*(BID<& ANODEBID)	Depends on 1 2 3	
5 E	0		

Because the structure and endpoint model have been changed, we must Evaluate the tree again. Selecting multiple rather than single plots under the Plot option of the Analyze menu (Figure 3–9), we obtain the probability distribution for all the alternative bid decisions (Figure 3–10). The staircase appearance is a result of the discrete approximation used in constructing the tree. If more branches had been used, the curves would be smoother. The data in Figure 3–10 show the "risks and rewards" associated with each of the alternatives. The decision-maker now has the data needed to make the decision.

─────────────────────── **Figure 3–9** ───────────────────────

Screen Display for Plotting Cumulative Probability Distribution

```
Present Order of Nodes:
  1 2 3
New Order of Nodes:
  1 2 3
Node at which to plot the probability distribution or distributions? 1

Cumulative or histogram plot? CUMULATIVE
Single or multiple distributions? MULTIPLE
Label for axis? Profit ($000)

Smallest and largest values in distributions are: -300.0 500.0
Enter lower and upper limits for display: -400 600

>> Distribution Plotted    6/1/90  12:00  BIDDING TREE
```

─────────────────────── **Figure 3–10** ───────────────────────

Probability Distribution on Profits for Alternative Bid Decisions

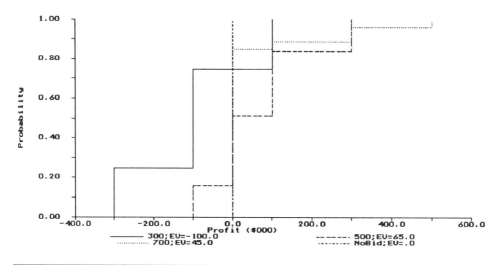

Which alternatives are risky and which are conservative? Often, the high bids ($700,000 in this case) are considered safer or more conservative because there is no possibility of losing money. However, we could also view the high bid as being the less conservative course of action: we are seeking to make a great deal of money, but since we probably will not make any money at all (because we probably will lose the bid), we are undertaking a great risk.

Notice the ambiguities in the preceding paragraph. "Risk" has so many ill-defined meanings that it is often better to avoid the word entirely. We will, however, use it in several well-defined contexts such as "risk attitude" and "risk penalty," as discussed in Chapter 5. Another problem word is "conservative," the meaning of which depends on our viewpoint and on the relevant values. When applied to estimates, conservative means a number the estimator thinks will result in a safe or conservative decision—according to his or her viewpoint. There is no point in giving "conservative" estimates for chance variables; they give an inaccurate estimate of the total uncertainty and often distort the results in unanticipated ways. It is much better to put in the best information through the probability distribution and to let the decision-maker make the decision.

Decision Criterion

How do we make decisions under uncertainty? For a simple tree with a single decision node (such as Figure 3–5), the decision-maker can stare at the probability distribution on value associated with each of the alternatives and make the decision. Figure 3–10 shows the results of combining all the information logically and consistently.

However, for more complicated trees with multiple decision nodes, this procedure is impractical. We need a decision criterion that enables Supertree to indicate the best decisions and that helps the decision-maker choose consistently. The decision-maker's true decision criterion is embedded in the values he or she brings to the decision. Thus, the decision criterion is highly personal. But there are common characteristics that can help the decision-maker (and the decision analyst) model these values and obtain a systematic decision criterion.

In most business and personal financial decisions, money is the primary value and maximizing wealth is the principal decision criterion. To express the value function completely in monetary terms, however, we must be able to express nonmonetary items in monetary terms. To do this, we must deal with the following three subjects:

- The value of nonmonetary, intangible goods

- The value of future money

- The trade-off between certainty and uncertainty.

The Value of Nonmonetary, Intangible Goods

When the principal value function of a tree is given in monetary terms, all values to be included in the tree must also be in monetary terms, including such intangible items as goodwill, worker safety, and laying off workers. Usually, obtaining estimates of monetary equivalents for these so-called intangibles is not difficult, though the decision-maker might not want the value needlessly publicized.

Many items that are referred to as intangibles are not really intangible, but rather are difficult to put a value on. For instance, increased goodwill may result in direct economic effects from increased sales or decreased transaction costs. This is not an intangible but rather an effect that is difficult to estimate. After this has been separated out, you can address the intangible part of the value that stockholders and managers attach to goodwill.

Establishing values for intangibles is not an attempt to disguise moral or social irresponsibility. Moral and social responsibility should be built into the initial choice of acceptable alternatives. Nor are intangible value trade-offs an attempt to put a price on intangibles such as happiness. The goal is to appropriately represent the trade-offs people make in practice in order to include them in economic decision-making.

In most business decisions, intangibles with even the most generous trade-offs have little effect on the value of the decision alternatives. In the rare case in which intangibles are important in the problem, the decision-maker must examine his or her values with much more care than outlined here.

In societal decisions, determining the value function is much more difficult. Societal decisions, such as road design or worker safety legislation, typically involve a trade-off between resources measured in monetary terms and in terms of human life and welfare. While there are a number of ways to deal with these decisions rationally, they are beyond usual business decision analysis practice.

The Value of Future Money

In the previous section, we expressed the value function in monetary terms. This reduces multiple time-varying uncertain results to a single time-varying uncertain result. This result is typically expressed as a stream of money stretching many years into the future. The value of money received in the future is not the same as that of money received today. Some people have immediate, productive uses for their capital while others do not; and if they do not, they can always lend (invest) their money to someone else for a fee (interest). Banks and other financial institutions establish a marketplace between present and future funds. The relationship between present and future funds is expressed in terms of a discount rate or an interest rate. The present value of cash, c_i, received years i from now is:

$$\frac{c_i}{(1+d)^i} \qquad (3\text{--}1)$$

where d is the discount rate the decision-maker wishes to use when trading off between present and future. (We discuss in Chapter 4 values that might be appropriate for the discount rate.) Using the present value formula, we can reduce the time series of cash extending m years in the future to a net present value (NPV):

$$\text{NPV} = \sum_{i=1}^{m} \frac{c_i}{(1+d)^i} \qquad (3\text{--}2)$$

thus eliminating time from the decision criterion.

Our decision criterion is to maximize the NPV of future cash flows. We could also maximize the NPV of other monetary measures, but cash flow is ordinarily a very good measure of the net change in wealth of a company or an individual. Other monetary measures (net income, earnings per share, dividends, payback period, return on investment) tend to focus only on parts of the problem and can lead to bad decisions if used as criteria without sufficient care.

The internal rate of return (IRR) criterion, although similar to the NPV criterion, is difficult to apply meaningfully in an uncertain situation. This criterion can be used to choose the best alternative given certainty (i.e., the same choice as from an NPV), but it does not show how much more valuable this preferred alternative is than the others—and in choices under uncertainty, we *must* be able to balance how much we might win against how much we might lose.

The Trade-off Between Certainty and Uncertainty

In the preceding two steps, we have reduced multiple time-varying uncertain outcomes to an uncertain NPV. As we saw in Figure 3–10, uncertainty means that there are many possible NPVs with associated probabilities. How can we now choose between alternatives with different probability distributions on NPV?

In Chapter 2, we discussed the expected value: the sum of probabilities multiplied by their respective values. The expected value represents the average return we would expect to receive if we were engaging in many identical but uncorrelated ventures. If the stakes are not very high, it makes sense to use the expected value as the value of a probability distribution. As the stakes go up, most people begin to show risk-averse behavior: the value they assign to a probability distribution is less than its expected value. (This behavior is discussed in Chapter 5.) Most business decisions, however, are not really that large relative to the total value of the company, and maximizing the expected value of the NPV of cash flow is a good approximation of the actual decision criterion.

The president of Positronics had become rather befuddled during the discussion of values and trade-offs. It had been a long time since he had been forced to examine just what he was trying to accomplish in running Positronics. However, it turned out that the simple value function used in the tree was substantially correct. Winning the bid would not greatly alter the probability of obtaining future work with MegaCorp, so there was no follow-on value to be added. Losing the bid would not entail any layoffs, because managing the normal labor turnover would be sufficient. The job was routine enough that no intangibles, such as added reputation, were attached to winning the bid. The job would be done within a year, so discounting was not a problem. Finally, at least for the time being, the president was willing to use expected value of profit as a decision criterion. After all, the possible profits or losses from the job were not that important to the company's long-term success.

Analyzing the Tree

The default decision criterion in Supertree is to maximize the expected value of the values given at the endpoints. Hence, we can use the Rollback option of the Analyze menu to find the expected value of the tree (Figure 3–11).

Figure 3–11

Screen Display for Rollback Option

```
Present Order of Nodes:
  1 2 3
New Order of Nodes:
  1 2 3
>> Expected Value: 65.0
>> Tree Rollback      6/1/90  12:00   BIDDING TREE
```

We can also use the Display option of the Analyze menu to see the whole of this small tree (Figure 3–12). Note the > to indicate the chosen alternative is to bid $500,000.

For large trees, it is impractical to display the entire tree to find out which scenarios lead to which values. Often, however, it is interesting to find a scenario that leads to a given value—either because the value is suspect or because we need a representative scenario to explain the results. The Trace option of the Analyze menu performs this task for you. Of course, the task is trivial in a tree as simple as this. (See Figure 3–13 for screen display.)

——————————————————— **Figure 3–12** ———————————————————

Decision Tree Showing Preferred Decision

Present Order of Nodes:
  1 2 3
New Order of Nodes:
  1 2 3
First Node: 1
Last Node: 3
Single or double spacing? SINGLE


```
      BID     EXP VAL    PROBS ANODEBID  EXP VAL    PROBS COST  EXP VAL

                                              _0.250_200_____100.0
                      _0.350_400_____-100.0_C_0.500_400____-100.0
                      |                         |_0.250_600____-300.0
                      |                          _0.250_200_____100.0
    _300_____-100.0_C_0.500_600_____-100.0_C_0.500_400____-100.0
    |                 |                         |_0.250_600____-300.0
    |                 |                          _0.250_200_____100.0
    |                 |_0.150_800_____-100.0_C_0.500_400____-100.0
    |                                           |_0.250_600____-300.0
    |                                            _0.250_200_____.0
    |                 _0.350_400_____.0_C_0.500_400_____.0
    |                 |                         |_0.250_600_____.0
    |                 |                          _0.250_200_____300.0
    |>500_____65.0_C_0.500_600_____100.0_C_0.500_400_____100.0
    |                 |                         |_0.250_600____-100.0
    |                 |                          _0.250_200_____300.0
    D                 |_0.150_800_____100.0_C_0.500_400_____100.0
    |                                           |_0.250_600____-100.0
    |                                            _0.250_200_____.0
    |                 _0.350_400_____.0_C_0.500_400_____.0
    |                 |                         |_0.250_600_____.0
    |                 |                          _0.250_200_____.0
    |_700_____45.0_C_0.500_600_____.0_C_0.500_400_____.0
    |                 |                         |_0.250_600_____.0
    |                 |                          _0.250_200_____500.0
    |                 |_0.150_800_____300.0_C_0.500_400_____300.0
    |                                           |_0.250_600_____100.0
    |_NOBID_____.0_____
```

>> Tree Drawn   6/1/90 12:00 BIDDING TREE
>> Expected Value: 65.0

--- **Figure 3–13** ---

Screen Display for Trace Option

```
Value to be traced? 500
THE CLOSEST VALUE IS =      500.0
PATH:
BID = 700
ANODEBID = 800
COST = 200
```

We have said that there is no such thing as a "correct" probability. The only worry is whether the probability assessment adequately reflects the decision-maker's state of knowledge. Nevertheless, there is a natural desire to know how important a probability assessment is in the choice of the alternatives in the decision problem. To show this, the Analyze Sensitivity Probability option performs probabilistic sensitivity analysis (also known as stochastic sensitivity analysis). As indicated in Figure 3–14, the horizontal axis is the probability assigned to the first (top) branch of node 3; the rest of the probability is assigned to the bottom branch, and the middle branch is given zero probability. This two-branch approximation is used for ease of interpretation. If the probability at node 3 depended on another node, that dependency would have been overridden in this option.

The plot in Figure 3–15 shows that when the probability of low cost ($200,000) is high, the $500,000 bid (alternative 2) is preferred. Below about 40 percent probability of low cost, the $700,000 bid (alternative 3) becomes preferred because the losses associated with the $500,000 bid become much more likely.

--- **Figure 3–14** ---

Screen Display for Sensitivity to Probability Option

```
Present Order of Nodes:
  1 2 3
New Order of Nodes:
  1 2 3
For which node do you want the sensitivity to probability? 3
Label for axis? Profit ($000)
Because the sensitivity requires multiple tree evaluations,
      it may take some time to run.
Smallest and largest values encountered are: 300.0 195.0
Lower and upper limits for vertical axis: 300 200
If the first node is a decision, the sensitivity will be shown for all branches.
The vertical axis is the expected value.
      The horizontal axis is the probability of the first branch of node 3;
      the last branch of node 3 has the remainder of the probability.

>>Probability Sensitivity  6/1/90  12:00  BIDDING TREE
```

────────────────────── **Figure 3–15** ──────────────────────

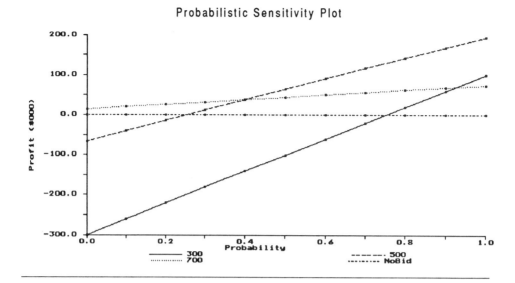

Probabilistic sensitivity to two nodes can be evaluated by systematically changing the probabilities by hand at one node and then using `Analyze Sensitivity Probability` at the other node to determine the probability at which the decision choice switches.

Positronics felt that the relative likelihoods of the $800,000 and $600,000 values for the Anode bid were reasonable. The staff was much less certain about the probability of the low bid ($400,000). Some thought a bid this low was not typical of Anode; others thought Anode had enough experience in this area that it could hold costs very low and hence afford to bid low. To see how changes in the relative likelihood of the $800,000/$600,000 bid level and the $400,000 bid level affected their decision, they decided to do a probability sensitivity analysis with the constraints shown in equations 3-3 and 3-4.

We use the notation $p(X | S)$ to indicate the probability that X occurs, given the state of knowledge S. However, in performing probabilistic sensitivity analysis, we are continuously varying probabilities—implying that we are similarly varying the underlying state of knowledge S on which a probability depends. Because the state of knowledge is varying, we have replaced the S notation here by S' to indicate that a different state of knowledge is implied by each different probability.

$$\frac{p(\text{Anode Bid} = 600 | S')}{p(\text{Anode Bid} = 800 | S')} = \frac{.5}{.15} \tag{3-3}$$

$$p(\text{Cost} = 400 | S') = 0 \tag{3-4}$$

——————————————————— **Figure 3–16** ———————————————————

Sensitivity of Preferred Decision to Changes in the Probability
Assessments for Cost and Anode Bid

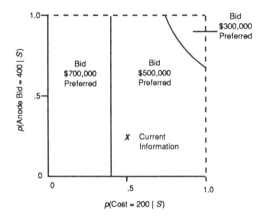

In the display of sensitivity results (Figure 3–16), the *X* marks a point corresponding to the current state of information. [Since Cost has been changed from a three-branch node to a two-branch node, we have set $p(\text{Cost} = 200 \mid S') = .5$ to get the same expected value as the original tree.]

The graph shows that when $p(\text{Cost} = 200 \mid S')$ is less than .4, bidding \$700,000 is preferred. When $p(\text{Cost} = 200 \mid S')$ and $p(\text{Anode Bid} = 400 \mid S')$ are both high, bidding \$300,000 is preferred.

Probabilistic sensitivities are often useful to settle arguments or to obtain consensus. If the same decision alternative is optimal for everyone's set of probabilities, then there is really no argument about what to do. If someone's probability indicates that he or she would choose a different alternative, then the plots show how much is "lost" by choosing the "wrong" alternative.

The Value of Perfect Information

The president of Positronics was satisfied by the results he had seen so far. He requested that the analysts add more branches to the tree so he could zero in on the optimal bid. However, the analysts suggested that they first examine other insights available from the tree: the value of information and the value of control.

One of the powerful features of decision analysis is the ability to show the value of resolving an uncertainty *before* making the decision. The simplest approach is to calculate the value of perfect information (also called the value of clairvoyance). Imagine that we had some means of obtaining information to completely resolve an uncertainty before we made our decision. (Perhaps a clairvoyant's services were available.) What is the maximum we should pay for this information? This value, which turns out to be easy to calculate, is the upper limit of the amount we should

─────────────── **Figure 3–17** ───────────────

Decision Tree to Determine the Value of Perfect Information on Anode's Bid

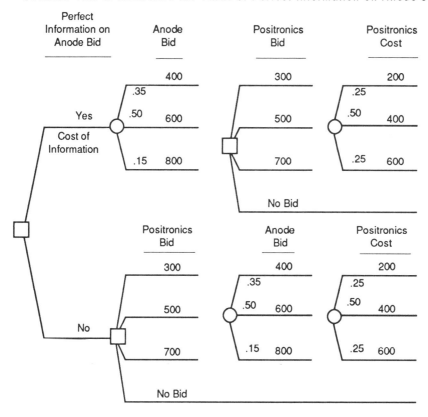

be willing to spend on any information-gathering effort, which generally yields imperfect rather than perfect information. Incidentally, we often find companies spending more on information-gathering than it is worth.

To calculate the value of perfect information on Anode's bid, Positronics introduced a new decision at the front end of the tree (Figure 3–17). The first node in this tree is the decision whether or not to obtain the perfect information. If Positronics does not obtain the information, it faces the tree following the "No" branch, which is identical to the tree evaluated in Figure 3–12. Thus, for the "No" branch, Positronics already knows it should choose to bid $500,000, resulting in an expected value of $65,000.

If the company decides to obtain the information (the "Yes" branch), it must pay the cost of the information, which could be entered in Supertree as a negative reward. It then faces a tree similar to the original one, but with the first and second nodes reversed, because Anode's bid is known before the decision is made. Note that the probabilities for Anode Bid are the same as before—if we thought there is a 35 percent chance of Anode's bid being $400,000, then we should think there is a

35 percent chance that the perfect information-gathering activity (or the clairvoyant) will reveal that Anode's bid is $400,000. This tree could be entered in Supertree and evaluated for varying costs of information until the expected value of the "Yes" (obtain information) alternative is equal to the expected value of the no-information alternative. This would then reveal the value of obtaining the (perfect) information—the maximum cost Positronics would be willing to incur to obtain it. However, Supertree provides a simpler approach. Use the `Rollback` option and give the new order of nodes as `2 1 3`.

———————————————— **Figure 3–18** ————————————————

Expected Value with Anode Bid Node Before Positronics Bid Node

```
Present Order of Nodes:
  1 2 3
New Order of Nodes:
  2 1 3
>> Expected Value: 95.0
>> Tree Rollback      6/1/90  12:00   BIDDING TREE
```

The resulting expected value of $95,000 is the expected value for the subtree at the end of the "Yes" branch in Figure 3–17; the new order of nodes specified in the `Rollback` option puts node 2 (Anode Bid) before node 1 (Positronics Bid). A way to represent this subtree at the end of the "Yes" branch is to add an arrow from the Anode Bid node to the Positronics Bid node in the influence diagram (Figure 3–19). This indicates that the uncertainty on Anode's bid is resolved before the Positronics bid decision is made.

———————————————— **Figure 3–19** ————————————————

Adding an Arrow from Anode Bid to Positronics Bid

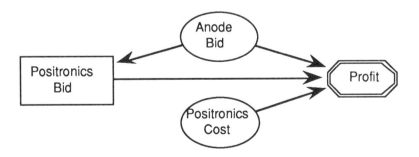

This expected value of $95,000 is the value of the venture with perfect information. We can then calculate the value of the perfect information as follows:

Value of Information   = Value with Information – Value Without Information
                        = $95,000 – $65,000
                        = $30,000   (3–5)

The Rollback option can be used to show that value of the venture with perfect information on Positronics' cost is $85,000 (Figure 3–20). The value of perfect information on Positronics' cost can be calculated to be $85,000 – $65,000 = $20,000.

Figure 3–20

Expected Value with Cost Node Before Positronics Bid Node

```
Present Order of Nodes:
  1 2 3
New Order of Nodes:
  3 1 2
>> Expected Value: 85.0
>> Tree Rollback    6/1/90   12:00   BIDDING TREE
```

Finally, the value of perfect information on both Anode's bid and Positronics' cost is $116,300 – $65,000 = $51,000 (Figure 3–21).

Figure 3–21

Expected Value with Anode Bid and Cost Nodes Before Positronics Bid Node

```
Present Order of Nodes:
  1 2 3
New Order of Nodes:
  2 3 1
>> Expected Value: 116.3
>> Tree Rollback    6/1/90   12:00   BIDDING TREE
```

Note that the value of information on two or more variables is *not* the sum of the values of information of each variable separately—it can be smaller or greater. In this case, the sum of the values of information on both variables separately is $30,000 + $20,000 = $50,000. This is smaller than $51,300, the value of information on both variables simultaneously.

We can gain further insight into the value of information by examining the portion of the tree as it would appear for the "Yes" branch of Figure 3–17. This subtree is displayed in Figure 3–22. Note that the only change that Positronics would make would be to change its bid from $500,000 to $700,000 if it knew that Anode were going to bid $800,000. Making this change in bid changes the expected value in that case

——————————————————— **Figure 3–22** ———————————————————

Subtree for "Yes" Branch of Figure 3–17

Present Order of Nodes:
  1 2 3
New Order of Nodes:
  2 1 3
First Node: 2
Last Node: 3
Single or double spacing? SINGLE

```
    PROBS ANODEBID  EXP VAL    BID     EXP VAL   PROBS COST  EXP VAL

                                                 _0.250_200_____100.0
                                  _300_____-100.0_C_0.500_400____-100.0
                                  |                |_0.250_600____-300.0
                                  |                 _0.250_200_____.0
                                  |>500_____.0_C_0.500_400_____.0
     _0.350_400_____.0_D  |                |_0.250_600_____.0
     |                            |                 _0.250_200_____.0
     |                            |>700_____.0_C_0.500_400_____.0
     |                            |                |_0.250_600_____.0
     |                            |>NOBID_____.0_____
     |                                             _0.250_200_____100.0
     |                           _300_____-100.0_C_0.500_400____-100.0
     |                           |                |_0.250_600____-300.0
     |                           |                 _0.250_200_____300.0
     |                           |>500_____100.0_C_0.500_400_____100.0
    C_0.500_600_____100.0_D  |                |_0.250_600____-100.0
     |                           |                 _0.250_200_____.0
     |                           |_700_____.0_C_0.500_400_____.0
     |                           |                |_0.250_600_____.0
     |                           |_NOBID_____.0_____
     |                                             _0.250_200_____100.0
     |                           _300_____-100.0_C_0.500_400____-100.0
     |                           |                |_0.250_600____-300.0
     |                           |                 _0.250_200_____300.0
     |                           |_500_____100.0_C_0.500_400_____100.0
    |_0.150_800_____300.0_D  |                |_0.250_600____-100.0
     |                           |                 _0.250_200_____500.0
     |                           |>700_____300.0_C_0.500_400_____300.0
     |                           |                |_0.250_600_____100.0
                                 |_NOBID_____.0_____
```

>> Tree Drawn   6/1/90 12:00 BIDDING TREE
>> Expected Value: 95.0

─────────────────────────── **Figure 3–23** ───────────────────────────

Determining the Value of Perfect Control

```
Present Order of Nodes:
  1 2 3
New Order of Nodes:
  3 1 2
First Node: 3
Last Node: 2
Single or double spacing? SINGLE


    PROBS COST  EXP VAL    BID    EXP VAL   PROBS ANODEBID  EXP VAL

                                          _0.350_400_____100.0
                              _300_____100.0_C_0.500_600_____100.0
                              |              |_0.150_800_____100.0
                              |               _0.350_400_____.0
                              |>500_____195.0_C_0.500_600_____300.0
    _0.250_200_____195.0_D   |              |_0.150_800_____300.0
    |                         |               _0.350_400_____.0
    |                         |_700_____75.0_C_0.500_600_____.0
    |                         |              |_0.150_800_____500.0
    |                         |_NOBID_____.0
    |                                         _0.350_400_____-100.0
    |                            _300_____-100.0_C_0.500_600____ ____-100.0
    |                         |              |_0.150_800_____-100.0
    |                         |               _0.350_400_____.0
    |                         |>500_____65.0_C_0.500_600_____100.0
    C_0.500_400_____65.0_D   |              |_0.150_800_____100.0
    |                         |               _0.350_400_____.0
    |                         |_700_____45.0_C_0.500_600_____.0
    |                         |              |_0.150_800_____300.0
    |                         |_NOBID_____.0
    |                                         _0.350_400_____-300.0
    |                            _300_____-300.0_C_0.500_600_____-300.0
    |                         |              |_0.150_800_____-300.0
    |                         |               _0.350_400_____.0
    |                         |_500_____-65.0_C_0.500_600_____-100.0
    |_0.250_600_____15.0_D   |              |_0.150_800_____-100.0
    |                         |               _0.350_400_____.0
            |>700_____15.0_C_0.500_600_____.0
                         |              |_0.150_800_____100.0
                         |_NOBID_____.0

>> Tree Drawn    6/1/90  12:00  BIDDING TREE
>> Expected Value: 85.0
```

from $100,000 to $300,000, for a net improvement of $200,000. But there is only a .15 chance of finding that Anode will bid $800,000. Therefore, the expected improvement in value is .15×200,000 = $30,000. This is the value of the information for Anode Bid—the same answer as obtained above.

Thus, information has value if knowing the results could lead us to change our decision. If none of the possible information-gathering results change the decision, there is no value to the information.

The value-of-information tree illustrates a number of powerful concepts. We believe that for many people, a change in perspective must occur before they understand the value of information calculation. ("Oh, is that what you mean?!") Understanding the concepts behind value of information is crucial to understanding and effectively using decision trees.

Positronics' president was impressed with the ideas implied in calculating the value of information. Since new information on Anode's bid was not obtainable by any ethical means, value of information was of only academic interest; most sources of information, such as information on prior bids, publicly available information on Anode's backlog, etc., had already been used in the probability estimates. Some information on what Positronics' cost might be was obtainable for considerably less than the value of perfect information of $20,000. This information would be obtained by using some off-the-shelf components to build a prototype instrument. The president encouraged production to go ahead with its prototype, provided the cost of the program was well under $20,000.

The Value of Perfect Control

Decision trees produce one more piece of information: the value of control (also called the value of wizardry). If a clairvoyant (someone who can foresee the future) is valuable to us, a wizard (someone who can change the future) is even more valuable. The effect of perfect control is that we could pick which one of the future (or otherwise unknown) possibilities (branches) we wanted to happen. Thus, the value with perfect control for Positronics' cost can be obtained by inspecting the tree with the Positronics Cost node moved to the front of the tree (Figure 3–23).

Inspecting the top branch shows that if there were some way to force Positronics' cost to be $200,000, it would yield an expected value of $195,000. (A more straightforward but time-consuming way of obtaining this result is to change the probability that Positronics' cost is $200,000 to 1.0 and then use the Rollback command.) The calculation of the value of perfect control is similar to the calculation of the value of information.

Value of Perfect Control   = Value with Perfect Control
                               − Value Without Perfect Control
                             = $195,000 − $65,000
                             = $130,000   (3–6)

How can we interpret the value of perfect control? The probabilities for cost were obtained under the assumption that Positronics would use its normal cost control procedures. Control might, therefore, correspond to the alternative of instituting some extraordinary cost control procedures to make sure costs stay as low as possible. The value of perfect control gives an upper limit on the amount Positronics should be willing to spend on such cost control procedures.

Summary

Given our understanding of uncertainties and their different possible outcomes, it is possible to define a good decision as one that is logically consistent with the information, alternatives, and values brought to the decision.

We introduced a decision on the bid level into the Positronics example and showed the probability distributions on profits for each bid level. It is clear that whatever bid level is chosen, there is some possibility of a bad outcome; and yet it would seem wrong to characterize a bid of $500,000 or $700,000 as a bad decision. The problem is choosing the better of the two levels.

We then discussed criteria for making a decision, including the value of nonmonetary, intangible goods; the value of future money; and the trade-off between certainty and uncertainty. (The trade-off between certainty and uncertainty is discussed at greater length in Chapter 5.)

By defining these valuations and trade-offs, we were able to calculate the preferred decision for the Positronics decision tree and to examine the sensitivity of the value of the preferred decision to changes in the probability assessment.

The analysis was expanded by the introduction of the value of perfect information and of perfect control. As illustrated by the modified trees used to calculate these values, information or control only has a value when it changes the preferred decision from what it otherwise would have been.

For Positronics, a small information gathering exercise on cost appeared justified. Much more valuable would be a cost control program.

Problems and Discussion Topics

3.1 It is very common for people to judge the quality of a decision by looking at its outcomes. Is this an unbiased point of view? How can you best deal with uncertainty to make a decision?

3.2 A good decision is defined as one that is logically consistent with the information, alternatives, and values brought to the decision. Give an example from your own experience (or perhaps from history) of a good decision/bad outcome and bad decision/good outcome. How could the bad decision have been improved? Remember that a good decision only has to be consistent with the information available at the time of the decision, though value of information should reveal the importance of the things you do not know.

Possible examples from history are: good decision/bad outcome—sailing on the Titanic (Who would have thought that the safest ship afloat would sink on its maiden voyage?); bad decision/good outcome—assigning Michelangelo to paint the Sistine Chapel (Who would have thought that a sculptor could paint on such a vast scale?).

3.3 Describe the information, alternatives, values, and logic you used in deciding where to eat dinner the last time you went out. Afterwards, were you satisfied with the decision? Was the outcome good or bad?

3.4 How is getting the expected value different for decision trees than for probability trees?

3.5 Net present value (NPV) and expected value are abstract concepts in that people usually will not get the NPV of a cash flow (unless they are buying or selling an annuity) or the expected value of a lottery. NPV is usually understood as the result of a trade-off between future value and present value; expected value is regarded as a way to deal with or evaluate an uncertainty that is unresolved.

Write a short definition of each term. How are these concepts implemented in decision tree calculations?

3.6 List two radically different alternatives to getting your homework done (other than doing it yourself). Are these alternatives worth pursuing further? Why or why not? (Relate them to your values, the probability of getting caught, and the consequences of getting caught; to the effect when you take the midterm exam; etc.)

3.7 Today, liability for damages is usually settled with a cash sum, whereas in the past, the rule was often blood for blood. (Consider Oedipus, for instance.) One rationale is not that the victim is being bought off (i.e., that money is equivalent to his or her pain), but rather that given that the incident has already occurred, the victim can use the money for some purpose whose value to him or her can help compensate for any losses. In addition, there are sometimes punitive damages to punish the malefactor.

Do you agree with this concept of trading money for pain and suffering? Do you find it more, less, or just as moral as the earlier method of compensation? Another alternative is no compensation. Suppose you are a victim. Do these two types of compensation mean anything different for you? Why or why not?

3.8 Anyone lending money at interest is establishing a marketplace between present and future money. The relationship between present and future is described by the interest rate. The marketplace works because some people have capital that would otherwise be unproductive if they did not lend it to people with a better use for it. List at least three reasons why people (or companies) might have different time values of money (discount rates).

3.9 As with discount rates, people can have different attitudes to trading off certainty and uncertainty. List at least three reasons why people might have different attitudes toward risk. For instance, some people have dependents and some don't. Why might a person's risk attitude change over time? Can education play a role in this?

3.10 List some of the principal values that must be considered in making decisions in a profit-making, publicly held hospital. Suggest the structure of a value model that establishes trade-offs between the values (at a deterministic level). State the limitations of the model. Are there ethical questions that cannot be simply resolved?

3.11 Explain how (if at all) the purpose of an influence diagram is different from that of a decision tree. Would it ever make sense to draw a tree and *then* the influence diagram? If so, when?

3.12 Can an equivalent decision tree *always* be drawn from an influence diagram and vice versa, or are there structural and/or informational differences that would make it impossible to do so without changing the problem or adding information? If there are differences, illustrate them with examples.

3.13 There are two main reasons for doing probabilistic sensitivity analysis in a decision-making process. First, probability assignments could change because of new information or could be different if there is more than one decision-maker. In each case, we need to know how the decision will change given changes in probabilities (information).

Second, probability sensitivity can distinguish the major uncertainties that are most influential to the decision from those that are less influential. This may increase understanding of the decision, provide directions for further information-gathering activity, etc.

Interpret Figure 3–15, the probabilistic sensitivity plot. If there are crossover points between alternatives, how do you interpret the corresponding crossover probabilities?

3.14 Draw an influence diagram that corresponds to the tree in Figure 3–17. (Hint: Introduce a deterministic node called Information Learned About Anode Bid.)

3.15 Suppose you are going skiing this weekend for the first time. However, you are worried about the possibility of breaking your leg during your first time out. Your alternative is to go to the beach. After thinking about the possibilities, you have decided that you value a weekend of skiing with no mishaps at $1,000 and that you value a broken leg at –$5,000. Going to the beach instead is worth $500 to you. Finally, after talking to other people, you peg the chance of breaking your leg at 1 in 100.

a. Draw the influence diagram for this problem.

b. Structure the decision tree for this problem. What is the preferred decision and expected value?

c. Calculate the values of information and control on breaking your leg. To do this, you will have to symmetrize the tree so that the uncertainty on breaking your leg follows both the ski and beach alternatives. (Supertree does this automatically.)

d. What impact might the values of uncertainty and control have on your choice of weekend?

e. For what probabilities of breaking your leg do you prefer going to the beach?

3.16 You are considering four different restaurants for dinner with a group of friends tonight. However, before deciding whether or not to eat at a restaurant, you'll want to look at the menu and see what they have. At that point, you can either stay and eat or move on to the next restaurant. You value the cost of gathering everybody up and driving to the next restaurant at $20.

When you look at a menu, you have a scale in mind for rating it. You'll assign a score of A, B, or C and value the scores for their contributions to the evening's enjoyment as follows.

Score	Value
A	$100
B	$50
C	$0

You judge your four possible choices as equally likely to get any of the three scores.

a. Draw the influence diagram and decision tree for this problem.

b. What is the best strategy for picking a restaurant, and what is the overall expected value?

c. Suppose you can buy a restaurant guide for $20 that will alert you to any C restaurants. Modify your influence diagram and tree to reflect this choice. Should you buy it?

3.17 Raquel Ratchet is working on a Volkswagen Beetle to be sold at a collectors' car sale on Saturday. If she finishes it in time, she'll be able to sell it for $1,000, at a cost of $100 in parts. (She got the car from a junkyard.) She thinks there's a 60 percent chance of being able to do this.

She also has the option of installing a turbocharger and intercooler in the car, which would quadruple the horsepower and enable her to sell it for $10,000. This would cost an additional $1,000 in parts. She thinks there's only a 20 percent chance of being able to finish this amount of work by Saturday. If she misses the collectors' sale on Saturday, Raquel figures she can only sell the car for $400 ($1,400 with turbocharger and intercooler).

Suddenly, the Wizard appears in the form of a good salesman and tells her that he can increase the selling price to $20,000 if she installs the turbocharger and intercooler. What is the maximum Raquel should be willing to pay the Wizard to do this? What is the maximum amount she should be willing to pay him on a contingency basis (if he makes the sale)?

a. Draw the influence diagram and tree for this problem.

b. How much should Raquel pay in advance (nonrefundable) if there's only a .8 probability of his making the sale?

3.18 Samuel Steelskull is thinking about whether or not to wear a helmet while commuting to work on his bicycle. He figures his chances of dying in an accident during the coming year without the helmet are about 1/3,000. The odds of dying go down to 1/5,000 with the helmet.

Sam figures it is worth about $80 to him for his hair not to be messed up when he gets to work during the coming year, and he is pretty much indifferent between wearing and not wearing the helmet.

a. Draw the influence diagram and tree for this problem.

b. What's the implicit value Sam is putting on his life (i.e., a value that might be used in very small probability situations)?

3.19 Your company has recently developed Chewsy, a new sugar-free gum that contains fluoride. Not only does it taste good, it's also good for your teeth. You are faced with the decision of whether or not to introduce Chewsy to the market.

The total sales of chewing gum are expected to be about $200 million over the next 10 years.

Your marketing personnel feel that with their best efforts and with a front-end marketing expenditure of $4 million, your company could capture from 2 percent to 10 percent of the chewing gum market with Chewsy. They have given you the following probabilities.

Market Share	Probabilities
High (10%)	.30
Medium (6%)	.50
Low (2%)	.20

Your financial advisors point out that the profit margin on Chewsy is quite uncertain because of unusual manufacturing requirements. They say that there is a 40 percent chance that the profit margin will be only 25 percent of sales revenue and a 60 percent chance it will be 50 percent of sales revenue. The manufacturing requirements will be known before the marketing decision needs to be made.

a. Draw the influence diagram for this problem.

b. Structure the decision tree for Chewsy. What is the preferred decision and expected value?

c. Plot the probability distribution for profit for the Chewsy decision. What are the expected values for both alternatives?

d. What is the value of information on market share? On profit margin? On both?

e. What is the value of control on market share? On profit margin? On both? Are there any possible ways of achieving further control over either of these uncertainties?

f. Does the preferred decision vary with the probabilities for market share or margin? What decisions are preferred for what ranges of probability?

3.20 The Southern Power Company is planning to submit a major rate increase request to the state Public Utilities Commission. The Commission has assured Southern Power that it would approve a request for a moderate rate increase. With this moderate rate increase, Southern would receive $40 million in additional revenues during the next few years (relative to no rate increase).

However, the company is also considering a riskier course of action—requesting a high rate increase that would yield $100 million in additional revenues, if approved. If the high rate increase is not approved, there is still some chance the Commission would grant Southern a low rate increase, which would mean $30 million in additional revenues. Of course, the possibility exists that the Commission would simply refuse any rate increase whatsoever if Southern asks for the high increase.

The best information within the company indicates a 70 percent probability the Commission would disapprove the high rate increase request. Given that it does so, the chance it would then grant a low rate increase is believed to be 60 percent.

a. Draw the influence diagram for Southern's problem.

b. Draw the decision tree for Southern's decision problem.

c. Find the expected value of each alternative.

d. Draw the probability distribution on profit for each alternative.

e. Calculate the value of perfect information on:

- Whether or not the Commission approves the high rate increase

- Whether or not the Commission would grant a low rate increase given that it does not approve the high rate increase

- Both of the above.

3.21 Your company markets an all-purpose household glue called Easystick. Currently, a sister company in another country supplies the product at a guaranteed delivered cost of $2.00 per unit. You are now thinking about producing Easystick locally rather than continuing to import it. A staff study indicates that with a projected sales volume of 4 million units over the product's life, local production would cost an average of $1.50 per unit.

However, two things could significantly affect this cost. First, the government in your country is considering imposing a heavy tax on the primary raw material of Easystick. This would increase the average production cost of Easystick to $2.25 per unit. You think there is a 50/50 chance the government will impose the tax.

The second factor is a newly developed improvement in the production process that uses the expensive raw material more efficiently. This new process would reduce the average production cost of Easystick as shown below.

Average Cost Per Unit

	Old Process	New Process
No tax on raw material	$1.50	$1.25
Tax on raw material	$2.25	$1.75

Unfortunately, local conditions may make it impossible to implement the new process. Your staff estimates a 60 percent chance of being able to use the new process.

Should you continue to import or switch to local production?

a. Draw the influence diagram for this problem.

b. Draw the decision tree for this problem and calculate the expected value for each option. (For the outcome measure, use the total savings in cost relative to importing Easystick.)

c. Draw the probability distribution on profit for each option.

d. Calculate the values of perfect information and control on:

   • Whether or not the tax will be imposed on the raw material

   • Whether or not the new production process can be used

   • Both of the above.

e. Do a probability sensitivity analysis to determine the preferred decision for different ranges of probabilities.

3.22 It is 1986 and Shipbuilder, Inc., has decided to take a long, hard look at its telephone needs. Its present system has one major problem: it is very costly to make moves or changes. A task force has identified the most attractive alternative: Fone-Equip can install a system that will enable moves and changes to be made at almost no cost.

The five-year lease on the current system is up for renewal for the period 1987–1991. Another renewal of the lease would be made in 1991 for the period 1992–1996. Fone-Equip's system is available only for outright purchase. Under any alternative, Shipbuilder will be in the same position in 1996 (a completely new phone system will be needed), so costs beyond 1996 can be neglected.

Shipbuilder is planning a shipbuilding program called Program A, which will entail considerable phone moves and changes in the years 1987–1991. Under the present system, these changes would cost $2 million per year. However, if Program A does not materialize, there will be very little in the way of phone moves and changes in this period.

Similarly, Program B would entail $4 million per year in costs for phone moves and changes in the years 1992–1996. However, if Program B does not materialize, there will be very few moves and changes in this period.

All costs were estimated in 1986 dollars, with the effects of inflation removed. The costs for the present system are $1.5 million per year lease and $0.5 million per year recurring costs. Fone-Equip's system has a purchase price of $14 million (including installation) and $1.0 million per year recurring cost.

Shipbuilder judged that Program A has a 50 percent chance of occurring. The 1986 telephone decision will be made before Program A's fate is known.

Program B is judged to have a 60 percent chance of occurring if Program A does occur, but only a 30 percent chance of occurring if Program A does not occur. If there is a telephone decision to be made in 1991, it will be made before Program B's fate is known.

There is also a 20 percent uncertainty on what Fone-Equip's system would cost in 1991.

The decision-maker insisted on using a discount rate of 10 percent. At this rate, the net present value in 1986 is:

- $1 expense in 1987—$0.91
- $1 expense in 1992—$0.56
- $1 expense per year for 1987–1991—$3.79
- $1 expense per year for 1992–1996—$2.12.

a. Draw the influence diagram and decision tree for this problem.

b. What is Shipbuilder's best strategy? Show the probability distribution on costs for the alternatives.

c. What is the value of delaying the 1986 decision until Project A's fate is known?

d. What is the value of delaying the 1991 decision until Project B's fate is known?

e. Suppose Shipbuilder could obtain perfect information on Project A and Project B before the 1986 decision is made. What would this information be worth?

f. Show how the expected values associated with the 1986 decision vary with the probability of Project A occurring.

3.23 The pharmaceutical division of Dreamland Products has been the world leader in the area of soporific drugs. Its major product, Dozealot, is approaching the end of its patent life, and already sales have fallen significantly from the peak because of the inroads of new and superior competitive products. However, Dozealot sales are still quite significant and are considered to be of strategic importance for maintaining the sales of the entire product line of soporific drugs. Therefore, the research and development (R&D) department has defined two alternative approaches to improve the product quality and, thus, future sales prospects.

One approach, which is quite conventional, is simply to reformulate the product to minimize an undesirable side effect that exists in the current galenical form. The manager in charge of galenical development has created a number of new formulations since the original introduction of Dozealot that have the desired characteristic, but even such a simple change in the formulation will require a development expenditure of 500,000 Swiss francs. By estimating the increase in sales of both Dozealot and the rest of the soporific product range, the product manager for soporific drugs has estimated the value of this improvement. Taking into account the production cost of the new formulation and the minor investments required, the improvement in Dreamland's cash flow would be substantial and yield a net present value (NPV) of 2.5 million Swiss francs (not including the cost of development).

The second approach, which is riskier but potentially more rewarding, involves a new controlled-release technology based on differential microencapsulation. This approach, if successful, would not only eliminate the undesired side effects but would also substantially improve the product efficacy. Market forecasts and cash-flow analyses indicate that this product, B, would be four times as profitable to produce and market as the more conventional product A, described above. The drawbacks, however, are that the microencapsulation development project would cost 3 million Swiss francs and still might fail because of an inability to control the differential layering process within tolerances specified by Good Manufacturing Practice. After a recent review of the microencapsulation process development efforts, the R&D director concluded that there is 1 chance in 2 of being technically successful within the deadlines imposed by the patent life of Dozealot.

a. Draw the influence diagram and decision tree for Dreamland Products considering it could separately pursue the development of A or B or even pursue both to reduce the risks involved in B. In the latter case, it would naturally market B and not A if B were a technical success.

b. Compute the expected value of each alternative, assuming B has 1 chance in 2 of being successfully developed. Based on the criterion of expected value, what should Dreamland do?

Since the probability of successfully developing product B is difficult to determine, Dreamland's managing director would like to know how sensitive the best decision is to this probability assignment.

c. Compute the expected NPV of developing B alone and of developing A and B simultaneously as a function of p_B, the probability of technical success of B.

d. Graphically represent the expected value of the three alternatives as a function of p_B and determine for what range of values of p_B each alternative is best.

Resolving the technical uncertainties surrounding the microencapsulation project early could be achieved by immediately conducting a few critical experiments at an additional cost of 1 million Swiss francs.

e. Compute the expected value of perfect information on whether microencapsulation could be successfully accomplished, assuming an initial probability of success of .5.

f. Compute and graphically represent the expected value of the entire project given perfect information about whether or not microencapsulation would be feasible as a function of the initial probability of success p_B. Graphically show the expected value of perfect information and determine over what range of initial probability of success p_B this value exceeds 1 million Swiss francs.

3.24 The internal rate of return (IRR) of a venture is the value that, if substituted for the discount rate, makes the net present value (NPV) zero. There are several difficulties in using IRR as the sole criterion in choosing between alternatives.

Consider the following two ventures:

A: Invest I in year 0, receive positive cash flow, C, in all years from year 1 to infinity

B: Invest I in year 0, receive positive cash flow, K, in year 1, nothing in succeeding years.

a. Solve for $c = C/I$ and $k = K/I$ in terms of $n = NPV/I$ and d, the discount rate. Use the sum

$$\sum_{i=1}^{\infty} \frac{1}{(1+d)^i} = \frac{1}{d}$$

b. Assume that both ventures have the same investment and the same NPV. Plot the IRR value against n for the two ventures. (Take the discount rate d to be .1.)

c. For equal n (equal value to the decision-maker), how do the IRR values of long-term and short-term investments (A and B) differ? Is IRR an adequate decision criterion? What assumptions do you have to make concerning use of funds after year 1 for investment B?

3.25 A venture with an NPV of zero is acceptable to the decision-maker. Why is this true? What problems in interpretation does this cause for the decision-maker unfamiliar with the concept? What steps would alleviate these problems?

3.26 If financing is available at an interest rate equal to the decision-maker's discount rate, a venture with a positive NPV can be transformed into a venture with an infinite IRR.

a. How can this be done?

b. Does a similar situation exist for leasing alternatives?

c. For existing businesses, one alternative usually involves no major new investments. What is the IRR for this strategy? Compare the type of results you might expect for NPV and for IRR for "Invest" and "No New Investment" strategies. In what situations might you prefer NPV or IRR as a decision criterion?

4

Probabilistic Dependence

Dependence and Independence

The probabilities in the preceding chapters were simpler than those one finds in most real decision problems. There was no probabilistic dependence; it made no difference to the the person providing the probabilities at one node if he or she learned what happened at another node. Real decision problems usually start with a set of variables for which the probabilities are very interdependent. One of the subtler skills in influence diagram and decision tree construction is finding a set of variables for the nodes that have independent probabilities and that are natural and meaningful. But it is not often that this can be done for all the variables in the problem.

Usually the analyst faces a situation described by variables that are far from independent. How are uncertainties related? How will resolving uncertainty on one variable affect the uncertainty in another area? Questions like these frequently lie just below the surface of many deliberations, but they can be extremely difficult to enunciate. One of the advantages of influence diagrams and decision trees is that they provide a language that makes dialog in this area possible and relatively easy.

This chapter deals with three related topics. First, the Positronics case is used to demonstrate why and how dependent probabilities are used in real decision problems. Second, dependent probabilities are used to combine new information with prior information. The process for doing this is called Bayes' Rule. Third, Bayes' Rule and decision trees are used to show how to calculate the value of imperfect information.

Dependent Probabilities _____

Obtaining the Data

Dependent probabilities are often important, particularly when information from different people needs to be combined. This is illustrated in the Positronics example.

After a presentation on the MegaCorp bid, the Positronics production manager came to the decision analyst. After seeing the presentation and learning more about how the probabilities were used, he had reconsidered the probabilities that he had provided for Positronics' costs. If he knew what Anode's bid was, he would assign different probabilities to Positronics' costs. He had great respect for the production staff at Anode and had heard it had much more experience than Positronics in making instruments of the type being bid on. Thus, Anode should have higher quality information and much less uncertainty about costs than Positronics. Positronics should have the same costs as Anode, except that Anode's experience would give it a small cost advantage. The analyst tentatively drew an arrow from the Anode Bid node to the Positronics Cost node to show this influence (Figure 4–1a). Using this diagram, the production manager would provide the probabilities for the distribution tree and the marketing department would give the probabilities for Anode Bid.

After some thought, however, the analyst realized they had it backwards. It was the probabilities for Anode's bid that should be reassessed. The original assessment on Anode's bid was done without any real input on Anode's cost and would be a meaningless starting point for an assessment of anyone's cost. However, the production manager had added two crucial pieces of knowledge: Anode will know its costs accurately when it makes its bid, and Anode and Positronics both have approximately the same costs because they use the same process. Thus, given a particular level of cost, the real uncertainty is how much over cost Anode would bid. The people who would best know how much Anode wanted the business and how much of a margin it would figure in were in marketing. Accordingly, the arrow was reversed, and the probabilities in Figure 4–1b for Anode's bid were obtained from the marketing department.

A discussion such as this would be very difficult without the language of influence diagrams and probability trees. Most people untrained in probability theory or decision analysis find it difficult to communicate information concerning uncertainty; interdependence among uncertain factors is almost impossible to talk about. The graphical structures of influence diagrams and trees give a visual, simple, and systematic way of discussing structure and data in this area.

Entering the Data

When we have chosen the order of nodes and assessed a set of dependent probabilities, we will have a set of probabilities that depends on (is influenced by) the branch or outcome of another node. The latter node is called the "conditioning" or "influencing" node and is the one at the base of the arrow in the influence diagram.

It is easy to input these dependent probabilities in Supertree. First, clear the tree by using the `Clear` option of the `Structure` menu. (Supertree could deal with the nodes in the order we originally entered them, but for the beginner, it is less confusing to reenter the tree in the order shown in Figure 4–2.)

Figure 4–1

Structuring the Problem and Identifying Data Requirements

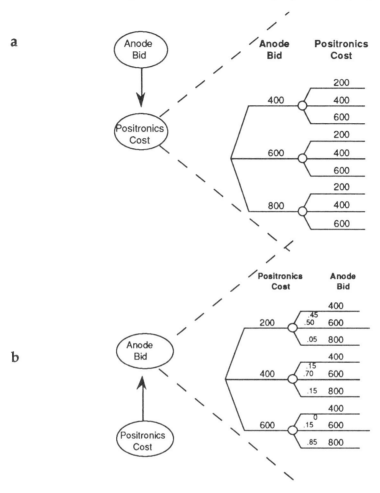

Use Input to enter BID as node 1, COST as node 2, and ANODEBID as node 3. Make the probabilities for ANODEBID depend on COST, node 2.

Select the area where the screen for node 3 says SELECT TO ENTER/REVIEW PROBABILITIES and press Return to produce the screen in Figure 4–3.

The conditioning node or nodes are shown on the left of the screen. The current conditioning outcome or combination of outcomes is highlighted and preceded by an arrow (>). We can advance through the combinations with the Tab key and go back with Shift Tab. Use the Return or cursor (arrow) keys to enter a set of probabilities for each outcome or outcome combination.

When through, press F1 to return to the main node screen, and then press F1 again to save the changes.

—————————————————————— **Figure 4–2** ——————————————————————

Supertree Node Input

NODE NUMBER:1

TYPE:DECISION   OUTCOMES DEPEND ON NODES:
NUMBER OF BRANCHES:4
NODE NAME:BID

```
                                                    SUCCESSOR
           OUTCOME           REWARD                 NODE

       __300_____0_____2__
        |
        |__500_____0_____2__
       D
        |__700_____0_____2__
        |
        |__NoBid_____0_____5__
```

NODE NUMBER:2

TYPE:CHANCE   OUTCOMES DEPEND ON NODES:
NUMBER OF BRANCHES:3   PROBABILITIES DEPEND ON NODES:
NODE NAME:COST

```
                                                    SUCCESSOR
       PROBABILITY    OUTCOME        REWARD         NODE

     __.25_____200_____0_____3_
       |
     C__.50_____400_____0_____3_
       |
     |__.25_____600_____0_____3_
```

NODE NUMBER:3

TYPE:CHANCE   OUTCOMES DEPEND ON NODES:
NUMBER OF BRANCHES:3   PROBABILITIES DEPEND ON NODES:2
NODE NAME:ANODEBID
```
           SELECT TO                                SUCCESSOR
           ENTER/REVIEW   OUTCOME        REWARD     NODE
           PROBABILITIES
       _____400_____0_____4_
         |
       C_____600_____0_____4_
         |
       |_____800_____0_____4_
```

──────────────────── **Figure 4–3** ────────────────────

Screen Displays for Probabilities Dependent on Costs of
200, 400, and 600

```
    COST              PROBABILITY FOR ANODEBID

   >200               _.45_____
    400               |
    600               C_.50_____
                      |
                      |_.05_____


    COST              PROBABILITY FOR ANODEBID

    200               _.15_____
   >400               |
    600               C_.70_____
                      |
                      |_.15_____




    COST              PROBABILITY FOR ANODEBID

    200               _0_____
    400               |
   >600               C_.15_____
                      |
                      |_.85_____
```

Use the Show option of the Structure menu to see the dependent probabilities exhibited in tree form (Figure 4–4).

Since we have reentered the tree, we need to Evaluate it again before analyzing it. (This would not be necessary if we had only changed the probabilities.) After evaluating, go to the Plot option of the Analyze menu and plot the cumulative distribution (figures 4–5 and 4–6). Comparing this with the previous cumulative plot (Figure 3–10), we see that the risk has been intensified: there is a larger probability of losing money if Positronics wins the bid. This makes sense, because the dependent probabilities tell us that if Anode bids high, Positronics wins the bid but its costs are likely to be high.

This effect would have been missed if the probabilistic dependency were missed. A common pitfall for the novice decision analyst is missing the interdependence between uncertainties. These interdependencies can often dramatically increase or decrease the uncertainty in the value measure. The use of influence diagrams helps avoid this problem; arrows indicate probabilistic dependence, and most people deal naturally and easily with these arrows.

Figure 4–4

Display of Supertree Data with Dependent Probabilities

Tree name: Bidding Tree

STRUCTURE	NAMES	OUTCOMES	PROBABILITIES
1 D 2 2 2 5	BID	300 500 700 NoBid	
2 C 3 3 3	COST	200 400 600	.25 .50 .25
3 C 4 4 4	ANODEBID	400 600 800	Depends on 2
4 E	B$(BID-COST)*(BID<&	Depends on 1 2 3	
	ANODEBID)		
5 E	0		

COST	PROBABILITY, NODE 3
_200_	0.45 0.5 0.05
C_400_	0.15 0.7 0.15
|_600_	0 0.15 0.85

The distributions for the two cases (independent and dependent probabilities, Figures 3–10 and 4–6) can be plotted on the same graph by using the Storedist and Recalldist options of the Utilities menu. Storedist is used to store on disk the distributions associated with any particular tree, either for use with external programs or for use with the Recalldist option. The Recalldist option can be used to plot stored distributions on the same graph.

Dependent Outcomes

Obtaining the Data

The next morning, the marketing people returned to the decision analyst and said they were really uncomfortable with the probabilities they had supplied the previous day (the dependent bid probabilities shown in Figure 4–1). After thinking about them, they wanted to be able to systematically change the outcomes rather than the probabilities. They presented the decision analyst with the distribution tree shown in Figure 4–7.

Dependent outcomes are another way of representing dependencies among uncertainties. In this case, it is not the probability of an outcome that changes, but the outcome itself.

Having dependent outcomes is another way of representing probabilistic dependence for continuous variables. In our discrete approximation, we chose ranges and then assigned probabilities to those ranges. Probabilistic dependence means that the probabilities assigned to these ranges change depending on which branch of the conditioning node we are on. Alternatively, we can readjust the ranges (as we move from branch to branch of the conditioning node) to keep the probabilities the same.

—————————————— **Figure 4–5** ——————————————

Screen Input for Plotting Cumulative Probability Distribution

```
Present Order of Nodes:
  1 2 3
New Order of Nodes:
  1 2 3
Node at which to plot the probability distribution or distributions? 1
Cumulative or histogram plot? CUMULATIVE
Single or multiple distributions? MULTIPLE
Label for axis? Profit ($000)
Smallest and largest values in distributions are: -100.0 300.0
Enter lower and upper limits for display: -400 600


>> Distribution Plotted    6/1/90  12:00   BIDDING TREE
```

—————————————— **Figure 4–6** ——————————————

Probability Distribution on Profits Given Dependent Probabilities

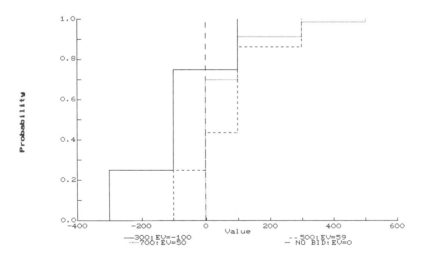

In our experience, using dependent outcomes is frequently a sign of systematic considerations in the thought process of the person supplying the data. To promote clarity of thought and communication, we can use the deterministic value model (rather than probabilistic dependence) to capture this systematic consideration in a deterministic way. For instance, dependent outcomes might result from a thought process like "Shift the value up by X in that case and then put a 10 percent uncertainty in either direction." Remembering our divide and conquer technique, we can improve the accuracy of the assessment by separating these two effects and assessing them individually.

Figure 4–7

Structuring the Problem on the Basis of Dependent Outcomes

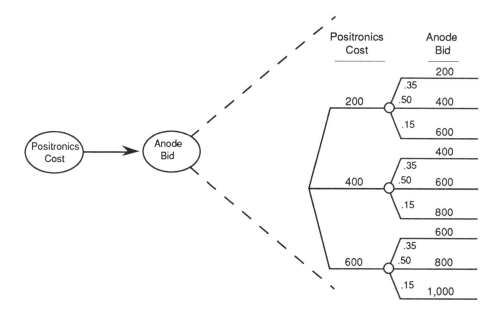

Entering the Data

Entering dependent outcomes in Supertree is easy. Supertree even allows dependent outcomes and dependent probabilities for a node (though it would take an unusual problem to need them both). Using the Input option for node 3 (Input is used to change nodes as well as add them), enter a blank for Probabilities depend on nodes and a 2 for Outcomes depend on nodes; then reenter the probabilities.

To enter dependent outcomes, select SELECT TO ENTER/REVIEW OUTCOMES and press Return. Then enter the dependent outcomes, as shown in the sequence of screens in Figure 4–8.

The Show option lets us review the current information in the tree (Figure 4–9).

We could then try the Plot option of the Analyze menu. However, if we did try, Supertree would inform us that we have made changes that require running the Evaluate command again. We have the option of using the old data, which might be desirable if we had made a change and then decided to change back to the original data. Supertree would have no way of knowing that there had been no net change.

─────────────────────────────── **Figure 4–8** ───────────────────────────────

Entering Dependent Outcomes in Supertree

NODE NUMBER:3

TYPE:CHANCE	OUTCOMES DEPEND ON NODES:2
NUMBER OF BRANCHES:3	PROBABILITIES DEPEND ON NODES:
NODE NAME:ANODEBID	

	PROBABILITY	SELECT TO ENTER/REVIEW OUTCOMES	REWARD	SUCCESSOR NODE
	__.35_____		0_____	4_
	|			
	C__.50_____		0_____	4_
	|			
	|__.15_____		0_____	4_

COST	OUTCOME FOR ANODEBID
>200	_200_____
400	|
600	C_400_____
	|
	|_600_____

COST	OUTCOME FOR ANODEBID
200	_400_____
>400	|
600	C_600_____
	|
	|_800_____

COST	OUTCOME FOR ANODEBID
200	_600_____
400	|
>600	C_800_____
	|
	|_1000_____

In this case, we want to use the Evaluate option and then Plot the distribution (Figure 4–11).

We see now that the risk has intensified (as indicated by the higher probabilities of low and high outcomes), and the even larger probabilities of losing money lead to an expected value of only 38.8. To better understand why this change has occurred, Display the tree (Figure 4–12). The preferred alternative has shifted from a bid of $500,000 to one of $700,000. The $500,000 option has an expected value that has dropped to 18.8

—————————————————————— **Figure 4–9** ——————————————————————

Supertree Data with Dependent Outcomes

Tree name: Bidding Tree

STRUCTURE	NAMES	OUTCOMES	PROBABILITIES
1 D 2 2 2 5	BID	300 500 700 NoBid	
2 C 3 3 3	COST	200 400 600	.25 .50 .25
3 C 4 4 4	ANODEBID	Depends on 2	.35 .50 .15
4 E	B$(BID-COST)*(BID<& ANODEBID)	Depends on 1 2 3	
5 E	0		

```
  COST   OUTCOME, NODE 3
 _200_   200 400 600
C_400_   400 600 800
|_600_   600 800 1000
```

—————————————————————— **Figure 4–10** ——————————————————————

Supertree Warning Message About Old Values

>>Input changes have occurred since the last evaluation of the endpoints of
   the tree. The old values (if there are any) may not be consistent with the
   present structure.
Do you wish to attempt to use the old values? NO

Nature's Tree _____

Dependent probabilities are important in dealing with a problem we address informally in our daily lives: How do we incorporate new information into our current
information base?

Indicators and States of Nature

In the section "Dependent Probabilities" (page 76), we stressed the importance of
drawing the influencing arrow correctly when encoding dependent probabilities.
There is one type of situation in particular where correct ordering is imperative and
where people frequently make mistakes, both in daily life and in decision analysis:
when people describe the relationship between an imperfect indicator and the state
of nature (e.g., the relationship between medical symptoms and the actual state of
health). To establish this relationship correctly, we follow a two-step process. First, we
track the indicator to see how accurate its predictions are. Second, these results are
incorporated into a tree, which is used to predict the state of nature, given an indicator
result.

——————————————— **Figure 4–11** ———————————————

Probability Distribution on Profits Given Dependent Outcomes

```
Present Order of Nodes:
  1 2 3
New Order of Nodes:
  1 2 3
Node at which to plot the probability distribution or distributions? 1
Cumulative or histogram plot? CUMULATIVE
Single or multiple distributions? MULTIPLE
Label for axis? Profit ($000)
Smallest and largest values in distributions are: -300.0 300.0
Enter lower and upper limits for display: -400 600


>> Distribution Plotted     6/1/90  12:00  BIDDING TREE
```

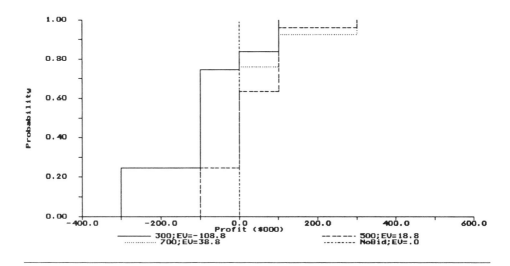

The following are examples of state of nature/indicator pairs that occur in business situations.

State of Nature	*Indicator*
Market size	Market survey
Number of future competitors	Articles in business journals
Amount of recoverable oil	Seismic study
Economic climate	Leading indicators
Production costs	Prototype costs
Drug safety and efficacy	Clinical trials
Software stability	Beta tests

_____ **Figure 4–12** _____

Decision Tree Given Dependent Outcomes

Present Order of Nodes:
  1 2 3
New Order of Nodes:
  1 2 3

First Node: 1
Last Node: 3

Single or double spacing? SINGLE

```
    BID     EXP VAL   PROBS COST  EXP VAL   PROBS ANODEBID  EXP VAL


                                            _0.350_200_____.0
                      _0.250_200_____65.0_C_0.500_400_____100.0
                      |                    |_0.150_600_____100.0
                      |                    _0.350_400_____-100.0
    _300_____-108.8_C_0.500_400_____-100.0_C_0.500_600_____-100.0
    |                 |                    |_0.150_800_____-100.0
    |                 |                    _0.350_600_____-300.0
    |                 |_0.250_600_____-300.0_C_0.500_800_____-300.0
    |                 |                    |_0.150_1000_____-300.0
    |                 |                    _0.350_200_____.0
    |                 _0.250_200_____45.0_C_0.500_400_____.0
    |                 |                    |_0.150_600_____300.0
    |                 |                    _0.350_400_____.0
    |_500_____18.8_C_0.500_400_____65.0_C_0.500_600_____100.0
    |                 |                    |_0.150_800_____100.0
    |                 |                    _0.350_600_____-100.0
    D                 |_0.250_600_____-100.0_C_0.500_800_____-100.0
    |                 |                    |_0.150_1000_____-100.0
    |                 |                    _0.350_200_____.0
    |                 _0.250_200_____.0_C_0.500_400_____.0
    |                 |                    |_0.150_600_____.0
    |                 |                    _0.350_400_____.0
    |>700_____38.8_C_0.500_400_____45.0_C_0.500_600_____.0
    |                 |                    |_0.150_800_____300.0
    |                 |                    _0.350_600_____.0
    |                 |_0.250_600_____65.0_C_0.500_800_____100.0
    |                 |                    |_0.150_1000_____100.0
    |_NoBid_____.0_____
```

>> Tree Drawn   6/1/90   12:00   Bidding Tree
>> Expected Value: 38.8

An Example from Medicine

Let us use a simple medical example. Through either experience or a controlled test, we track the number of people with and without measles who have spots on their face. Using this and other data, we can find the probability that someone who has spots on his or her face has measles. Unfortunately, people make mistakes all too often when they try to go through this process. The problem is that they do not correctly combine their prior information with the indicator data. For instance, assume that most people with measles have spots on their face and that few people without measles have spots on their face. If you know (prior or general information) that there is a measles epidemic, spots on a person's face would lead you to put a high probability on measles. If, on the other hand, there has not been a case of measles in the city for months, spots on a person's face would lead you to put a much lower probability on measles.

How do we correctly mix our prior or general information with the data (indicator results and track record of the indicator)? The rule for performing this process correctly is to first construct Nature's tree. In the influence diagram corresponding to Nature's tree, the indicator result node is influenced by the state-of-nature node. The data then supply the probabilities for the indicator results, given the state of nature. We have to supply our subjective (prior, general information) probabilities for the state-of-nature node.

Suppose a doctor has tracked the correlation between the state of health and the indicator for her patients. Suppose she has come up with the Nature's tree in Figure 4–13. (The probabilities in this distribution tree are for illustration only.)

Now let us assume there has been a measles epidemic, and the doctor judges that the next patient who walks into her office has a 20 percent chance of having the measles (Figure 4–14).

In the probability tree (Figure 4–15), the column of joint probabilities (that is, the probability that both events will occur) has been calculated by multiplying the probabilities at each branching for a path through the tree. For instance, the topmost path (Measles, Spots on Face) has a probability of .19 (20 × .95).

Bayes' Rule

To find the probabilities in the order needed for most decision-making, we use Bayes' Rule to reverse the order of nodes, putting the indicator node first and the true state of nature second. Thus, we can read off the probability of the true state of nature given an indicator result.

To apply Bayes' Rule to trees, we first calculate the joint probabilities from Nature's tree. Second, we draw the tree with the nodes in reversed order and transcribe these probabilities to the ends of the appropriate paths in the reversed tree. Then we can find the probabilities for the node on the left by adding the probabilities of all paths passing through that branch. The probabilities for the branches of the node on the right are found by dividing the joint probability at the end of the branch by the probability for the branch of the node on the left. The process is fairly simple but tedious. Supertree performs Bayes' Rule revisions automatically.

Figure 4–13

Probabilities for Indicator

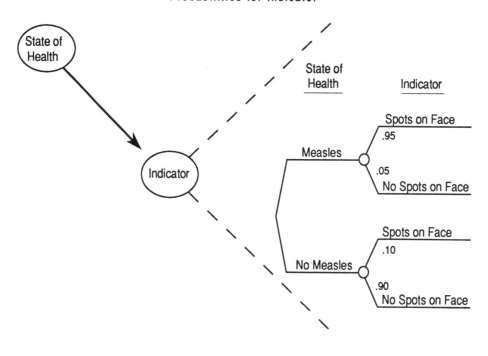

For the measles example, we can use this process to reverse Nature's tree (Figure 4–16). Thus, we see that if a patient with spots on his or her face walks into the doctor's office, there is a 19/27 = .70 chance the patient has measles. There is a 27 percent chance that the next patient who walks in will have spots on his or her face.

The probabilities in Nature's tree have traditional names (Figure 4–17). In Nature's tree, the probabilities of the state of nature are called the prior probabilities; the probabilities of the indicator (the second, influenced node) are called the likelihood function. The rule for reversing the order of nodes in the tree is called Bayes' Rule. Reversing the order of nodes in the tree is indicated in the influence diagram by reversing the arrow between the nodes. The probabilities of the second node of the reversed tree (the state of nature) are called the posterior probabilities; the probabilities of the first node in the reversed tree are called, believe it or not, the preposterior probabilities.

Why is Bayes' Rule so important? It gives the method for correctly adding data and new information to an existing subjective state of information (the prior). This information can then be used to construct the posterior distribution, which represents an updated state of information. People commonly make mistakes in using new information. Although it appears rather formal, Bayes' Rule is the best method for avoiding mistakes in judgments that often have great importance.

———————————— **Figure 4–14** ————————————

Probabilities for State of Nature

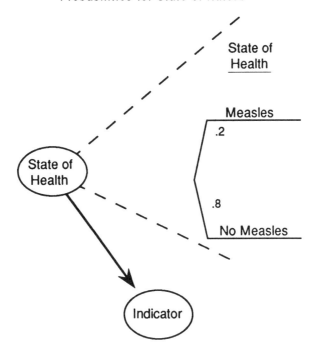

———————————— **Figure 4–15** ————————————

Probability Tree for Medical Example

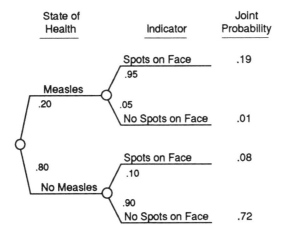

In summary, when dealing with indicators, first draw Nature's tree: the tree with the state of nature first and the indicator second. Then, enter the data into this tree. Only in this way will we be able to correctly separate our expectations about what the future will bring from how good the indicator is. The process of reversing the tree is important when we wish to find out how knowledge of an indicator result changes our expectations of what the future will bring. This procedure will become clearer in the next section, "The Value of Imperfect Information."

A Prototype As an Indicator

The production engineer suggested that Positronics could resolve some of the uncertainty on production costs by building a prototype instrument and carefully monitoring the cost of the steps that went into building it. The cost of the prototype would be an indicator for the state of nature, the actual costs. In Nature's tree for this procedure, the first node is the actual costs and their probabilities, as used earlier. The next node is the prototype cost, which was felt to be best described as inexpensive or expensive. (The production engineer gave a technical specification for these rather vague terms.) Given the difference between prototypes and real production, the engineer estimated the probabilities for prototype cost, as shown in Figure 4–18.

We emphasize that the probabilities must be assessed in this order, although there is a real and constant temptation to assess them in the reverse order. The reason for using this order is that it clearly separates expectations about what the future will bring (the probabilities on the first node) from the reliability of the test (the probabilities of the second node). Assessing probabilities with the nodes in the opposite order completely mixes the two sets of ideas.

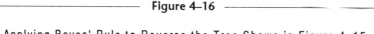

—————————— Figure 4–16 ——————————

Applying Bayes' Rule to Reverse the Tree Shown in Figure 4–15

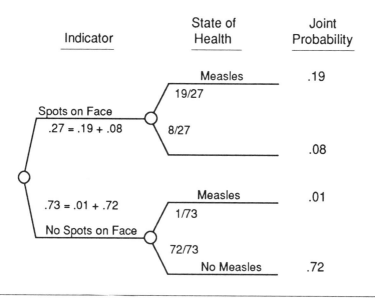

Figure 4–17

Names of Probabilities in Nature's Tree

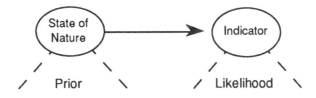

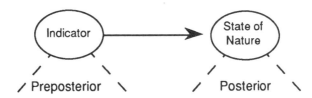

Letting Supertree Do the Work

Reversing trees by hand is a tedious and error-prone process. Supertree can perform the calculations automatically. The tree in Figure 4–18 can be entered into Supertree, as shown in Figure 4–19. The information for this tree from the Show option of the Structure menu is shown in the first screen in the figure. The probabilities for Positronics' cost are assessed in Chapter 2. Since we are not really interested in values here, we have entered an endpoint node with value 0.

Before analyzing the tree, we still have to use the Evaluate option. We can then use Display to examine the tree in its original order (Figure 4–19b), confirming that we have entered the data correctly.

We can use the Display option to show the tree with the nodes reversed (Figure 4–19c). We now see the probability for the various Positronics costs, given, for instance, that the prototype turned out to be inexpensive. These probabilities are a mixture of two values: the probabilities we assigned to the costs prior to knowing the prototype costs and the likelihood that the prototype costs would occur, given the costs.

The Value of Imperfect Information

One of the most important uses of Bayes' Rule and Nature's tree is in obtaining the value of imperfect information. If we obtain imperfect information, we know the outcome of the imperfect indicator before we make a decision—and before we learn the true state of nature. This order requires reversing Nature's tree.

The president of Positronics was well aware that perfect information is seldom available. Most often, the choice is whether or not to undertake a study to reduce the uncertainty.

─────────────────── **Figure 4–18** ───────────────────

Influence Diagram for Cost of a Prototype

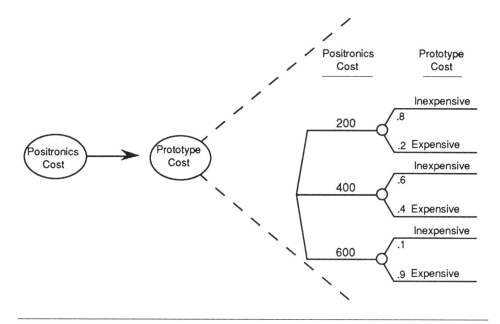

Figures were now available (Figure 4–18) that would permit more quantitative analysis of the value of building the prototype instrument to reduce the uncertainty on cost (see Chapter 3, "The Value of Perfect Control").

One way to represent this extended decision problem is shown in Figure 4–20.

The Construct Prototype node contains the alternatives "Yes" and "No." The distribution tree contained in the Prototype Cost Information node is show in Figure 4–21.

The decision tree (Figure 4–22) is constructed according to the rules given in the section "Recasting the Problem as a Decision Problem" in Chapter 3. Note the difficulty in representing the probabilities in this tree. We could reverse the arrow between Positronics Cost and Prototype Cost Information (see Appendix B) and use the results shown in Figure 4–19c. Instead, we will let Supertree do the work for us.

This tree could be entered into Supertree and evaluated in its entirety. However, the easiest way to find the value of imperfect information is by just evaluating the subtree following the "Yes" branch. We can do this by adding the node on Prototype Cost onto the front of the existing tree and by then comparing its value with that of the original tree (the subtree at the bottom of Figure 4–22). After renumbering and adding the new node, we obtain the Show display in Figure 4–23. Note that Supertree will allow you to input the probabilities in the Nature's tree order.

We then need to Evaluate the tree before using the Display option (Figure 4–24).

The expected value with the imperfect information is $73,000. We follow the same calculation method we used for the value of perfect information.

———————————————— **Figure 4–19** ————————————————

Prototype Information

a   Tree name: NATURE'S TREE

STRUCTURE	NAMES	OUTCOMES	PROBABILITIES
1 C 2 2 2	COST	200 400 600	.25 .50 .25
2 C 3 3	PROTOTYPE	INEXPENSIVE EXPENSIVE	Depends on 1
3 E		0	

```
  COST  PROBABILITY, NODE 2
 _200_  0.8 0.2
C_400_  0.6 0.4
|_600_  0.1 0.9
```

Nature's Tree for Prototype Information

b   Present Order of Nodes:
          1 2
        New Order of Nodes:
          1 2
        First Node: 1
        Last Node: 2
        Single or double spacing? SINGLE

```
        PROBS COST  EXP VAL   PROBS PROTOTYPE   EXP VAL

                             _0.800_INEXPENSIVE_____.0
        _0.250_200_____.0_C_0.200_EXPENSIVE_____.0
        |                    _0.600_INEXPENSIVE_____.0
        C_0.500_400_____.0_C_0.400_EXPENSIVE_____.0
        |                    _0.100_INEXPENSIVE_____.0
        |_0.250_600_____.0_C_0.900_EXPENSIVE_____.0

        >> Tree Drawn    6/1/90  12:00  NATURE'S TREE
        >> Expected Value: .0
```

———————————————— **Figure 4–19 (continued)** ————————————————

Prototype Tree in Reversed Order for Decision-Making

c   Present Order of Nodes:
              1 2
           New Order of Nodes:
              2 1
           First Node: 2
           Last Node: 1
           Single or double spacing? SINGLE

              PROBS PROTOTYPE   EXP VAL   PROBS COST   EXP VAL

                                             _0.381_200_____.0
              _0.525_INEXPENSIVE_____.0_C_0.571_400_____.0
              | |_0.048_600_____.0
              C   _0.105_200_____.0
              |_0.475_EXPENSIVE_____.0_C_0.421_400_____.0
                                           |_0.474_600_____.0

           >> Tree Drawn   6/1/90   12:00   NATURE'S TREE
           >> Expected Value: .0

Value of Imperfect Information = Value with Imperfect Information
                               − Value Without
                               = \$73,000 − \$65,000

                               = \$8,000   (4-1)

Thus, the prototype program should not be undertaken if it costs more than \$8,000.

As with perfect information, there is an alternative method for calculating this value. From Figure 4–24, you can see that about half the time (probability .475) the prototype information will lead you to switch your bid (hence, the information has value). If the prototype is expensive, we switch the bid from \$500,000 to \$700,000. This improves the value by \$33,900 − \$17,100 = \$16,800. The expected improvement is then \$16,800 × .475 = \$8,000.

Figure 4–20

Influence Diagram Depicting the Positronics Prototype Build Decision

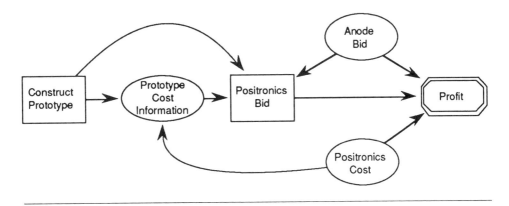

Figure 4–21

Distribution Tree of Prototype Cost Information Node

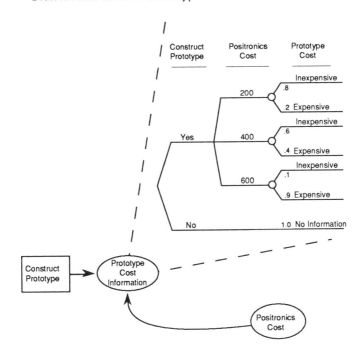

─────────── **Figure 4–22** ───────────

Decision Tree of Prototype Construction Question

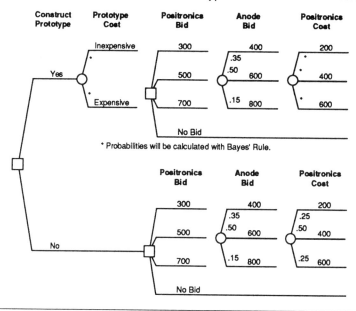

* Probabilities will be calculated with Bayes' Rule.

─────────── **Figure 4–23** ───────────

Data to Determine the Value of Imperfect Information

Tree name: BIDDING TREE

STRUCTURE	NAMES	OUTCOMES	PROBABILITIES
1 C 2 2	PROTOTYPE	INEXPENSIVE EXPENSIVE	Depends on 4
2 D 3 3 3 6	BID	300 500 700 NOBID	
3 C 4 4 4	ANODEBID	400 600 800	.35 .50 .15
4 C 5 5 5	COST	200 400 600	.25 .50 .25
5 E	B$(BID-COST)*(BID<& ANODEBID)	Depends on 2 3 4	
6 E	0		

```
  COST  PROBABILITY, NODE 1
 _200_  0.8 0.2
C_400_  0.6 0.4
|_600_  0.1 0.9
```

The Value of Imperfect Control

The value of imperfect control is much simpler to calculate. Assume that a feasible cost control program is put into effect. Obtain the probabilities for Positronics' costs given this cost control program. Presumably, the probability of the high-cost branch is smaller than before. Find the expected value of the tree using these new probabilities. This is the value with control for this (imperfect) cost control program. As before, the value of control is the improvement in value.

$$\text{Value of Imperfect Control} = \text{Value with Imperfect Control} \\ - \text{Value Without Imperfect Control}$$

(4-2)

Common Interpretive Problems with Reordering the Tree

When reordering the tree, Supertree sometimes produces puzzling messages or results. These messages or results are normally concerned with decision-dependent probabilities, decision-dependent outcomes, or rewards. The information in this section will help you in these cases.

Decision-Dependent Probabilities

Probabilities can depend on a decision node. For instance, suppose we introduced a decision on whether or not to institute stringent cost control measures. The probabilities for Positronics' costs would then depend on which branch of the cost control decision node we were on (Figure 4–25).

Suppose we now decide to move the cost node in front of the cost control decision node in the decision tree. This would be equivalent to drawing an arrow from the Positronics Cost node to the Cost Control node. Decision analysis theory (and Supertree) would object that this was not a valid order for the tree because of decision-dependent probabilities.

There are three ways to understand why the reordering is not allowed. The first way is operational. To reverse the order of nodes with dependent probabilities, Supertree uses Bayes' Rule. However, a decision node has no probabilities to insert into Bayes' Rule!

The second, more fundamental way of understanding the problem is to realize that this would create a loop in the influence diagram. Since influencing arrows represent a flow of information, a loop makes no sense. This conclusion is reinforced by the chronology implied by arrows into and out of decision nodes. (See Appendix B.)

The third way of understanding the problem is the second way reexpressed in decision tree language. If the Positronics Cost chance node occurs before the Cost Control decision node, it means we know what our costs are going to be before we make the decision. However, knowing that costs were low, for instance, would argue that we are probably going to make the decision to implement the stringent cost controls, which will make costs low. This gets us into a logical loop. No matter how we put it, decision trees will not allow us to interchange the order of a decision node and a chance node whose probabilities depend on the decision node.

--- **Figure 4–24** ---

Value with Imperfect Information (Section 1)

```
Present Order of Nodes:
 1 2 3 4
New Order of Nodes:
 1 2 3 4
First Node: 1
Last Node: 4
Single or double spacing? SINGLE
     PROBS PROTOTYPE   EXP VAL   BID   EXP VAL   PROBS ANODEBID  EXP VAL   PROBS COST  EXP VAL
                                                                  _0.381_200_____100.0
                                        _0.350_400_____-33.3_C_0.571_400____-100.0
                                        |                         |_0.048_600____-300.0
                                        |                          _0.381_200_____100.0
                      _300_____-33.3_C_0.500_600_____-33.3_C_0.571_400____-100.0
                      |         |                         |_0.048_600____-300.0
                      |         |                          _0.381_200_____100.0
                      |         |_0.150_800_____-33.3_C_0.571_400____-100.0
                      |                                   |_0.048_600____-300.0
                      |                                    _0.381_200_____.0
                      |          _0.350_400_____.0_C_0.571_400_____.0
                      |         |                         |_0.048_600_____.0
                      |         |                          _0.381_200_____300.0
                      |>500_____108.3_C_0.500_600_____166.7_C_0.571_400_____100.0
                      |         |                         |_0.048_600____-100.0
                      |         |                          _0.381_200_____300.0
   _0.525_INEXPENSIVE____108.3_D |         |_0.150_800_____166.7_C_0.571_400_____100.0
   |                  |                                   |_0.048_600____-100.0
   |                  |                                    _0.381_200_____.0
   |                  |          _0.350_400_____.0_C_0.571_400_____.0
   |                  |         |                         |_0.048_600_____.0
   |                  |         |                          _0.381_200_____.0
   |                  |_700_____55.0_C_0.500_600_____.0_C_0.571_400_____.0
   |                  |         |                         |_0.048_600_____.0
   |                  |         |                          _0.381_200_____500.0
   |                  |         |_0.150_800_____366.7_C_0.571_400_____300.0
   |                  |                                   |_0.048_600_____100.0
   |                  |_NOBID_____.0
```

Decision-Dependent Outcomes

For chance nodes whose outcomes depend on a decision node, we would expect the same problem as with decision-dependent probabilities. After all, dependent probabilities and dependent outcomes are both ways of characterizing dependent probability distributions. However, there is an interpretation of dependent outcomes that allows us to interchange the nodes, and Supertree assumes we intend this interpretation.

The interpretation is that we learn whether we are on the high branch, the middle branch, or the low branch (assuming there are three branches) before we make the decision. We do not know the value of the outcome, only whether we are on the top branch, the second branch, or the third branch. This interpretation is consistent with the observation that dependent outcomes often represent a deterministic shift combined with uncertainty in estimation. The information gained in interchanging the

─────────────── **Figure 4–24** ───────────────

Value with Imperfect Information (Section 2)

```
|                                                          _0.105_200_____100.0
|                                      _0.350_400_____-173.7_C_0.421_400____-100.0
C                                     |                    |_0.474_600____-300.0
|                                     |                    _0.105_200_____100.0
|                        _300_____-173.7_C_0.500_600_____-173.7_C_0.421_400____-100.0
|                       |             |                    |_0.474_600____-300.0
|                       |             |                    _0.105_200_____100.0
|                       |             |_0.150_800_____-173.7_C_0.421_400____-100.0
|                       |                                  |_0.474_600____-300.0
|                       |                                  _0.105_200_____.0
|                       |              _0.350_400_____.0_C_0.421_400_____.0
|                       |             |                    |_0.474_600_____.0
|                       |             |                    _0.105_200_____300.0
|                       |_500_____17.1_C_0.500_600_____26.3_C_0.421_400_____100.0
|                       |             |                    |_0.474_600____-100.0
|                       |             |                    _0.105_200_____300.0
|_0.475_EXPENSIVE_____33.9_D       |_0.150_800_____26.3_C_0.421_400_____100.0
|                       |                                  |_0.474_600____-100.0
|                       |                                  _0.105_200_____.0
|                       |              _0.350_400_____.0_C_0.421_400_____.0
|                       |             |                    |_0.474_600_____.0
|                       |             |                    _0.105_200_____.0
|                       |>700_____33.9_C_0.500_600_____.0_C_0.421_400_____.0
|                       |             |                    |_0.474_600_____.0
|                       |             |                    _0.105_200_____500.0
|                       |             |_0.150_800_____226.3_C_0.421_400_____300.0
|                       |                                  |_0.474_600_____100.0
|                       |_NOBID_____.0
```

```
>> Tree Drawn    6/1/90  12:00  BIDDING TREE
>> Expected Value: 73.0
```

nodes is on the uncertainty in estimation. This interpretation is illustrated in the influence diagram in Figure 4–26.

Whenever a node with dependent outcomes occurs before its conditioning node, the outcomes are shown in the Display option as asterisks. There is no way to show the outcome values in a tree display in this order because they depend on a node that comes afterwards. However, all calculations are done with the correct combinations of outcome values because Supertree keeps track of which outcomes are associated with which scenarios (tree paths) regardless of how the nodes are reordered for display purposes.

Rewards

Supertree gives us the option of figuring the rewards into the endpoints or of keeping rewards at the node and figuring them into the values at that point. This makes a difference in the results of the Display option (and the Plot option, if you are plotting a distribution at a node other than the first node in the tree).

——————————————— **Figure 4–25** ———————————————

Influence Diagram Showing Probabilities Dependent on a Decision Node

In moving a node with rewards, there are two ways to interpret the reordering. First, we could be rearranging the order of events that make up the tree, in which case the rewards should move with the node to the new order. Second, we could be performing a value of information calculation, in which case the rewards should stay where they are and be incurred when the event happens, rather then when you get information on it. (Recall that node reordering is a shortcut to obtain the value of information.)

An unexpected effect can arise when nodes are reordered in an asymmetric tree with rewards. The reordering can force Supertree to put the tree into a more symmetric form. With this symmetrization, figuring in rewards at the nodes can cause surprising changes to endpoint values. These changes occur because figuring in rewards at a node may mean adding the node (and its rewards) on a path in the symmetrized tree where it was not present in the original asymmetric tree. To keep the net value the same, Supertree must also subtract the reward from the endpoint value for that path, resulting in the unexpected endpoint values. The net change in the value of the scenarios (tree paths) is zero.

——————————————— **Figure 4–26** ———————————————

Influence Diagram Illustrating Handling of Uncertainty in Estimation

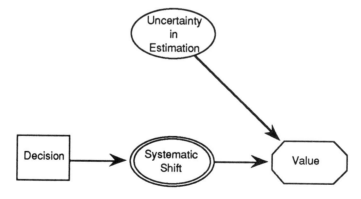

Summary

A dependency can be expressed with dependent outcomes or with dependent probabilities. These forms are equivalent, and the selection of form usually depends on how the source of information thinks about the uncertainty. This was illustrated in a probabilistic dependence that increased the riskiness of Positronics' bid decision.

We also discussed how correctly handling dependencies is a common problem that arises when dealing with tests or information gathering (Nature's tree). We then applied this to the calculation of the value of the imperfect information that could be obtained if Positronics were to build a prototype.

Finally, we discussed some interpretive difficulties that commonly arise when reordering trees with decision-dependent probabilities, decision-dependent probabilities, or rewards.

Problems and Discussion Topics

4.1 What are joint probabilities? How are these different from conditional probabilities?

4.2 Suppose your interview with a decision-maker has revealed a dependency between two uncertainties. How do you determine which uncertainty depends on the other for assessment purposes? What does this imply for the order of assessment?

4.3 "Flipping the tree" refers to reordering the nodes in a tree or part of a tree (reversing them if there are only two nodes). Since the flipped tree represents the same state of knowledge (uncertainties) as the original tree, the principle of flipping a tree is that the probability of any event derived from the original tree should be the same as the probability of the same event represented by the flipped tree.

Consider the medical example on page 87. Suppose a medical expert assigns a probability that 50 percent of the total population currently has measles, and that given a person has measles there is a chance of 85 out of 100 that the person has spots on his or her face. If a person does not have measles, there is a .95 chance that the person has no spots on his or her face.

What is the conditional probability that someone who has spots on his or her face has measles? What is the conditional probability that someone who does not have spots on his or her face has measles?

The procedure used to answer this question is exactly what Supertree does when we change the order of nodes.

4.4 We already know that changing the order of two chance nodes (called flipping the tree) does not change the knowledge represented by that tree. What happens if we move a chance node from the right of a decision node to the left of it? And vice versa?

4.5 The radiator in your car tends to overheat, but you have not fixed it because it is still winter and cold outside. The radiator overheats only 5 percent of the days it is used in cool weather. However, it overheats 70 percent of the time in warm weather. The weather report has just predicted a 1 out of 5 chance of warm weather today.

a. Draw the influence diagram for these relationships.

b. What is the chance your radiator will overheat today?

4.6 After having had pizza delivered at 11 p.m. several times a week for a number of years, you decide that there is a 70 percent chance that a pizza with a visible amount of cheese has a visible amount of pepperoni. You also figure that the probability that a randomly selected pizza will have visible amounts of cheese and pepperoni is .40.

a. Draw the influence diagram for these relationships.

b. What is the probability that a randomly selected pizza has a visible amount of cheese?

4.7 Using first dependent probabilities and then dependent outcomes, write down your probabilities on the temperature outside given that it is 9 a.m. or 9 p.m. Assume a .5 probability that the observation is made at either time and make your chance node on temperature have three branches.

Compare the expected temperature from each method (dependent probabilities or outcomes). How different are they? Which method enabled you to give the better estimate and why? What does this tell you about the underlying process affecting the temperature? What does it tell you about your thought process?

4.8 An expected-value decision-maker faces the following short-term investment in a given stock:

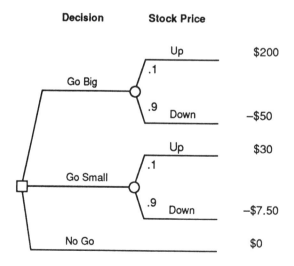

a. Draw the influence diagram. Do you have enough information to do so?

b. Calculate the expected value of this decision.

c. What is the maximum amount the decision-maker should pay for perfect information on the stock price?

d. Suppose there is a test that can predict the stock price with an accuracy of .9. Draw the influence diagram for this. What is the maximum amount the decision-maker should pay for this test?

e. Suppose the test says the stock will rise and this information is given to the decision-maker for free. Now what is the value of perfect information on the stock price?

f. Suppose a wizard comes along. He can make any possible outcome happen the decision-maker desires. Draw the influence diagram for the value with the wizard. What is the maximum amount the wizard should be paid?

4.9 Ursa Major Movies (UMM) has been trying a blind test on all its movies before releasing them. The test labels a movie as a "Hit" or a "Dud." To make the test blind, UMM released all movies regardless of the test result. The test result and the actual history of the movies are shown in the table on the next page.

	Test Result	
	"Hit"	"Dud"
Broke box office records	5	1
Run of the mill	13	7
Disaster	8	9

a. Draw the influence diagram for the test and movie results. Is it in the order of Nature's tree? Why or why not?

b. What is the probability that a film chosen at random out of the studio's past movies was a disaster? Run of the mill? Broke records?

c. What is the probability that a disaster had previously been labeled a "Hit"? What is the probability that a box office record breaker had been labeled a "Dud"? Is the test better at detecting good or bad movies?

d. The producer thinks that a new movie is really quite good (a 5 in 10 chance of being a box office hit, a 3 in 10 chance of being run of the mill). After learning that the test came up "Dud," how should the producer revise her probabilities?

e. The president thinks that this new movie is like all the others, meaning that the historical frequencies above apply. What should he think after learning that the test result for this movie was "Dud"?

f. Assume a record breaker gives the company a net profit of $20 million; a run of the mill, $2 million; and a disaster, a net loss of $2 million. What value would the producer place on the new film before learning the test results? After learning the test results? How about the president?

4.10 C. Thompson, the credit manager of IJK Industrial Products, considered extending a line of credit to Lastco Construction Company. Lastco was a new company and was definitely considered a credit risk. Drawing on his experience, Thompson said, "There is about a 30 percent chance Lastco will fail within the year, which means a severe credit loss. And the way these construction companies operate, I would say there is another 25 percent chance Lastco will run into serious financial trouble." After being further questioned about other possibilities, Thompson said, "If they don't run into financial problems, there still is less than a 50/50 chance of Lastco becoming a regular customer. I would say the odds are about 5 to 4 that Lastco will end up being a sporadic customer." Thompson also made the following predictions:

If Lastco failed completely, it would average purchases of $1,500 before failing but leave an average unpaid balance of $800, which would be totally lost.

If Lastco had severe financial troubles, it would lose its credit but only after purchases of $2,000, including an unpaid balance of $1,000, of which $500 would ultimately be collected.

As a sporadic customer, Lastco would average purchases of only $500 (with no credit losses). However, as a good customer, it would average purchases of approximately $6,000.

IJK was concerned about granting credit to Lastco. On the one hand, if it did not extend credit to a potential customer, business was lost. On the other hand, there was a substantial risk of nonpayment (as described above), and since IJK made an average profit (price minus variable cost) of only 20 percent of sales, this exacerbated the problem. In addition, there were collection costs of $100 per customer for those that failed or were in financial trouble.

a. Draw the influence diagram for this case.

b. Construct the decision tree for this case.

c. Should IJK grant credit to Lastco?

d. Suppose a credit rating company could somehow provide perfect information on a potential customer for $200. Should IJK buy it?

e. Suppose the fee of the credit rating company was only $50, but the company could provide only "good opinions" (not perfect information) about potential customers. Suppose also that Thompson has

some experience with credit rating companies, which he says applies
to the Lastco decision. His rating experience is summarized below.

Credit Ratings by Customer Classiciation (percent of total)

Rating	Failed	Financial Troubles	Sporadic Customer	Good Customer
Good	0	10	40	40
Medium	40	50	50	50
Poor	60	40	10	10
	100	100	100	100

Note: The table should be interpreted as follows: For example, in
similar situations of companies that failed, none had been rated good,
40 percent had been rated medium, and 60 percent had been rated bad.

Would it be worthwhile to use the credit rating company? Illustrate
your answer with a revised influence diagram.

4.11 Most market surveys give imperfect information. The example below shows a
symmetric situation—a fraction, q, of product successes had positive survey
results, and a fraction, q, of failures had negative survey results. The prior
probability of a product success is given as p.

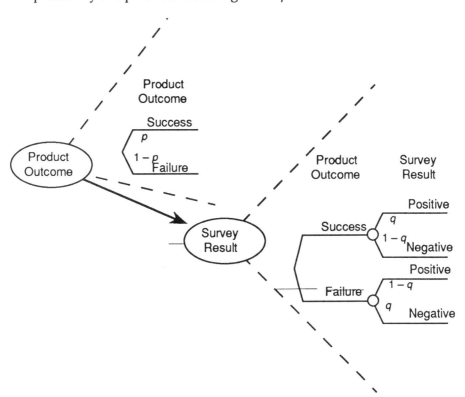

a. Flip the tree and calculate the posterior probabilities for Product Outcome and the preposterior probabilities for Survey Result in terms of p and q.

b. Plot the probability of a product success given a positive survey result against the value of p. Do this for $q = .5, .6, .7, .8, .9$, and 1.0. Why are values of q less than .5 and greater than 1 not needed?

c. How useful is the survey result for values of p near 0, .5, and 1.0? How does this depend on the value of q? Explain qualitatively what this means in terms of uncertainty and certainty and the accuracy of surveys.

5

Attitudes Toward Risk Taking

The Inadequacy of Expected Values

As noted previously, the expected value is not always an adequate decision criterion, especially for decisions that involve uncertainty and that are truly important to people or companies. Usually (but not always) people shy away from risk and uncertainty.

For example, in seminars to upper-level executives from many of the country's largest companies, participants were asked to bid for the rights to toss a coin where the prize was $200. Because we are dealing with a coin toss, the expected value is, of course, $100. It is surprising how few people bid anywhere close to $100. Most bid in the $40 to $60 range—and these were not the people who objected in principle to gambling.

The exercise shows how easy (but often wrong) it is to think of expected value as an adequate decision criterion. When there is money on the table, we find we are anything but expected-value decision-makers. The seminar also revealed that few people behave consistently when making decisions involving risk. If they carried the attitude used in the coin toss over into other decisions, they would be very conservative investors indeed!

Most people and companies exhibit an aversion to risk taking. While they are willing to play the averages for small stakes, they are willing to give up a part of the expected value to avoid the uncertainty and risk for larger stakes. Thus, this attitude should be incorporated in the decision criterion. The effects of risk attitude can be quantified in terms of the certain equivalent, which, as we recall, is the certain amount the decision-maker would accept in exchange for the uncertain venture. This certain amount of cash is thus the venture's minimum selling price.

One way to see the effect of a risk-averse attitude is to look at the risk penalty (or risk premium)—the difference between the expected value and certain equivalent. As the amount at risk increases (e.g., as the prize in the coin toss increases), the risk penalty increases and the certain equivalent becomes a smaller fraction of the expected value (Figure 5–1).

Figure 5–1

Relationship Between Risk Penalty and the Amount at Risk

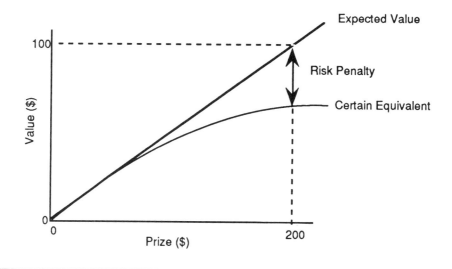

Furthermore, the decision criterion should have the certain equivalent decreasing the most (relative to the expected value) when the uncertainty is greatest. For instance, experience shows that if we hold the prize constant, but vary the probability (p) of winning the prize, we will see the greatest difference between the expected value and the certain equivalent in the region where the uncertainty is greatest (p around .5). (See Figure 5–2.)

Toward a Consistent Risk Attitude

The decision-maker could, in principle, stare at the probability distribution on value for each alternative of each venture, arrive at a set of certain equivalents, and then make the decision. Indeed, this is what we all do informally when faced with a decision under uncertainty. However, this approach has three problems. It is virtually impossible to be consistent from decision to decision, it is difficult to delegate effectively, and it is time-consuming and exhausting when many decisions must be made.

For these reasons, the decision criterion should enable the decision-maker to make explicit this most personal of values. The criterion should be applicable to all decisions, simple to apply in calculations, simple to communicate, and based on solid grounds—not just a rule of thumb of limited applicability.

Fortunately, we can take a series of certain equivalents the decision-maker has given for different ventures and produce a criterion for making other decisions consistently. The argument goes as follows:

- If we choose to behave according to a few reasonable behavioral rules, there is a utility function that describes our attitude toward risk taking.

- This utility function can be used in a simple way to obtain our certain equivalent for any probability distribution.

- The utility function is obtained by asking what our certain equivalent is for a few simple uncertain ventures.

- Over a reasonable range of outcomes, most people's and companies' utility functions for money can be fit by a function with one parameter, the risk tolerance. This makes it simple to speak of and compare attitudes toward risk.

───────── **Figure 5–2** ─────────

Relationship Between Certain Equivalent and Uncertainty

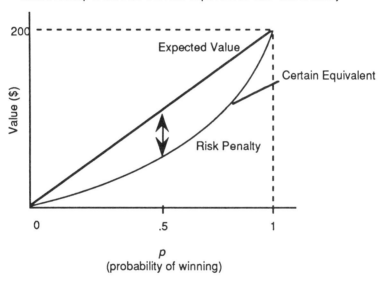

The behavioral rules are shown below. We give a mathematical formulation for each rule and then explain how each relates to the way we actually behave—or wish to behave. Note that in the context below > means preferred to and an arrow in the tree drawing indicates this preference.

Order Rule

If A > B and B > C, then A > C.

The order rule states that if we prefer A to B and B to C, then we prefer A to C. For instance, if we prefer a Mercedes to a Ford and a Ford to a Volkswagen, then we prefer a Mercedes to a Volkswagen. If we were to violate this rule, an unscrupulous car dealer could turn us into a "money pump": have us trade in our Volkswagen and buy a Ford; trade in our Ford and buy a Mercedes; trade in our Mercedes and buy (at a higher price) a Volkswagen. In the end, we have returned to our original state, but are poorer. Objections to this rule usually err in focusing on only one attribute of the outcomes.

Equivalence Rule

If A > B > C, then there is some value, p, for which the decision-maker is indifferent between the alternatives shown in the tree below. (The double arrow means indifference between the two alternatives.)

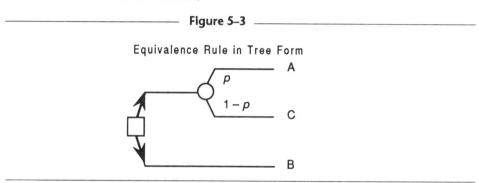

——————— **Figure 5–3** ———————

Equivalence Rule in Tree Form

The equivalence rule says there is some value for the probability, p, at which we are indifferent between choosing a Ford and choosing the alternative where we might win a Mercedes or we might win a Volkswagen.

Substitution Rule

Given this indifference, B can be substituted for the uncertain venture in the top branch of the tree shown in Figure 5–3 without changing any preferences.

The substitution rule is really here for mathematical purposes. In behavioral terms it means, "Do you really mean it?" Are you willing to use the value p obtained in the preference statement of the equivalence rule as a probability in calculations? You must be able to substitute a certain venture for an uncertain venture with the same certain equivalent without changing any preferences.

Choice Rule

If A > B, then the choice shown in Figure 5–4 is true only if p is greater than q.

The choice rule says that we prefer the venture with the greater probability of winning the Mercedes.

Probability Rule

The decision-maker is indifferent between the two alternatives shown in Figure 5–5. (Note that the probabilities of outcomes A and B are the same for both alternatives.)

The probability rule is fundamental in that it says that we wish to act rationally

Figure 5–4

Choice Rule in Tree Form

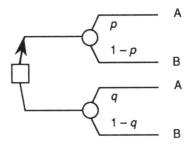

and consistently, at least to the level of being willing to use probabilities in our decision-making.

This rule is sometimes called the "no fun in gambling" rule. It states that multiple ventures can be replaced by equivalent single ventures because the decision-maker finds no intrinsic value in the ventures themselves. Much of the "fun in gambling" occurs because multiple ventures spread the excitement out over time. If we can put this entertainment value of gambling into the value function, then even the gambler may be able to satisfy this rule.

We can prove that if we subscribe to these rules, a utility function exists that can be used to find our certain equivalent for any uncertain venture. We will postpone the proof for the existence of the utility function until the end of this chapter.

For convenience, we will restrict the values to a single continuous variable (money), although the utility function can treat discrete variables and multiple attributes. As we discussed in Chapter 3, this restriction will cause no problem for most business decisions.

Figure 5–5

Probability Rule in Tree Form

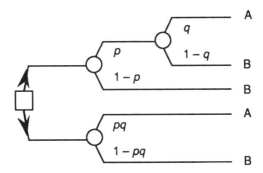

What Is a Utility Function?

A utility function is a means of describing how much a particular outcome is worth to you. For instance, winning $1 million probably means something different to you than it does to the Sultan of Brunei (unless you are the Sultan of Brunei), and this difference would be reflected in your respective utility functions. A utility function measures worth by translating values (such as $1 million) into a measure called utiles or utility values.

Your utility function has the following two properties that, as we will see in a moment, make it useful in establishing a decision criterion:

- You prefer the alternative with the largest expected utility.

- Because utility values have no intrinsic meaning, you can arbitrarily assign the utilities of any two outcomes. This allows you to set a scale that determines the utility value of any other number, much like the way water freezing at 0 °C and boiling at 100 °C sets the centigrade scale.

These two properties can be seen in the proof of the existence of a utility function in the section "Deriving the Existence of a Utility Function " (page 126).

Before it can be used, a utility function must first be created. For example, let us continue with the case of someone who is willing to bid a maximum of $60 for the chance to flip a coin for a prize of $200. Using tree notation, we can illustrate a very similar situation where the decision-maker is indifferent between accepting a sure $60 and accepting the coin flip (Figure 5–6). Another way to state the situation would be to say that the decision-maker's certain equivalent for the coin flip is $60—sixty percent of the expected value of $100.

Figure 5–6

Tree Showing Coin Flip Decision

	Value	Utility Value
Win	$200	$u(\$200)$
.5 Lose	$0	$u(\$0)$
Take the Sure Thing	$60	$u(\$60)$

Play (.5 / .5)

We can write the utility of an outcome, x, as $u(x)$. Then the (expected) utility of the second alternative is simply $u(\$60)$. The expected utility of the first alternative is computed in the same manner as the expected value: multiply the probabilities by the utility values and sum the results. Thus, the expected utility of the first alternative is $(.5 \times u(\$200)) + (.5 \times u(\$0))$.

If we always prefer the alternative with the largest expected utility, indifference means that the two alternatives have the same expected utility.

$$u(\$60) = (.5 \times u(\$200)) + (.5 \times u(\$0)) \qquad (5\text{--}1)$$

Using the second property from above, we can arbitrarily assign two utility values.

$$u(\$0) = 0 \qquad (5\text{--}2)$$

$$u(\$200) = 2 \qquad (5\text{--}3)$$

Now we can calculate $u(\$60)$.

$$u(\$60) = (.5 \times 2) + (.5 \times 0) = 1 \qquad (5\text{--}4)$$

We can then graph these three points and sketch in a smooth curve (Figure 5–7). (A procedure for assessing the curve more carefully is given in the section "Encoding a Utility Function," page 125.)

Figure 5–7

A Utility Function

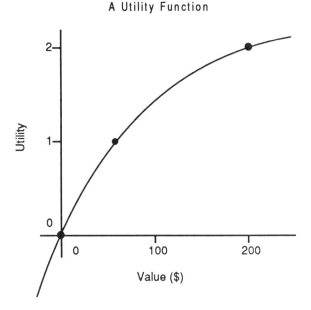

How can we interpret this curve? In the positive direction, the curve flattens out so that, for instance, going from $200 to $220 produces less increase in utility value than going from $0 to $20. In other words, going from $200 to $220 means less to us than going from $0 to $20. In the negative direction, the curve becomes ever steeper, indicating that additional decreases in value become ever more significant.

Utility curves have some general properties that help in understanding them.

- Utility curves should generally be monotonically increasing. A utility function that sometimes decreases would mean that getting more of what you want would sometimes be undesirable!

- It is the curvature of the utility function that is important. The shape of the curve in Figure 5–7 (concave downward) indicates that the certain equivalent is less than the expected value. Upside potential means less (the curve flattens in the positive direction) than downside risk (the curve grows steeper in the negative direction). Having a certain equivalent smaller than the expected value is characteristic of risk-averse behavior. The more risk averse you are, the more curved (concave downward) your utility function is.

- The reader can easily verify that risk-neutral behavior (with the certain equivalent equal to the expected value) is described by a straight-line utility function. Utility curves for expected-value decision-makers are straight lines.

- Risk-seeking behavior is possible. Risk seeking implies certain equivalents greater than expected values. Utility curves for risk-seeking individuals would be concave upward. Significant risk seeking (not just buying a state lottery ticket) is ordinarily found in individuals whose aspirations are blocked by lack of fair markets. For instance, a man who needs $100,000 to start a small business and cannot find any backing may be willing to risk all his $50,000 capital in a desperate gamble whose net expected value is much less than $50,000, but which has a possible outcome of $100,000. Clearly, this type of behavior is very special and will not be considered further in this book.

Using a Utility Function

How do we use the utility curve? Suppose, for instance, that the person whose utility curve we plotted above is faced with a venture with smaller stakes, such as a coin flip for only $100. We can use the utility curve to determine this person's certain equivalent (maximum bid) for the new coin flip. As in equation 5–1, the utility of the maximum acceptable bid is equal to the expected utility of the coin flip. We could draw a tree similar to the one for the first flip, but the following steps more directly accomplish the same calculation (finding the certain equivalent):

1. Use the utility curve to find the utility values of the outcomes.

2. Calculate the expected utility.

3. Use the utility curve to find the certain equivalent value corresponding to the expected utility.

This calculation is illustrated in the tree in Figure 5–8 describing a coin flip for a $100 prize. The values used in this tree are obtained from the utility curve shown in 5–9.

─────────────────────────── **Figure 5–8** ───────────────────────────

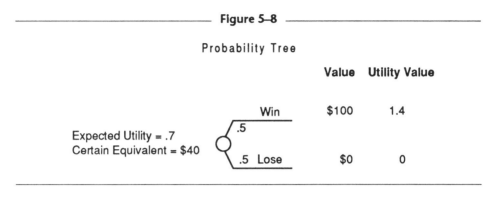

Probability Tree

		Value	**Utility Value**

Expected Utility = .7
Certain Equivalent = $40

Win $100   1.4

.5

.5 Lose $0   0

─────────────────────────── **Figure 5–9** ───────────────────────────

Reading Values from a Utility Curve

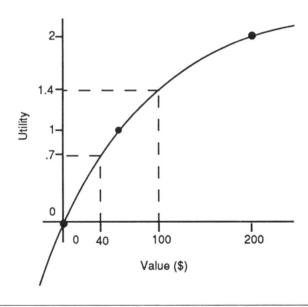

Value ($)

Note that with an expected value of $50, the certain equivalent is now 80 percent of the expected value, whereas in the first coin flip the $60 certain equivalent was only 60 percent of the $100 expected value. With smaller amounts at stake, the certain equivalent becomes a higher percentage of the expected value. Another result the reader can verify is that the certain equivalent value becomes equal to the expected value as the probability of winning (or losing) approaches 1.0.

After some discussion, the president of Positronics consented to an interview in private by the decision analysts. In the interview, the analysts assessed a utility curve for the president. Reluctantly, he allowed his utility curve (Figure 5–10) to be shown the next day at the analysis group meeting that had by now begun to be scheduled on a regular basis. At first, he was a little hesitant to allow people to see what his attitude to risk was. The analysts also presented a few examples to show some implications of the utility curve. Upper level management was a bit surprised that the examples showed the president willing to take much greater risks than they had thought he would. They had previously discarded ventures as too risky that they now perceived might be interesting to him. Some rather frank discussion revealed that although the president was willing to take risk, he frequently rejected ventures not because of the risk but because he thought the optimists who presented the decision to him had overstated the probability of success.

Figure 5–10

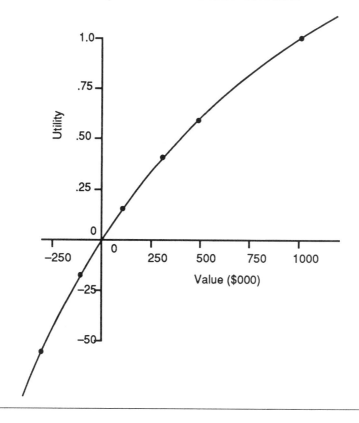

Utility Curve of Positronics' President

By examining the curve (Figure 5–10), we can see that, like most people, the president is risk averse. As mentioned above, this means that his utility values drop off ever more sharply for large negative numbers and flatten out for large positive numbers.

We saw above how to use a utility function in a simple situation. A similar procedure is used for more complicated situations (and more complicated trees). As the proof in the section "Deriving the Existence of a Utility Function" (page 126) shows, the procedure for using the utility function starts by first converting all the values at the endpoints of the tree into utiles. Then, in the rollback procedure, chance nodes are replaced by their expected utility (instead of expected value) and decision nodes by the alternative with the greatest (expected) utility. The utility curve can then be used in reverse to convert the expected utility into the certain equivalent of the overall tree, or even to convert the expected utility into the certain equivalent at any point in the tree.

Positronics applied this procedure to the decision tree (Figure 5–11). The utility values at the end of the tree were calculated and rolled back through the tree to obtain the expected utility at each node.

The choice is still to bid $500,000, with a utility of .088. Although it is difficult to tell from the encoded utility function (one reason why we will go to a computerized function), we can estimate that the certain equivalent corresponding to the utility is quite close to the expected value of $65,000.

Value of Information with an Encoded Utility Function

One thing to remember when using a directly encoded utility function is to be particularly careful about doing value of information calculations. To calculate the value of information, you should use the full value of information tree (Figure 3–17) rather than just reorder the nodes.

To find the value of information, put in different information costs as (negative) rewards on the "Yes" branch until you have found a cost level for which the value of the two alternatives is equal. This cost is the value of information. This iterative procedure is necessary because different costs shift us to different regions of the utility curve where the utility/value trade-off may be different.

However, when using an exponential utility function (such as the one built into Supertree and discussed below), we can calculate the value of information as we did for expected-value decision-makers—there is no need for this iterative procedure.

An Exponential Utility Function _____

Within a reasonable range of values, many personal and corporate utility curves can be approximated well by an exponential function:

$$u(x) = a - be^{-x/R} \tag{5-5}$$

where x is the value (such as dollars), R is the risk tolerance, and a and b are parameters set by the choice of two points in the utility curve. The parameter b must be greater than zero. The risk tolerance is the parameter that describes the curvature of the utility curve and is expressed in the same units as the values. One sometimes sees reference to the risk-aversion coefficient, which is defined as $1/R$.

Figure 5–11

Using the Utility Function in the Positronics Tree

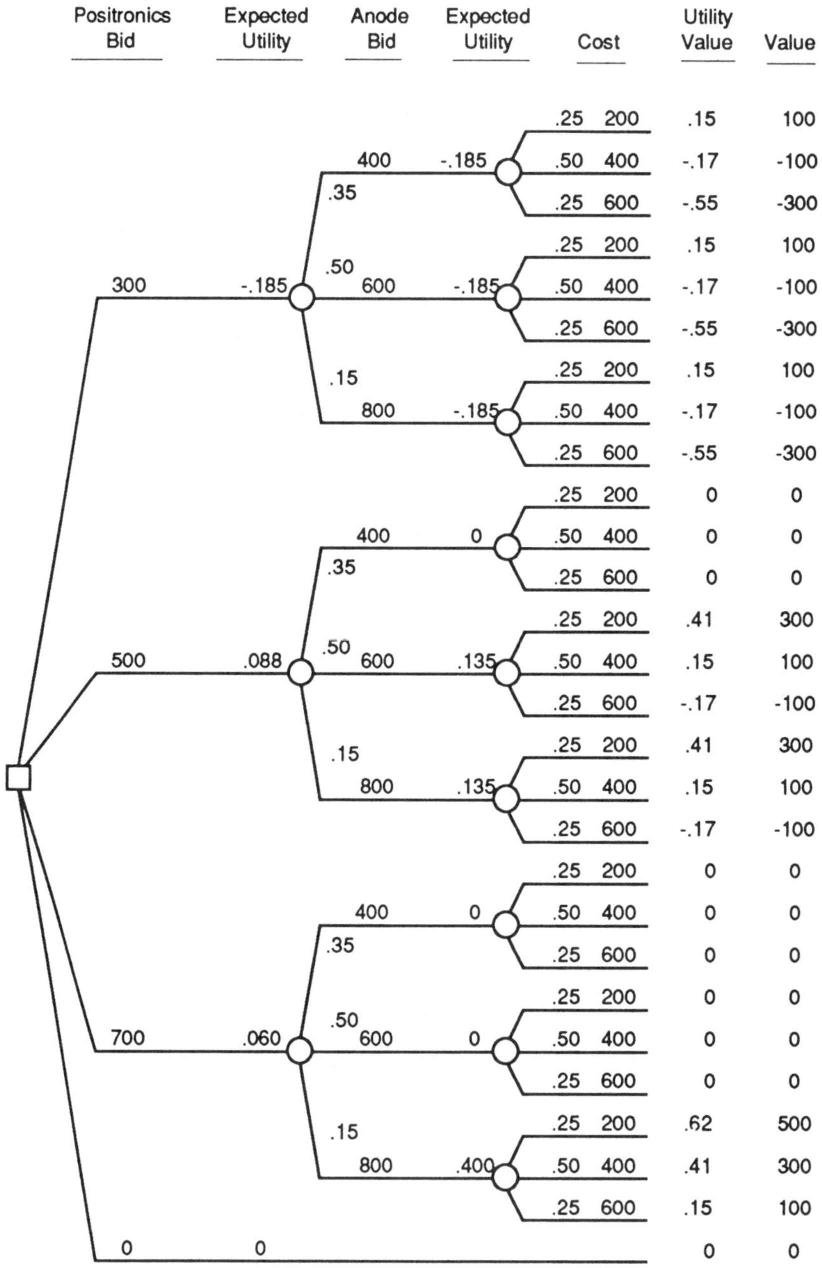

Positronics Bid	Expected Utility	Anode Bid	Expected Utility	Cost		Utility Value	Value
				.25	200	.15	100
		400	-.185	.50	400	-.17	-100
		.35		.25	600	-.55	-300
				.25	200	.15	100
300	-.185	.50 600	-.185	.50	400	-.17	-100
				.25	600	-.55	-300
		.15		.25	200	.15	100
		800	-.185	.50	400	-.17	-100
				.25	600	-.55	-300
				.25	200	0	0
		400	0	.50	400	0	0
		.35		.25	600	0	0
				.25	200	.41	300
500	.088	.50 600	.135	.50	400	.15	100
				.25	600	-.17	-100
		.15		.25	200	.41	300
		800	.135	.50	400	.15	100
				.25	600	-.17	-100
				.25	200	0	0
		400	0	.50	400	0	0
		.35		.25	600	0	0
				.25	200	0	0
700	.060	.50 600	0	.50	400	0	0
				.25	600	0	0
		.15		.25	200	.62	500
		800	.400	.50	400	.41	300
				.25	600	.15	100
0	0					0	0

The analyst graphed exponential utility functions* for several different values of risk tolerance and compared these functions with the curve encoded from the president of Positronics. As he saw in Figure 5–12, the utility function encoded from the president was well described by an exponential utility function with a risk tolerance of about $1 million. Further, within the range over which the curve was encoded, he saw that Positronics was not far from an expected-value decision-maker (which would mean a straight-line utility function and imply infinite risk tolerance).

─────────────────────── **Figure 5–12** ───────────────────────

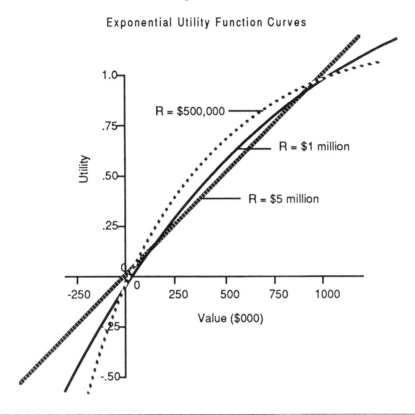

Exponential Utility Function Curves

Supertree has the exponential utility function built in. Using the Attitude-to-Risk option of the Analyze menu, we set the risk tolerance to $1 million (Figure 5–13). (A frequent error involves using different units for risk tolerance and for values.)

───────────────

* The two arbitrary points in the encoded curve were $u(\$0) = 0$ and $u(\$1\ \text{million}) = 1$. The exponential utility function that goes through these points is

$$u(x) = \frac{1 - exp(-x/R)}{1 - exp(-1{,}000/R)}$$

where R is the risk tolerance and x and R are expressed in units of thousands of dollars.

─────────────────────── **Figure 5–13** ───────────────────────

Screen for the Exponential Utility Function

```
Do you wish to use the exponential utility function? YES
Input the value for the Risk Tolerance: 1000
```

We can then use the Display option to draw the tree (Figure 5–15) and see that the results are, indeed, very similar to those calculated by hand above. The other options of the Analyze menu also now show certain equivalents when appropriate, with decisions in the tree being made to maximize the certain equivalent.

As the analyst saw from the tree drawing, the certain equivalents for each alternative were quite close to the expected values. The difference is small because none of the possible outcomes in this decision problem posed a significant risk to the business. The risk premium was only $65,000 − $57,600 = $7,400.

There are several quick ways of estimating risk tolerance.* First, you can consider the uncertain venture illustrated by the chance node in Figure 5–14. To make it more concrete, imagine that an acquaintance needs backing to start a small business and offers to "double your money in a short period." You judge there are 3 chances in 4 he will be able to pay off.

─────────────────────── **Figure 5–14** ───────────────────────

Use of a Venture to Estimate Risk Tolerance

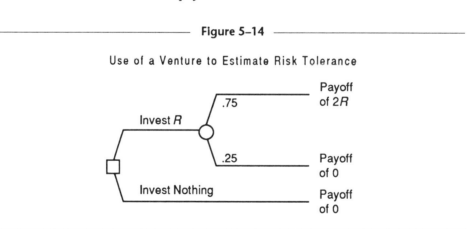

The question, then, is what is the largest sum of money you would be willing to lend your friend? In other words, what is the largest investment, R, you would consider making in a venture that has a .75 chance of paying $2R$ in return and a .25 chance of paying nothing in return?

An equivalent way of posing this question is shown below. Suppose you had an opportunity to take the chance illustrated in Figure 5–16 or pass. What is the largest value R for which you will accept a .75 chance of winding up R richer and a .25 chance

─────────────

*The proofs of these estimating techniques are in problems 5.14 and 5.15.

─────────────── **Figure 5–15** ───────────────

Positronics' Decision Tree with a Risk Tolerance of One Million Dollars

```
Present Order of Nodes:
  1 2 3
New Order of Nodes:
  1 2 3
First Node: 1
Last Node: 3
Single or double spacing? SINGLE

    BID    CERT EQ    PROBS ANODEBID  CERT EQ    PROBS COST  CERT EQ
   -----  --------    ----- --------  --------    ----- ----  --------
                                                  _0.250_200_____100.0
                      _0.350_400_____-110.0_C_0.500_400____-100.0
                      |                         |_0.250_600____-300.0
                      |                          _0.250_200_____100.0
   _300_____-110.0_C_0.500_600_____-110.0_C_0.500_400____-100.0
   |                  |                         |_0.250_600____-300.0
   |                  |                          _0.250_200_____100.0
   |                  |_0.150_800_____-110.0_C_0.500_400____-100.0
   |                                           |_0.250_600____-300.0
   |                                            _0.250_200_____.0
   |                  _0.350_400_____.0_C_0.500_400_____.0
   |                  |                         |_0.250_600_____.0
   |                  |                          _0.250_200_____300.0
   |>500_____57.6_C_0.500_600_____90.0_C_0.500_400_____100.0
   |                  |                         |_0.250_600____-100.0
   |                  |                          _0.250_200_____300.0
   D                  |_0.150_800_____90.0_C_0.500_400_____100.0
   |                                           |_0.250_600____-100.0
   |                                            _0.250_200_____.0
   |                  _0.350_400_____.0_C_0.500_400_____.0
   |                  |                         |_0.250_600_____.0
   |                  |                          _0.250_200_____.0
   |_700_____38.5_C_0.500_600_____.0_C_0.500_400_____.0
   |                  |                         |_0.250_600_____.0
   |                  |                          _0.250_200_____500.0
   |                  |_0.150_800_____290.0_C_0.500_400_____300.0
   |                                           |_0.250_600_____100.0
   |_NOBID_____.0_____

>> Tree Drawn    6/1/90  12:00  BIDDING TREE
Certain Equivalent: 57.6
```

———————————————————— Figure 5–16 ————————————————————

Would You Take the Chance or Pass?

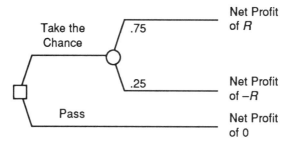

of winding up R poorer? (This question just combines the investment and return from the Figure 5–14.) R is approximately your risk tolerance and should be the same in both cases.

You can also use another venture (Figure 5–17) to estimate your risk tolerance without having to consider the possibility of such severe losses.

———————————————————— Figure 5–17 ————————————————————

Use of Another Venture to Estimate Risk Tolerance

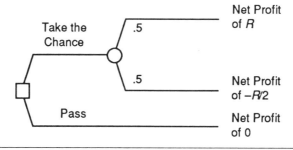

What is the largest value of R for which you will accept a .5 chance of winding up R richer and a .5 chance of winding up R/2 poorer? Once again, R is approximately your risk tolerance.

In assessing corporate risk tolerances from top management in the corporation, we normally use the encoding methods described at the end of this chapter rather than the quick estimates discussed above. However, there are several rules of thumb for estimating risk tolerance. One rule of thumb is to set risk tolerance about equal to net income for companies that generally take moderate risks. Another rule of thumb is to set the risk tolerance equal to one-sixth of equity, or to one-fifth of market value. Compare these rules to the figures in the following table, which shows the risk tolerance obtained in the 1970s from the top management in three real companies.

Measure ($ millions)	Company		
	A	B	C
Net Sales	2,300	16,000	31,000
Net Income	120	700	1,900
Equity	1,000	6,500	12,000
Market Value	940	4,600	9,900
Risk Tolerance	150	1,000	2,000

These three companies are large capital-intensive oil and chemical companies. Individual companies and different types of companies vary widely in the ratio of risk tolerance to net income, company size, stockholders' equity, or other measures. The ratio of risk tolerance to equity or market value usually translates best between companies in different industries.

Once we have assessed a risk tolerance, the following formula is a quick way to approximate the certain equivalent for a given probability distribution:

$$\text{Certain Equivalent} = \text{Expected Value} - \frac{1}{2} \frac{\text{Variance}}{\text{Risk Tolerance}} \qquad (5\text{–}6)$$

This approximation comes from the Taylor series expansion of the utility function and of the probability distribution (problem 5.22). The variance characterizes the width (uncertainty) of the probability distribution, and the risk tolerance characterizes the risk attitude embodied in the utility function. The second term on the right is just the risk penalty. To estimate the variance, take the width from the .1 to the .9 points on the cumulative probability curve, square it, and then divide by 6.6. This works because that width is 2.56 times the standard deviation for a normal (Gaussian) distribution. (This value can be seen in the graph of the normal distribution at the end of Appendix A.) Since the variance is the square of the standard deviation, when we square the width, we get $(2.56)^2 = 6.6$ times the variance. For distributions that are not normal distributions, this is, of course, only an approximation of the variance.

What is a reasonable range of values for which the exponential function is adequate? Normally, a reasonable range is one for which none of the values (positive or negative) are much larger than the risk tolerance. There are a number of other functional forms that fit well to utility functions with a wider range of values but that are not as convenient to work with. Furthermore, our experience shows that probability distributions should be explicitly examined by the decision-maker when they involve a range of values so great that the exponential utility function is inadequate, because decision-makers will not rely solely on the decision implied by a utility function when so much is at stake.

The president of Positronics had tried all these techniques and obtained values for the company risk tolerance that, although well within an order of magnitude of each other, varied considerably. Part of the problem was that he had never worked with an explicit representation of uncertainty, so he was on unfamiliar ground. Furthermore, risk attitude is difficult to express quantitatively because it involves very personal values. To help him with his decision, the president asked the analysts to evaluate the tree for a number of values of risk tolerance and see if it changed the preferred decision.

Supertree has an automatic way of performing sensitivity analysis to risk attitude. The results from selecting the Analyze Sensitivity Risk option are shown in Figures 5–18 and 5–19. The horizontal axis is linear in 1/risk tolerance, which is the risk-aversion coefficient. The leftmost values are for infinite risk tolerance, which is equivalent to the expected value. The certain equivalents are then plotted for each alternative for each value of the risk tolerance. We see that the $500,000 bid (branch 2) is optimal for all reasonable risk tolerances.

Figure 5–18

Entry Screen for Sensitivity to Risk Attitude

```
Present Order of Nodes:
  1 2 3
New Order of Nodes:
  1 2 3
Vary risk tolerance from infinity down to? 500
Label for axis? Profit ($000)
Because the sensitivity requires multiple tree evaluations,
        the program may take some time to run.
Smallest and largest certain equivalents are: -119.9 65.0
Lower and upper limits to be used for plot: -120 80
If the first node is a decision, the sensitivity is shown for all branches.
The vertical axis is the certain equivalent.
The horizontal axis is the risk tolerance;
    the scale is linear in 1/risk tolerance.


>> Risk Sensitivity    6/1/90  12:00  BIDDING TREE
```

Figure 5–19

Risk Attitude Sensitivity Graph

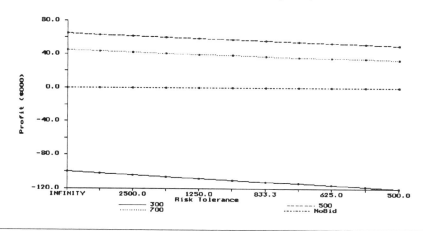

The risk attitude sensitivity is a very powerful tool. Frequently, decision-makers do not feel they have been consistent in encoding their risk tolerance and, thus, would not want an important decision to hang on such a difficult number. Also, in large companies, it is often difficult to interview decision-makers long enough to encode a utility curve. One approach is to estimate a risk tolerance for the company from the ratios above and then use the sensitivity to find out if a more exact determination of the risk tolerance is called for. The risk tolerance sensitivity frequently shows that, for any reasonable range of risk tolerances, the decision is clear.

Encoding a Utility Function

Encoding a utility function is not particularly complicated for a single continuous attribute such as money. First, arbitrarily set two points on the utility scale. A common practice is to set the utility of $0 value to be 0: $u(\$0) = 0$. Pick another point (say $10,000 for a personal utility curve) and let it be 1: $u(\$10,000) = 1$. Next, construct a simple two-branch venture with these two values as outcomes.

$$\text{———————— Figure 5–20 ————————}$$

Simple Two-Branch Venture

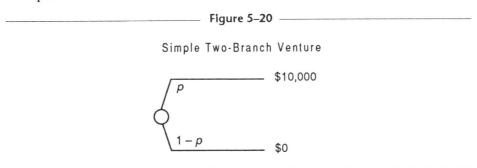

Choose a probability p and ask the decision-maker what his or her certain equivalent is. Suppose the probability p were .7 and the decision-maker responded with a certain equivalent of $5,000. We would then be able to plot a third point on the utility curve by using the basic utility property: indifference between the sure $5,000 alternative and the uncertain alternative means their expected utilities are equal.

$$u(\$5,000) = [.7 \times u(\$10,000)] + [.3 \times u(\$0)]$$
$$u(\$5,000) = (.7 \times .1) + (.3 \times 0)$$
$$u(\$5,000) = .7 \tag{5–7}$$

We can now either change the probability, p, or construct a new simple venture from the values for which we have utility values. We then request that the decision-maker furnish a certain equivalent for this venture, which is used to find the utility point of still another value.

The process of encoding the utility points is thus fairly straightforward. However, the process of giving the certain equivalents is very unfamiliar and difficult. The first try at a utility function may produce a set of points that do not fit on a smooth curve.

The person encoding should be alert for discontinuities in slope occurring at \$0. People frequently get unduly alarmed by numbers with a negative sign, no matter how small. One technique to iron out this problem is to ask the decision-maker to consolidate this venture with another (certain) venture. This does not change the problem, but it does shift the place where the zero occurs. By doing this several times, you should obtain smooth continuity through the zero point.

In corporate decision problems, the utility function should be encoded from the top management of the company—often the president or CEO. However, since top management time is valuable, it is often best to estimate an appropriate risk tolerance for the company, perhaps using the ratios mentioned earlier in this chapter. You can then find out if the problem requires going beyond the expected value and risk sensitivity. For many business decisions, expected value turns out to be adequate. Only the largest and most uncertain problems require careful use of the utility function.

Deriving the Existence of a Utility Function

The behavioral rules discussed in the section "Toward a Consistent Risk Attitude" (page 108) can be used to show that a utility function exists that has the desired property: decisions are made to choose the alternative with the greatest expected utility. The following seven-step proof derives this property from the rules. To keep things simple, we will present the proof for a finite number of discrete outcomes. The outcomes need not all be monetary and can represent a mix of different values.

1. The order rule is used to order the outcomes as $R_1, R_2, ..., R_n$, where $R_1 > R_2 > ... > R_n$.

2. Any uncertain venture, P, can be reduced by the probability rule to the form shown in Figure 5–21.

Figure 5–21

Representation of Uncertain Venture P

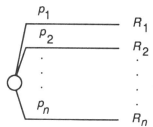

---

3. The equivalence rule is used to find, for each R_i, a probability u_i such that R_i is equivalent to the uncertain venture shown in Figure 5–22.

─────────────── **Figure 5–22** ───────────────

Using the Equivalence Rule

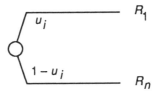

4. The substitution rule can be used to substitute the results of step 3 of the tree in step 2 and obtain the tree in Figure 5–23.

─────────────── **Figure 5–23** ───────────────

Using the Substitution Rule

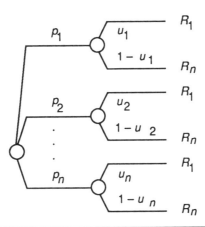

5. The probability rule can be used again to simplify this tree, as shown in Figure 5–24.

─────────────── **Figure 5–24** ───────────────

Probability Rule Used to Simplify the Tree

$$\frac{\sum\limits_{i=1}^{n} p_i u_i}{1} \qquad R_1$$

$$\sum\limits_{i=1}^{n} p_i (1 - u_i) \qquad R_n$$

6. Another uncertain venture, Q, can be represented by a tree (as P was in step 2),

Figure 5–25

Representation of Uncertain Venture Q

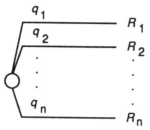

and, by the same procedure, put in the form shown in Figure 5–26.

Figure 5–26

Revised Form

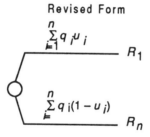

7. If P is preferred to Q, then the choice rule states that

$$\sum_{i=1}^{n} p_i u_i > \sum_{i=1}^{n} q_i u_i \tag{5-8}$$

Believe it or not, we have achieved the desired result. If we define u_i to be the utility of R_i, then we prefer the alternative with the larger expected utility. (Remember that p_i and q_i are the probabilities associated with the alternatives P and Q.) We have constructed a utility function with the desired property.

Incidentally, you can easily see that when the utility values are transformed by a linear transformation

$$u'_i = a + b u_i \tag{5-9}$$

(with $b > 0$), the decision criterion that P is preferred to Q if $\sum_i p_i u_i' > \sum_i q_i u_i'$ is still maintained. The two parameters a and b are set by arbitrarily choosing the utility of any two values (provided the utility of the preferred value is greater than the utility of the other value).

Risk-Free Discount Rates

The choice of a discount rate is important in almost any business decision. Making a proper choice involves finance and decision analysis and is one of the thornier questions an analyst faces. It is often difficult to find people who really understand the considerations in choosing a discount rate and who will commit themselves to a particular rate. In this section, we describe some of the considerations and pitfalls in choosing a discount rate.

In Chapter 3, we mentioned that we accounted for time in the value function by discounting future cash flows to obtain the net present value. In this chapter, we have shown how to account for risk. For this reason, a risk-free discount rate should be used in the evaluation. What is an appropriate value for a risk-free discount rate? One risk-free investment opportunity is U.S. Treasury bills. Examining interest rates on these bills over the last 50 years or so has shown that, in real terms (excluding inflation effects), these bills return less than 4 percent (Figure 5–27).

Figure 5–27

Real Average Annual Returns on Three Common Investments

Real Average* Annual Return (%)

Series	1926–1989	1940–1989	1960–1989	1980–1989
Common stocks	7.2	7.4	5.4	12.4
Long-term corporate bonds	2.1	0.4	2.0	7.9
U.S. Treasury bills	0.5	–0.2	1.4	3.8

* Geometric mean, net of inflation

Source: Roger G. Ibbotson and Rex A. Sinquefield, *Stocks, Bonds, Bills, and Inflation.* 1990 Edition. Institute of Chartered Financial Analysts, Charlottesville, Virginia.

In business evaluations, an internal rate of return (IRR) criterion is often used. To account for risk, a minimum acceptable value for the IRR is established. In Chapter 3, we showed why the IRR criterion is inappropriate for dealing with situations in which uncertainty is important.

Another commonly used decision criterion is to apply a risk-adjusted discount rate and then to check for a positive present value. This criterion addresses uncertainty and risk indirectly by adding several percent to the discount rate to account for risk. However, this approach contains many potential pitfalls, since it mixes considerations of time and risk, which are not necessarily connected.

In contrast to the risk-adjusted discount rate approach, the certain equivalent accounts for risk explicitly in the risk penalty, and the discount rate separately accounts for time with a risk-free rate. With the certain equivalent approach, when the certain equivalent for any uncertain venture falls below zero, the venture becomes undesirable (Figure 5–28). This is determined by the risk tolerance, a number that is determined once and then used for all decisions.

With the risk-adjusted discount rate approach, on the other hand, the venture is desirable for all values of the discount rate for which the NPV of some base case is greater than 0. The adjustment to the discount rate, however, has to be estimated for each alternative, taking into account the uncertainty of each venture. The Capital Asset Pricing Model (CAPM) is one approach to determining the discount rate for risky ventures.

The basic problem is that there is no intrinsic relationship between time and risk; thus, why try to evaluate risk by a discount rate? Several simple cases where blindly applying risk-adjusted discount rates produces spurious results illustrate this problem, as shown below. The certain equivalent method discussed in this chapter always works.

─────────────────────── Figure 5–28 ───────────────────────

Certain Equivalent and Risk-Adjusted Discount Rate Approaches

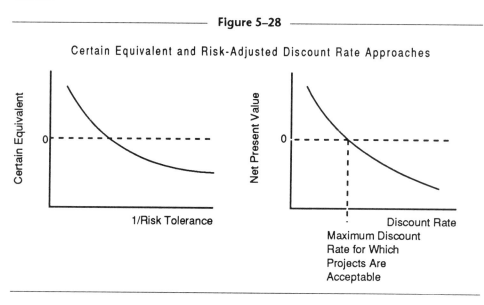

1. For any ventures where the uncertainty is resolved almost immediately, virtually no discount rate is high enough for the risk-adjusted discount rate method to make a risky venture appear undesirable. Ventures of this type include coin tosses, foreign currency exchanges, options, and opportunities arising because of acquisitions and divestitures.

2. For ventures with long time horizons, risk-adjusted discount rates tend to discourage ventures with any amount of uncertainty. This is one of the reasons why some companies spend too little money on long-term activities like research and development. Ironically, much of the uncertainty in research and development is usually resolved in the short term with the technical success or failure of a project.

3. For ventures with unconventional cash flows (profits occurring before payment), the higher we adjust the discount rate, the better the risky venture looks. However, higher discount rates are intended to discourage risky ventures! Examples of such "fly now, pay later" ventures occur in litigation (settle now or wait to see if the courts will declare you liable), in long-term financing, and in nuclear power plant construction (initial investment followed by operating profit followed by decommissioning costs).

4. A last example shows how the certain equivalent approach is sensitive to the size of the amounts involved, while the risk-adjusted discount rate approach is not. Consider Venture A and Venture B; B is identical to A except that it has all A's outcomes cut in half. B could be, for instance, a 50/50 joint venture of A. The certain equivalent approach shows that below some value of the risk tolerance, the larger venture A becomes too risky and B is preferred (Figure 5–29). (This is one of the reasons for engaging in joint ventures.) However, the risk-adjusted discount rate approach will always prefer the larger Venture A for values of the discount rate where the NPV is positive. Venture B is only preferred for discount rates for which the NPV of both A and B is negative—the "lesser of two evils." This characteristic depends only on the time pattern of the cash flow and not at all on the size of the alternatives, even though A is obviously riskier than B because it is bigger. Different risk adjustments must be used for the discount rates for Ventures A and B to make the risk-adjusted discount rate approach work.

─────────────── Figure 5–29 ───────────────

Sensitivity of Certain Equivalent and Risk-Adjusted Discount Rate
Approaches to Size of Amount at Risk

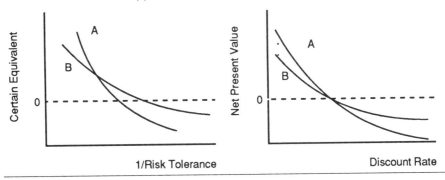

Summary

Expected values are often an inadequate criterion for decision-making. People often exhibit an aversion to risk that leads them to different choices than looking at expected values would indicate. This behavior can be accounted for by substituting certain equivalent values for expected values. Certain equivalent values can be assessed directly for each probability distribution, but this procedure is cumbersome and difficult to do consistently.

Certain equivalent values for a decision-maker can be calculated consistently and easily by using a utility function. If the decision-maker is willing to accept a reasonable set of behavioral rules, it can be shown that he or she has a utility function with the desired properties. The utility function can be used to translate a probability distribution on values into the certain equivalent value.

A utility function can be encoded directly. However, an exponential utility function often provides a good approximation of actual behavior for most individuals and corporations and is analytically much easier to use. An exponential utility function can be characterized by a single parameter, the risk tolerance.

Finally, we briefly discussed why it is better to account for risk by using a utility function and a risk-free discount rate rather than by using risk-adjusted discount rates.

Problems and Discussion Topics

5.1   Consider several decisions you have made, ranging from minor importance to major importance. Was there implicit or explicit risk aversion in the way you went about making these decisions? Do you think your risk attitude was consistent across these decisions? Give examples and say why or why not.

5.2   Do the behavioral rules adequately describe the way you would like to make certain types of decisions? Are there cases that do not fit the way you would like to make a decision? If so, give an example.

5.3   What factors contribute to the difference between using the expected value and using a utility function with risk aversion? Under what circumstances would the expected value and the certain equivalent value be the same?

5.4   Suppose you have a certain equivalent, CE, for a venture with probabilities $(p_1, p_2, ..., p_n)$ and prizes $(x_1, x_2, ..., x_n)$. The Delta Property states that if we add some arbitrary amount Δ to all the prizes such that the venture is now for prizes $(x_1 + \Delta, x_2 + \Delta, ..., x_n + \Delta)$, then your certain equivalent for the new venture will be $CE + \Delta$. Furthermore, if you subscribe to the Delta Property, then your utility function is exponential or linear.

Describe a situation where the Delta Property would not apply to you.

5.5   Use one of the two methods described in the text to assess a risk tolerance for yourself. Have the rewards or losses used in this assessment be paid immediately.

Now consider that the money you invest or lose can be paid monthly over a thirty-year period. For instance, at 10 percent you would pay roughly $1,000 each month for the next thirty years to pay off $100,000. Reassess your risk tolerance. Is it any different? Why or why not? What if interest were included on the balance?

5.6 Use the method described in the text to encode a utility function for a classmate. Then, directly assess his or her certain equivalent (minimum selling price) for a 1 in 5,000 chance of winning $10,000. Compare the result with the certain equivalent from using the utility function. What does this tell you about your classmate's risk attitude for this kind of opportunity?

5.7 Peter Portfolio faces a decision for a short-term investment based on the prospective movement of a stock. The possibilities are shown below.

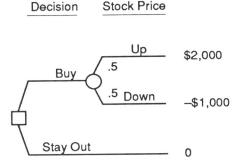

Peter has an exponential utility function with a risk tolerance of $5,000.

a. What is Peter's decision? What is his certain equivalent for the venture?

b. Peter is not sure if his risk tolerance is exactly $5,000. For what range of risk tolerance should he "Buy"?

c. Sheba Sisters brokerage firm has investigated the stock and offers Peter perfect information on whether the stock price will go up or down. What is the maximum he should pay for the information?

5.8 Your regular morning radio show has awarded you the uncertain venture shown below.

You have an exponential utility function with a risk tolerance of $2,000. You are indifferent to selling the venture for $700. What is the probability p?

5.9 J. K. Kay faces a short-term investment decision on stocks A and B whose performance is correlated.

a. If JK is an expected-value decision-maker, how much should he pay the clairvoyant for perfect information on whether stock B goes up or down?

b. If JK is risk averse and has an exponential utility function with a risk tolerance of $500, what is the most he should pay for the perfect information on stock B?

5.10 Compare the certain equivalents from using the exponential utility function for some problems in previous chapters with the certain equivalents obtained from the following approximation:

$$\text{Certain Equivalent} = \text{Expected Value} - \frac{1}{2}\frac{\text{Variance}}{\text{Risk Tolerance}}$$

where

$$\text{Expected Value} = \sum_{i=1}^{m} x_i\, p(x_i | S)$$

$$\text{Variance} = \sum_{i=1}^{m} (x_i - \text{Expected Value})^2 p(x_i | S)$$

5.11 Je has the following utility function:

$$u(x) = ln(1 + x/R)$$

where $R = \$200$. His utility is set so that outcomes x are measured as differences from his present wealth. There is an uncertain venture, L, shown below.

Assume that Je can borrow money at no cost.

a. Suppose that Je does not own the venture. What is the maximum he should be willing to pay for this venture?

b. Assume that he owns the venture. What is the lowest price that he should be willing to sell it for?

5.12 There are extreme situations in which people may behave differently than normal. Some of these situations can be explained by a special utility function.

Mr. Sam Spade, after a night of partying in San Francisco, suddenly realizes that he has only a $10 bill left in his pocket. Unfortunately, the train fare home for him is $15. Then he observes a wild gambler in the nearby corner who offers him the three opportunities shown below, each at a certain cost:

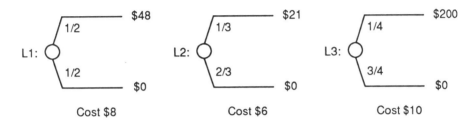

Right now, all Sam cares about is getting home. What is his special utility function for this situation? Which opportunity should Sam choose?

5.13 Missouri Tubing, Inc., is a manufacturer of specialty steel and copper tubing. Its production facility is located adjacent to the Missouri River and is protected from the waters by a 20-foot-high dike. Extremely heavy rains in recent weeks have raised the level of the river dangerously close to the top of the dike. Several other areas near the river have already been badly flooded and the weather forecast is for continued rain.

The risk manager of Missouri Tubing estimates that there is a 20 percent chance that the river will top the dike in the coming weeks and flood the factory. If the factory is flooded, there is a 50 percent chance the damage will be heavy, costing about $20 million to repair, and a 50 percent chance it will be light, costing about $10 million. Furthermore, flooding of the factory will force it to shut down while repairs are made. If damage is heavy, the factory will be closed for four months. If damage is light, there is a 60 percent chance the shutdown will last four months and a 40 percent chance it will last only two months. For each month the factory is closed, Missouri Tubing will lose $25 million in profits.

The risk manager now regrets that he recently cancelled the company's insurance policy covering flood damage. However, his insurance agent has decided to help him out by offering him a special emergency flood insurance policy. The policy provides coverage of both property damage and business interruption (i.e., lost profits) from flooding for a period of six months. The premium for the policy is $30 million. Another policy providing only the business interruption coverage is also available for a premium of $25 million.

a. Draw the influence diagram for Missouri Tubing's problem.

b. Structure the decision tree for Missouri Tubing's problem and calculate the expected value of each alternative.

c. Calculate the value of clairvoyance for an expected-value decision-maker on whether or not the Missouri Tubing factory is flooded.

d. Calculate the certain equivalent for each alternative assuming that Missouri Tubing's risk tolerance is $50 million.

e. Calculate the value of clairvoyance with risk aversion on whether the Missouri Tubing factory is flooded.

5.14 Suppose that a decision-maker agrees on the five utility rules. We then know that there exists a utility function for the decision-maker. If he or she also agrees on the Delta Property, then we know further that the utility function is exponential and can be characterized by a single number, the risk tolerance. (See problems 5.4 and 5.17.)

One way to approximate the risk tolerance is to find the largest number X for which the venture shown below is still acceptable to the decision-maker. Show that X is within about 4 percent of the true risk tolerance.

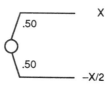

5.15 Show that the largest value X for which the venture shown below is acceptable is within 10 percent of the risk tolerance (assuming an exponential utility function).

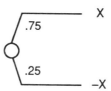

5.16 In general, the risk tolerance function can be defined as

$$\rho(x) = -u'(x) / u''(x)$$

where x is the increment to current wealth of the person in question (wealth = x + current wealth), u' is the first derivative of the utility function, and u'' is the second derivative. Some people agree that if they had more wealth, they would probably tolerate more risks. To a first approximation, this can be captured by:

$$\rho(x) = \rho_0 + Kx \quad \text{where } K \geq 0,$$

which says that risk tolerance would increase if wealth increased. At the current level of wealth, $x = 0$ and the risk tolerance is just ρ_0. What are the values of K and ρ_0 for the following utility functions?

a. $u(x) = a - be^{-x/R}$

b. $u(x) = a - \dfrac{b}{(1 + cx/R)^{(1-c)/c}}$

c. $u(x) = a + b \ln(1 + x/R)$

d. $u(x) = a + bx$ (expected-value decision-maker)

The utility functions in (b) and (c) go to negative infinity when $x \leq -\rho_0/R$. What does this mean behaviorally? Is it meaningful to use these utility functions for values $x \leq -\rho_0/R$?

5.17 If someone owns a venture, then the selling price for that venture should be such that the owner is indifferent between having the venture and having the selling price. The buying price should be such that the person is equally happy (has equal utilities) before and after giving up the buying price and getting the venture.

a. Show that for a particular person the selling price of a venture is, by definition, equal to the certain equivalent of that venture.

b. Show that if a person agrees to the Delta Property (which implies an exponential or linear utility function), then the selling price and buying price for a venture are the same for that person. (See problems 5.4 and 5.14 for a discussion of the Delta Property.)

Does this result make sense to you?

5.18 A decision-maker is confronted with an uncertain venture, A, with outcomes x_i and associated probabilities $p(x_i | S)$.

a. Justify the statement that if the decision-maker already owns A, then the minimum selling price, S, of the venture is equal to the certain equivalent.

b. Justify the statement that the maximum buying price, B, of the venture is a number such that if the decision-maker wishes to acquire A, his certain equivalent for A with outcomes set to $x_i - B$ is zero.

c. Show that $S = B$ for a linear utility function $u(x) = a + bx$.

d. Show that $S = B$ for an exponential utility function $u(x) = a - b\,e^{-x/R}$.

e. Explain why if the stakes are large enough, the decision-maker can logically have $S > B$.

5.19 Value of information can be viewed as the largest amount the decision-maker would be willing to pay to get the information. It is, therefore, really the buying price of the information. Show that the value of information is given by

Value of Information = Value with Information – Value Without Information

for a straight line or exponential utility function. Explain behaviorally why this is not generally the case.

5.20 Assume that you own two uncertain ventures, A and B, with outcomes x_i and y_j, respectively. There are no synergies between the ventures, so the net outcome to the company is the sum of the outcomes for each venture. The probability distributions for A and B are independent.

$$p(x_i, y_j | S) = p(x_i | S)\ p(y_j | S)$$

a. For a straight-line utility function $u(x) = a + bx$, show that the certain equivalent of A and B together is the sum of the certain equivalents for A and B separately.

b. Repeat (a) for an exponential utility function $u(x) = a - be^{-x/R}$.

c. Explain in behavioral terms why the certain equivalent for A and B together can logically be less than the certain equivalents for A and B separately (e.g., for cases when (a) or (b) above do not apply).

It is the property in (a) and (b) above that lets the decision analyst work on a decision problem without too much concern for the resolution of other decision problems within the company.

5.21 You are given an uncertain venture with outcomes $x_i (i = 1, 2, ..., n)$ and probabilities $p(x_i | S)$.

a. Show that if the utility function is straight line $u(x) = a + bx$, then the certain equivalent of A is equal to its expected value.

b. If the utility function is exponential $u(x) = a - be^{-x/R}$, show that the certain equivalent of A is

$$CE(A) = -R\ ln\left[\sum_{i=1}^{n} p(x_i | S)\ e^{-x_i/R}\right]$$

and is independent of the choice of values for a and b (provided that b is not equal to 0).

5.22 Given the results of the previous problem, prove that for an exponential utility function there is the following approximate expression for the certain equivalent.

$$Certain\ Equivalent = Expected\ Value - \frac{1}{2} \frac{Variance}{Risk\ Tolerance}$$

Hint: Use the following Taylor Series approximations, which are valid for x.

$$e^x = 1 + x + x^2/2! + x^3/3! + \ldots$$
$$ln(1 + x) = x - x^2/2 + x^3/3 - \ldots$$

5.23 You have the venture shown below and your certain equivalent is zero.

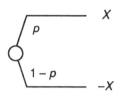

a. If your utility function is $u(x) = a - b\,w^x$, show that $w^x = p/(1-p)$. The value of $p/(1-p)$ is often called the odds.

b. If your utility function is $u(x) = a - b\,e^{x/R}$, show that your risk tolerance is $R = x\,/\,ln(p/(1-p))$.

6

The Complexity of Real-World Problems

Up to now, we have dealt with problems that are relatively simple and easy to structure and analyze. Actual decision problems, however, are usually complicated and thorny. Furthermore, they never come to the decision analyst in simple form. The professional decision analyst sees only the problems that are complicated and often poorly described; frequently, it is unclear what the problem is and what decisions need to be made.

Fortunately, the techniques for dealing with simple problems are virtually the same as those for dealing with complex problems. The most important rule for dealing with both kinds of problems is "Keep it simple!" Unnecessary complexity makes the analysis more difficult without offering additional insight.

Throughout this chapter, we use an example to illustrate how decision analysis applies to the complicated problems (and short time frames) typically encountered in practice. This example is based on an actual analysis performed in five days.

James Broderick is the director of Broderick Brokerage Ltd., a brokerage firm that manages investment portfolios for an assortment of pension funds and corporate customers. Since its founding, Broderick Brokerage has been leasing office space at the prestigious Modena Place office complex, which is owned and run by the Modena Land Company. While rents at Modena Place are among the highest in the area, the address is so prestigious that prospective tenants must wait years for an opening. Modena Place has thus been exceptional in its consistent zero vacancy rate (and accompanying high profits).

When Broderick Brokerage was formed, it purchased a small share in Modena Place as a hedge against the ups and downs of the brokerage business. This small share returned steady profits, but these profits became relatively unimportant as Broderick Brokerage prospered. Now, however, Broderick has an opportunity to increase its share in Modena Place. To raise money for the nearby Creighton-Chillingsborough College of Business and Economics, Modena is selling part of its majority share in Modena Place. Existing shareholders, such as Broderick Brokerage, can purchase an additional interest of up to half their current interest. For Broderick, this would mean an additional investment of up to $300,000. To encourage additional investment, Modena Land has prepared an informal prospectus that "conservatively" projects the revenues and expenses of Modena Place and predicts continued high profits.

However, James Broderick is not so sure Modena Place's future is inevitably golden. Other developers have long envied the success and zero vacancy rate of Modena Place, especially since the average vacancy rate for commercial office space in the area is 30 percent. As a result, one developer is building a similar prestige office complex nearby; another is remodeling a large, adjacent office building; while a third is acquiring a nearby former corporate headquarters and turning it into prestige space. Thus, James Broderick is not sure if Modena Place can retain its commanding market position in the face of an already glutted office space market and increased competition. Modena may be forced to endure vacancies or reduced rent increases (which have historically been several percentage points larger than inflation) or both.

Furthermore, Broderick is not sure if Broderick Brokerage should stay at Modena Place when it could enjoy a large rent reduction by moving a few miles away. However, if Broderick Brokerage leaves Modena Place, Broderick believes Modena Land will want him to sell the existing interest back to them. While James Broderick is not sure that he wants to increase the investment, he is not sure he wants to liquidate it either.

The attractiveness of investing in Modena Place is further complicated by a $19.3 million loan, which Modena Land took out several years earlier at a fixed interest rate of 12.25 percent. There are loan prepayment penalties until 1989, but then Modena Land plans to refinance the loan at a rate around 9 percent, resulting in lower interest payments and several hundred thousand dollars of additional profits per year. Of course, these additional profits are contingent on stable or declining interest rates.

A Cyclical Approach

To deal with complex real-world problems, decision analysis uses a cyclical approach (Figure 6–1). The phases of this approach are illustrated in detail in this chapter. In this section, we give an overview of the process.

To start with, we bring some initial knowledge to a problem. Then, in the basis development phase, we gather data, generate alternatives, and identify values for making the decision. In the deterministic structuring phase, we build a model of the decision, develop base-case input to the model, and perform deterministic sensitivity analysis to find the crucial uncertainties in the problem. (Many uncertainties are relatively unimportant.) Then, in the probabilistic evaluation phase, we encode probability distributions for these variables, construct the decision tree, and evaluate the alternatives. Finally, in the basis appraisal phase, we examine the results obtained from the decision tree, revisit the information, alternatives, and values used in the evaluation, and reexamine the model. Based on this appraisal, we decide whether to act or to return to the beginning and start the cycle again.

Drawing on years of experience using the approach, we have developed several rules of thumb for how many times to go through the cycle and for how long to spend on each phase of the cycle. In general, there should be at least two to three iterations through the decision analysis cycle. Through each phase, the analysis should be successively developed and refined until it reflects the best judgment and expertise of the analyst and personnel involved, keeping in mind that the level of effort should be commensurate with the size and importance of the problem.

Figure 6–1

The Decision Analysis Cycle

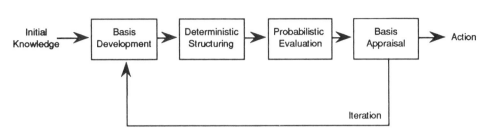

In an analysis lasting several months, a preliminary iteration should take place in the first weeks (possibly even in the first few days) to give a feeling for the overall scope and structure of the analysis. Depending on the situation (and to a certain extent on the analyst), another iteration might be performed before the full-scale analysis (when the major work is done). At the end, there should be time for a final iteration to recheck the problem formulation and results and make any final modifications.

Using the cyclical approach minimizes wasted time and effort. For instance, while the initial pass does not produce definitive results, it does give us a sense of how much additional information will be required and of how to further structure the model. And making multiple passes minimizes the practical errors that often arise: treating the wrong problem, focusing on the wrong factors, using the wrong model, gathering the wrong information, and using the wrong people.

Most of the hard analytical and data-gathering work is done during the main pass through the cycle, which, of course, varies tremendously in terms of time spent. In a typical analysis, the main pass might consume 50 percent of the time, with 25 percent of the time spent in the initial passes and 25 percent spent in a final pass and in preparing the presentations. (Typically, there is one presentation after the main deterministic structuring phase and one presentation at the end of the analysis. A presentation after the basis development phase, however, is often an excellent investment of time and resources.) During the main pass through the cycle, the effort is usually split fairly evenly between constructing the model and gathering the data to use in it.

The total amount of time and effort spent in each of the phases varies with the type of problem. Basis development ranges from 10 percent of the effort in a well-defined problem to 50 percent for a strategy project involving many people and complex alternatives. Basis appraisal can vary from 5 percent of the effort for clear problems with clear solutions and a single decision-maker to 25 percent for problems involving many people and many divisions within a company. Finally, deterministic structuring usually takes about twice the effort required for probabilistic evaluation.

For James Broderick, all the passes through the cycle had to take place in the five-day period between seeing the investment invitation (he had been out of town) and the next partners' meeting. Any recommendations would have to be presented for approval at that meeting. He therefore called in one of the investment analysts who had done decision analyses for him in the past, explained to him the need for fast turnaround, and sat down with him to start on the problem.

Basis Development: Starting the Process

The basis development phase determines the scope, method of approach, requirements, and objectives of the analysis. This phase is especially critical because all the successive phases depend on it. When something really goes wrong in analyzing a problem, the roots of the difficulty usually lie in the problem structure that came out of the basis development. Similarly, when a problem is exceptionally well analyzed, it is usually because the analysis was well structured from the beginning.

The most common errors in structuring are analyzing the wrong problem or analyzing the correct problem in an overly complicated manner. While there is unfortunately no procedure to follow that guarantees success in structuring a problem—problem structuring is a skill learned by doing—most successful analyses have a number of common elements.

First, the decision analyst must have sufficient authority and expertise to direct the analysis effort, though he or she may be relatively unfamiliar with the problem at hand (as is usually the case when acting as a decision consultant). Second, the analyst must have the courage to ask questions about the obvious and the perspective to see the forest, not just the trees. Furthermore, the analyst must have at least occasional access to the decision-maker.

The decision-maker should almost certainly be involved at some point in the basis development phase, because the analysis will be much smoother if from the start it addresses at least the alternatives the decision-maker sees as viable, the uncertainties or worries he or she thinks critical, and any special values that may be important.

As the effort progresses, initial meetings and interviews with key personnel should focus on identifying the key decision or decisions. All too frequently, the initial focus is on operational, tactical, or "how-to-do-it" decisions rather than on the underlying strategic or "what-should-we-be-doing" decisions. One way to identify the key decisions is to elicit a short description of the problem, such as, "Explain to an interested stranger what all the effort is about."

When the principal strategic decisions have been identified, a number of operational or tactical decisions can be dropped from the analysis. This must be done in a realistic manner. Usually, it should be assumed that these decisions will be made using the expertise available to the company. To avoid losing the goodwill of important personnel, the process of eliminating "how-to-do-it" decisions from the analysis must be done delicately.

Having identified the strategic decisions, the analyst needs to develop a range of significantly different alternatives. Finding really different alternatives can be a difficult and challenging task. One common problem is tunnel vision, where companies evaluate only a few fundamentally similar alternatives. By using processes ranging from simple heuristics to extensive group exercises, companies can stimulate the creativity needed to generate these alternatives. One simple exercise that often elicits creative responses is to imagine we are looking back from some future point (perhaps retirement) and critically examining this portion of our life.

Finally, the analyst should develop a list of the uncertainties that will probably be important. While this list will be revised during the analysis, it lays the groundwork for developing a deterministic model that considers these uncertainties. The model should contain as explicit variables the major uncertainties identified so far and should be suitable for analyzing the alternatives that have been developed.

Basis Development: Using Strategy Tables

In many problems, there are a bewildering number of alternatives simply because several decisions must be made, each with several alternatives. The strategy table is a convenient technique for dealing with this. The strategy table consists of a column for each decision, with all the alternatives for that decision listed in the column. A complete set of decisions (a strategy) for the problem can then be specified by picking an alternative for each decision.

In practice, forming a strategy table is often a group exercise. Different people contribute the decisions they feel are important and then help to list all the alternatives in that decision's column. Initially, all the decisions relevant to the problem are included, whether strategic or operational, important or unimportant. The group then discusses the different possible rationales for forming strategies.

Next, the group identifies a set of different strategies to be developed. Strategies begin with a strategy theme or with the choice of an alternative for a key decision. Then the strategy is developed by picking one alternative from each decision column. One strategy should describe how things would have happened on their own—this might be the "momentum" or "do nothing" strategy, depending on the context.

Tables for major strategic studies can have as many as 40 or 50 columns. For tables this large, explicitly identifying the elements of major strategies often shows that what at first appeared to be a good strategy is a poor or unfeasible one. In addition, some decisions may be perceived to be mainly tactical or operational. Finally, some decisions may have alternatives dictated by the decision made for a more important strategic decision. Through these kinds of considerations, the complexity of even large strategy tables can be reduced to a conceptually manageable level.

Although it is not a quantitative tool, the strategy table is a surprisingly effective way to apply intuition and experience to a highly complex situation. When done correctly, the table can also be used to eliminate most of the possible strategies that are inconsistent, inferior, or undesirable.

James Broderick started off by describing the situation to the analyst. As the analyst listened, he noted all the decisions and options James Broderick mentioned. He then organized these into a simple strategy table (Figure 6–2a) and presented it to Broderick, asking him if it fairly represented the choices faced.

———————————————— **Figure 6–2** ————————————————

Progressive Development of Broderick's Strategy Table

a

Key Decisions		
Interest in Modena Place	Tenancy at Modena Place	Tenancy Elsewhere
Increase	Continue	None
Decrease	End	Rent
Maintain		

b

Key Decisions		
Interest in Modena Place	Tenancy at Modena Place	Tenancy Elsewhere
Increase	Continue	None
Decrease	End	Rent
Maintain		Buy
		Build

c

	Key Decisions		
Strategy Theme	Interest in Modena Place	Tenancy at Modena Place	Tenancy Elsewhere
I. Invest	Increase	Continue	None
	Decrease	End	Rent
II. Status Quo	Maintain		Buy
			Build

Broderick agreed the table included the three decisions Broderick Brokerage faced. The analyst then continued by asking what else the firm could do. For instance, if it moved, was the only choice to rent elsewhere? Broderick said the firm could just as well buy or even build elsewhere. Further, these options had the advantages of possibly getting space more specifically tailored to the company's needs and growth plan and of eliminating the present annoyance of having space on two different floors. In response to Broderick's comments, the analyst then added these options to the strategy table (Figure 6–2b).

Using this table, Broderick and the analyst discussed the different possible strategies. Broderick stated that, upon reflection, he really did not feel the firm would want to leave Modena Place at this time. His growth plans included opening a second office within two years, and he did not believe the firm would want to put a lot of resources into a new primary office now when a second office was on the way. Further, the prestige of Modena Place had worked well for the firm and the high rent costs were partially ameliorated by the return on the investment in the complex. The lower rent elsewhere would be partially offset by the loss of investment income, assuming that Modena Land would indeed want Broderick to sell its interest if it moved.

As far as selling Broderick's interest and remaining at Modena Place, the firm would do this only if it had a dire need for cash or if another truly lucrative investment opportunity presented itself. Neither of these possibilities was considered very likely. Thus, Broderick and the analyst picked out two strategies (Figure 6–2c) as being consistent with the firm's values and objectives. These strategies, then, would be the ones analyzed in further detail (including different possible levels of increased investment).

Basis Development: Using Influence Diagrams

Earlier, we developed the basic tools and theory of influence diagrams. In this section, we focus on using influence diagrams in fairly complicated analyses involving people throughout an organization and, later, on how deterministic sensitivity analysis identifies the most crucial of these uncertainties.

There are two ways to begin an introductory session using influence diagrams. One way is to start from a simple influence diagram that the analyst is fairly sure represents the "backbone" of the problem. This has the advantage of cutting short the initial phases of the discussion and the disadvantage of not allowing the session participants' understanding to grow while the diagram grows.

The opposite approach is to start with the value function on one side of the page and a decision node on the other and to gradually break the value function uncertainty into its components; near the end of the process, the decision variable becomes connected to the growing diagram. The advantages of this approach is threefold.

1. It focuses attention and demands agreement on the value function at the outset. It is surprising how much confusion in a decision problem arises because the decision criterion is not explicit and agreed on.

2. It focuses attention on the future rather than on the immediate concerns of selecting and implementing an alternative.

3. It allows all the participants to join in the thought process. This is valuable for obtaining enthusiastic implementation of the alternative that is finally chosen.

Most often, a modification of the second approach is used. The analyst begins the process, creating several nodes. Fairly soon, the participants get the idea and begin to contribute. People who are not quantitative often find themselves contributing enthusiastically and productively at this stage of the analysis.

Occasionally, a tree is a more natural tool than an influence diagram for opening the structuring session. This can occur when the sequential nature of the problem is very important. For instance, some litigation and R&D problems are more readily described by trees in the early stages of structuring. (See Chapter 7.)

In using an influence diagram to structure their problem (Figure 6–3), Broderick and the analyst first created the right-most node (net present value of the investment decision made) as the fundamental uncertainty; in other words, if they knew the probability distribution on NPV for each alternative, it would be easy to make the decision. Since this was the value function, it was drawn as an octagon.

The next question was, given that they could not determine the distribution on NPV for each alternative directly, what would they most like to know to reduce the uncertainty on NPV? Broderick indicated that he would most like to know the NPV of the property and the level of Broderick's investment decision. The analyst classified Broderick's responses as an uncertainty and a decision, wrote them down as an oval and a box, and drew arrows from each to NPV.

The analyst next asked what Broderick would most like to know to reduce the uncertainty on the NPV of the property. Broderick responded with cap rate (the rate used to capitalize the cash flow) and cash flow from operations. The analyst wrote these factors down in ovals (since neither were decisions) and drew arrows from them to the oval representing the NPV of the property. At each point, the analyst also checked whether arrows should be drawn to other ovals or boxes. They repeated this process until all the important uncertainties and decisions had been drawn.

Broderick and the analyst were unsure about whether to think of Space Vacancy as influencing Rental Rates or vice versa; as a result, they indicated this by drawing a double-headed arrow with a question mark between the two ovals. The final direction of the arrow would be determined by a decision on how best to model the influence and assess information on it.

When do we stop adding to the diagram? When we reach a level of detail where we can use intuition and judgment to make meaningful assessments. In practice, we usually add another level of decisions and uncertainties beyond this point, which are discarded later on as too detailed. Typically, an influence diagram for a complex diagram can grow to 50 or 60 decisions and uncertainties, can then be reduced to 10 or 20 by general considerations, and can be finally reduced to 5 to 10 by sensitivity analysis. (See "Deterministic Structuring: Sensitivity Analysis," page 154.)

The chief value of constructing the influence diagram is that it forces people to think hard about the decisions and uncertainties and their interrelationships. Specifically, people can contribute their thoughts and argue with others' conceptions, areas of investigation can be identified and responsibility established, and probabilistic dependencies can be elicited and examined.

Figure 6–3

Influence Diagram of the Broderick Investment Decision

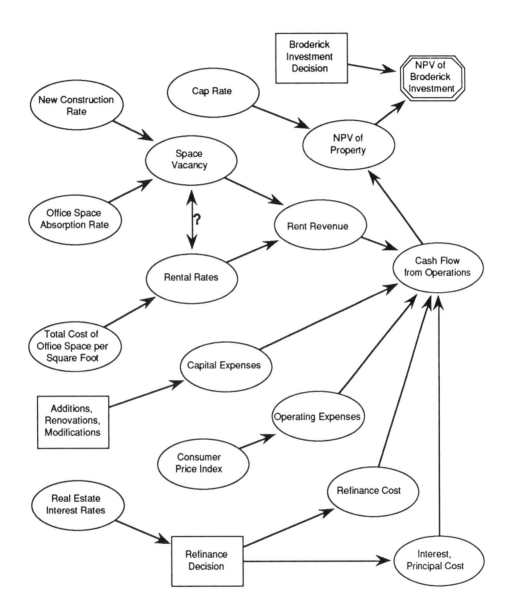

Deterministic Structuring: Modeling the Problem

Most corporate decision problems are complex enough to require using a model, usually implemented on a computer, to determine the value of each alternative. However, the models used today tend to be simpler than those used when decision analysis was first routinely applied to real-world problems. This change has come with the realization that the model does not need to depict the real world with absolute accuracy, but rather mainly needs to differentiate between the possible alternatives.

Preexistent corporate models are rarely useful for decision analyses. They tend to be too complex, take too long or are too expensive to run, and usually focus on quantities important to running the company but are not really relevant to making major decisions. For this reason, decision analysts almost always create a new "throwaway" model that simply and clearly describes the problem at hand. Once the decision is made, much of the model becomes irrelevant to future operations. What remains can sometimes be used as the core of a model for future business.

The primary criterion for the model is that it be accurate enough to distinguish between the alternatives. The large value differences caused by uncertainty will make the accuracy of the model relatively unimportant. The cyclical decision analysis approach enables us to successively refine the model as we go through iterations of the decision analysis cycle (Figure 6–1), which means the model does not have to be perfect the first time used.

One frequent comment is that "the model has to be complete and detailed enough to convince the decision-maker and others of its accuracy." Such logic is poor justification for building an overly complex model. To the contrary, decision-makers are often suspicious that very complex models are black boxes hiding all sorts of errors or incorrect assumptions. A well-wrought model is seldom rejected for being too simple. Because they are easier to understand, simple models also have the advantage of yielding insight into a problem that helps generate new alternatives.

Today's computing languages and packages (e.g., Lotus 1-2-3, Multiplan, Symphony, Microsoft Excel, Quattro, IFPS, APL, etc.) furnish the capability for simple logic and easy output, making it easy to understand and validate the model and to understand the results. The modeling language chosen should be accepted within the organization, familiar to those involved in the analysis, and compatible with the tools of decision analysis. The languages mentioned above are all compatible with the Supertree and Sensitivity software packages.

To analyze the options, the analyst built a spreadsheet model. The model had to relate together all the quantities indicated on the influence diagram (as either data inputs or calculation results) and had to be able to value all the different alternatives indicated in the strategy table. Most of these relationships could be expressed as simple financial calculations. The most difficult relationships to deal with were the relationship between New Construction Rate, Office Space Absorption Rate, and Space Vacancy (at Modena Place), and the relationship between Total Cost of Office Space per Square Foot and Rental Rates (at Modena Place). Presumably, Rental Rates could increase as office space costs increased, but, at some point, increased vacant space and price reductions in the local market would cause vacancies at Modena Place or force Modena Place to reduce its rates to keep tenants. How could these relationships be captured?

First, Broderick and the analyst agreed to have Rental Rates increase as office costs increased (as opposed to their historical faster-than-costs increases) and to use Space Vacancy to capture the market effects. (This decided the direction of the double-headed arrow on the influence diagram as pointing to Space Vacancy.) Then the analyst considered modeling a relationship between New Construction Rate, Office Space Absorption Rate, and Space Vacancy at Modena Place by establishing a market vacancy threshold below which Modena Place would continue at zero vacancy and above which vacancy at Modena Place would be a function of the market vacancy rate. However, given the lack of time and given Broderick's willingness to make quantitative assessments, they decided to assess the potential vacancy rates for Modena Place directly. The data inputs for the Lotus 1-2-3 spreadsheet are shown in Figure 6–4a. The first seven years of the final spreadsheet model are shown in Figure 6–4b; the actual spreadsheet goes out to 1995.

Note that the analyst separated the spreadsheet into a data inputs section and a calculations section. The data inputs section contains all the input numbers for the spreadsheet. The calculations section contains only equations, though, of course, the results of these calculations appear as numbers. By setting up the spreadsheet this way, the analyst has automatically parameterized the inputs for later analysis and made sure that he can easily scan down the complete list of data inputs.

Some programmers, especially those who use spreadsheets, are accustomed to entering a string of numbers to represent a time series, such as estimates of sales volumes for the next 10 or 20 years. To model the uncertainty and to help understand the results, these strings of numbers should be parameterized. For instance, for sales volume, we could enter an initial value and a growth rate instead of 10 or 20 numbers. Thus, decision analysis may require programmers to change their style of programming, especially if spreadsheets are used.

The following paragraphs contain modeling suggestions that may appear obvious to some. However, we have noticed that oversights in these areas are surprisingly frequent.

Modeling Profit

Care must be taken in modeling how revenue and cost change over time. Because profit is a small difference between these two larger numbers, it is extremely sensitive to the details of modeling. For many businesses, it is better to estimate costs and margin (or revenue and margin) rather than revenue and costs directly.

Sunk Costs

It is surprising how much confusion arises if investments have already been made in the area of the decision problem. This money is spent (it is a "sunk cost"), and the decision problem is what to do in the future, given present assets and experience. One approach is to exclude all sunk costs from the evaluation of the problem; the other approach is to include the sunk costs in all alternatives, including the "do nothing" alternatives.

─────────────────────────────── **Figure 6–4a** ───────────────────────────────

Spreadsheet Model of the Broderick Investment Decision

	A	B	C	D
1			Modena Land Company	
2			An Investment Analysis	
3	***PARAMETERS SECTION -- DATA INPUTS***			
4				
5	DESCRIPTION	VALUE	RANGE NAME	UNITS
6	Modena Vacancy Rate	5%	vacancy	annual rate
7	Initial Rent ($000)	$6,058	initrent	dollars/year
8	Annual Rent Escalation	3.5%	rentesc	annual rate
9	Inflation/Escalation Differenc	0%	realescalation	annual rate
10	Operating Expenses ($000)	$1,450		
11	Capital Expenses ($000)	$0		
12				
13	Loan Principal ($000)	$19,300	loanprinc	dollars
14	Interest Rate	12.25%	intrate	annual rate
15	Year Amortization Starts	1989	yramort	year
16	Years for Amortization	30	amortyears	length
17	Year of Refinancing	1989		
18	Interest Rate at Refinance	10.0%	refinance	annual rate
19	Points to Refinance	2.0%	points	
20	Min. Spread to Refinance	2.0%	spread	
21				
22	Inflation	3.5%	inflation	
23	Capitalization Rate	8.0%	caprate	
24	Discount Rate	8.5%	discount	
25	Risk Free Discount Rate	5.0%		
26	Broderick Purchase Share	0.5%	share	

Shutting Down the Business

Models should have a cutoff in them so that when margins are negative for more than a few years, the business shuts down. Models should also have checks to prevent unrealistic or impossible situations, such as a market share exceeding 100 percent. Remember that the decision tree will evaluate the model for a number of extreme cases and that unexpected values may occur in these cases, thus distorting the overall results.

—————————————— **Figure 6–4b** ——————————————

Spreadsheet Model of the Broderick Investment Decision

	A	B	C	D	E	F	G	H
41	***CALCULATIONS SECTION***							
42		1986	1987	1988	1989	1990	1991	1992
43	MODENA RENT REVENUE							
44	Rent Escalation	3.5%	3.5%	3.5%	3.5%	3.5%	3.5%	3.5%
45	Full Occupancy Rent	$6,058	$6,270	$6,489	$6,717	$6,952	$7,195	$7,447
46	Modena Vacancy Rate	5%	5%	5%	5%	5%	5%	5%
47	Net Rent After Vacancies	$5,755	$5,957	$6,165	$6,381	$6,604	$6,835	$7,074
48								
49	FINANCE COSTS							
50	Loan Principal	$19,300	$19,300	$19,300	$19,300	$18,657	$18,013	$17,370
51	Principal Payment	$0	$0	$0	$643	$643	$643	$643
52	Interest Rate Paid	12.3%	12.3%	12.3%	10.0%	10.0%	10.0%	10.0%
53	Interest Payment	$2,364	$2,364	$2,364	$1,930	$1,866	$1,801	$1,737
54	Total Finance Payments (w/pts)	$2,364	$2,364	$2,364	$2,959	$2,509	$2,445	$2,380
55								
56	INCOME STATEMENT ($000)							
57	Rent Revenue	$5,755	$5,957	$6,165	$6,381	$6,604	$6,835	$7,074
58	Operating Expenses	$1,450	$1,501	$1,553	$1,608	$1,664	$1,722	$1,782
59	Capital Expenses	$0	$0	$0	$0	$0	$0	$0
60	Finance Costs	$2,364	$2,364	$2,364	$2,959	$2,509	$2,445	$2,380
61		---						
62	Cash Flow from Operations	$1,941	$2,092	$2,247	$1,814	$2,431	$2,668	$2,912
63								
64	INVESTMENT VALUE ($000)							
65	Cap Rate Property Value	$24,261	$26,144	$28,094	$22,673	$30,390	$33,356	$36,397
66	Terminal Value (undiscounted)	$50,504						
67	NPV (Cash + Terminal Value)	$42,741						
68	Broderick Share of NPV	$214 npv						

Inflation

It is usually better to model in constant dollars, because you can then avoid simultaneously modeling both the systematic changes of prices and costs and the change from inflation. Remember, however, to deflate such items as interest payments, undepreciated capital, and working capital to account for the effects of inflation on them.

Terminal Value

Even when the model explicitly considers 10 to 15 years, as much as 50 percent of the net present value of a business may arise from the period beyond that modeled. This occurs especially for new product introductions and for research and development. It is therefore usually important to explicitly include a value for the business beyond the time period of the model. This value might be estimated as a sale value (perhaps expressed as a multiple of cash flow in the final year considered) or as a salvage value (estimated from assets, including working capital). In estimating this value of ongoing business, remember that no business lasts forever and that migrating to new forms of the business may require substantial new capital investments.

Broderick and the analyst had a number of value measures. They could have looked at the appreciation of Broderick Brokerage's investment in Modena Place over time and compared it with potential returns from other investments or they could have looked at the future value of Broderick's share and related it to future revenue needs of the firm. As is suggested for most decision analyses, they decided to focus on the NPV of cash flow from Modena Place (exclusive of taxes, because both Modena Land Company and Broderick Brokerage defer all their taxes). To model this profit, they projected rental rates and operating expenses directly, but they carefully controlled the difference between these numbers by having both increase at the rate of inflation and by having an explicit amount above or below the inflationary increase that rental rates change (the Inflation/Escalation difference). Rent revenue was further modified by vacancy rate projections.

Sunk costs were excluded from the calculations, including the cost of the initial Broderick investment. However, one further cost that was not in the spreadsheet but would be needed in the decision tree was the actual payment for the additional investment. There was no need to include a provision for shutting down the business, because Modena Place is so profitable that only a drastic event (such as an outbreak of Legionnaire's Disease at the complex) could cause it to turn unprofitable for a long period of time.

To eliminate inflation, Broderick and the analyst at first tried to model all flows in real terms. However, putting all flows in real terms made it difficult for Broderick to sort out and assess the relationship between inflation, interest rates, and cap rates. Therefore, the analysis was done in nominal dollars—which meant the discount rate used had to be the sum of a risk-free rate and the rate of inflation and had to be adjusted whenever the inflation assumption was changed.

The terminal value for the analysis was the cash flow from operations in the final year divided by the cap rate. Thus, the final NPV was calculated by adding the discounted terminal value of Modena Place to the discounted cash flow. In this case, the terminal value contributed about half of the NPV.

Deterministic Structuring: Sensitivity Analysis

One of the main tasks in the deterministic structuring phase is to sufficiently develop the model to produce credible base-case results. The base case is a set of input parameters used as a starting point for further analysis. If the decision alternatives are very different, it may be necessary to establish a base case for each alternative. If there is an underlying uncertainty of success or failure (as with a new product introduction), the base case should usually be estimated given success. Too much effort should not spent in establishing base-case values, since they are just a starting point. On the other hand, the values should be reasonable enough not to stir up unnecessary controversy.

Ideally, the base-case parameters should all represent a median value, which means that in most people's judgment there is a 50/50 chance that the true value will be above or below the value. In practice, however, base-case parameters are often developed from an unduly optimistic or pessimistic business plan. As the analysis progresses, some effort should be spent establishing a set of base-case parameters close to most people's median value.

For all important variables, a range of values should be established in early interviews: the base-case value, a low value (10 percent chance that the value will turn out to be lower), and a high value (10 percent chance that the value will turn out to be higher). The next task is to identify the crucial uncertainties, which is accomplished using deterministic sensitivity analysis. Frequently, this process shows that uncertainties originally thought to be important are relatively unimportant.

Deterministic sensitivity analysis starts by evaluating the model with all variables set to their base-case values, which gives the base-case value of the model. Then, for each of the variables in turn, the model is evaluated at the low value of the variable and then at the high value of the variable (with all other parameters kept at their base value), thus yielding low and high values of the model. The difference between the low and high value of the model is a measure of how sensitive the problem is to the uncertainty in that variable.

Supertree's companion program, Sensitivity, automates the deterministic sensitivity analysis. The program is especially valuable at this stage in the analysis because the model and base-case values are frequently revised, requiring a tedious reevaluation of the sensitivity analysis after each change.

Sensitivity is similar to Supertree. Refer to Appendix D for information on the PC-DOS/MS-DOS version of the Sensitivity software. This is the version used for the illustrations below; other versions have similar input and output.

James Broderick and the analyst listed the data inputs from the spreadsheet (Figure 6–4a) and developed ranges for them. That spreadsheet contained the base-case values for all inputs. They then input these data ranges into the Sensitivity program. For instance, by selecting the Add option from the `Structure` *menu, they input the information for Vacancy Rate (Cell B6), as in Figure 6–5.*

Figure 6–5

Screen Showing Sensitivity Variable Input

```
Name of variable: B6
Description: Vacancy Rate
Base value: .05
Variation type: VALUE
Low modifier: 0
High modifier: .30
```

The program allows for three variation types: Value [the low (high) modifier is substituted for the base value], Multiplicative [the base value is multiplied by the low (high) modifier], and Additive [the low (high) modifier is added to the base value]. Note that in the example, the variable being varied is the value of one of the cells in the data input section of the spreadsheet. Range names that refer to single cells could also be used as variable names.

The Joint option varies two or more variables together—all at their low (high) values simultaneously. The joint sensitivity input for inflation and refinance cost is shown in Figure 6–6.

Figure 6–6

Joint Sensitivity for Inflation and Refinance Cost

Enter a name for the joint sensitivity: J>INFL/FIN

Enter a description for this sensitivity: Inflation/Refinance

Joint variable name: J>INFL/FIN

Enter name at bottom line to add line; change name to blank to delete line.

Name	Base	Var Low	High
B22	.035	VAL .02	.1
B18	.10	ADD -.015	.05

The Show option (Figure 6–6) displays the data entered. The final column in this display, STATUS, is NEW for variations still to be performed and OLD for those that have already been evaluated.

The data used in the first pass at the sensitivity analysis were quite different from those displayed in Figure 6–7. Fortunately, the overall conclusions drawn from sensitivity analysis seldom change when the data are updated and refined. In the Broderick case, the sensitivity analysis conclusions remained substantially the same even after what appeared to be large changes in the data.

Just as in Supertree, the Evaluate option of Sensitivity uses the model to calculate results for each variation. The Analyze menu then displays the result of the evaluation through two options: List and Plot. The final column in the List display (Figure 6–8a) shows the swing, which is the largest of the absolute values of the differences between the high, low, and base values of the model for that variation. The variables are arranged so that those having the largest swing are at the top. The Plot option plots the swing (as shown in figures 6–8a and b); the base value is shown as the vertical line in the plot.

Those variables with the greatest swing are the crucial uncertainties that dominate the problem. As such, they will be treated as explicit uncertainties in the decision tree, while the remaining variables will be set to their base-case values (but may change with the decision alternatives). Several variables may tend to vary together and, even if they individually appear low in the sensitivity analysis table, their joint effect may be large enough for them to be included in the tree. These variables may be entered in the tree as separate nodes (with dependent probabilities) or as a single joint node that sets the values for two or more variables on each branch.

Figure 6–7

Sensitivity Input for Inflation and Broderick's Refinance Cost

Sensitivity name: Modena Sensitivity

Model name: L$MODENA$B68

VARIABLE	DESCRIPTION	BASE	TYPE	LOW	HIGH	STATUS
B6	Vacancy Rate	.05	VAL	0	.30	OLD
B9	Inflation/Escalation Diff.	0	VAL	-.03	.03	OLD
B18	Refinance Rate	.10	ADD	-.015	.05	OLD
B19	Refinance Points	.02	ADD	-.01	.01	OLD
B20	Spread to Refinance	.02	VAL	.015	.025	OLD
B22	Inflation	.035	VAL	.02	.1	OLD
B23	Cap Rate	.08	VAL	.065	.11	OLD
B24	Discount Rate	.085	VAL	.05	.1	OLD
B26	Broderick Purchase Share	.005	VAL	.0025	.01	OLD
J>INFL/FIN	Inflation/Refinance		JNT			OLD
J>INFL/REFIN/CAP	Inflation/Refinance/Cap Rate		JNT			OLD

JOINT SENSITIVITY DATA

NAME	VARIABLE	BASE	TYPE	LOW	HIGH
J>INFL/FIN	B22	.035	VAL	.02	.1
	B18	.10	ADD	-.015	.05
J>INFL/REFIN/CAP	B22	.035	VAL	.02	.1
	B18	.10	ADD	-.015	.05
	B23	.08	VAL	.065	.11

Some variables in the sensitivity analysis table may be decision or value variables (such as the discount rate). These variables may have been included in the sensitivity analysis for general interest, but they should not be confused with the critical uncertainties that will go into the tree as chance nodes.

──────────────────────────── **Figure 6–8a** ────────────────────────────

Crucial Variables in Broderick's Decision

Show variable description or name or both? DESCRIPTION

SENSITIVITY 1/1/86 12:00 Modena Sensitivity

Model: L$MODENA$B68

Base Value: 214

```
|-----------------------------|-----||---|-----|-----||--------|--------|-------|
|BRODERICK PURCHASE SHARE  | .005|| V |.0025| .01 ||   107|   427| 320.6|
|INFLATION                 | .035|| V |.02  | .1  ||   181|   402| 221.5|
|INFLATION/REFINANCE       |     || J |     |     ||   194|   385| 190.8|
|INFLATION/ESCALATION DIFF.| 0   || V |-.03 | .03 ||   130|   316| 186.0|
|VACANCY RATE              | .05 || V |0    | .30 ||   239|    90| 149.0|
|INFLATION/REFINANCE/CAPRATE|    || J |     |     ||   218|   317| 103.2|
|DISCOUNT RATE             | .085|| V |.05  | .10 ||   270|   194|  75.5|
|CAP RATE                  | .08 || V |.065 | .11 ||   241|   181|  60.3|
|REFINANCE RATE            | .10 || A |-.015| .05 ||   227|   196|  30.7|
|SPREAD TO REFINANCE       | .02 || V |.015 | .025||   214|   196|  17.8|
|REFINANCE POINTS          | .02 || A |-.01 | .01 ||   214|   213|   1.4|
|----------------------------------------------------------------------------|
```

JOINT SENSITIVITY DATA

NAME	VARIABLE	BASE	TYPE	LOW	HIGH
J>INFL/FIN	B22	.035	VAL	.02	.1
	B18	.10	ADD	-.015	.05
J>INFL/REFIN/CAP	B22	.035	VAL	.02	.1
	B18	.10	ADD	-.015	.05
	B23	.08	VAL	.065	.11

In reviewing the sensitivity results, Broderick and the analyst noted that the most sensitive variable was the Broderick Purchase Share, which would be included in the decision tree as a decision node. The next most sensitive variable was inflation, which, as Broderick suspected, could greatly change the compounded rate of rent escalation and thus the value of the property. The joint sensitivity on inflation and refinance rate was less sensitive because the

─────────────── **Figure 6–8b** ───────────────

Crucial Variables in Broderick's Decision—Screen to Plot Sensitivity

The low and high values for the sensitivity are: 90 427

Enter the low and high values for the plot: 0 500

Single or double spacing? DOUBLE

Show variable description or name? DESCRIPTION

Show low/high modifiers? YES

Label for axis? NPV ($000)

SENSITIVITY 1/1/86 12:00 Modena Sensitivity

Model: L$MODENA$B68

Base Value: 214

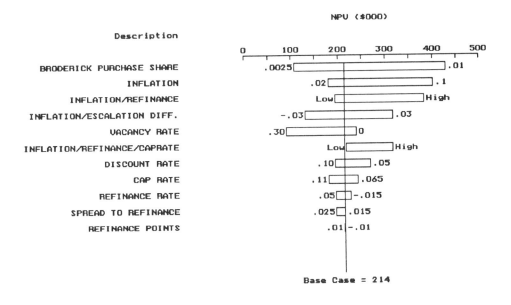

effects of high inflation and high refinance rate counteracted each other. Because of this counteractive effect, the joint sensitivity on inflation, refinance rate, and cap rate was even less sensitive than the joint sensitivity on inflation and refinance rate.

Vacancy rate was a sensitive variable, although the uncertainty was not as important as first expected. The discount rate was also sensitive, but, as mentioned earlier, Broderick and the analyst would handle that by linking the discount rate to the inflation assumption for each scenario—the underlying real discount rate is a matter of time preference, not an uncertainty. The remaining variables showed some sensitivity but not as much as the joint sensitivities, vacancy rate, or inflation.

Often, the largest uncertainties affect all the alternatives in the same way, causing the model result for each alternative to vary up or down about the same amount. Usually, the uncertainties that affect all the alternatives this way are underlying macroeconomic variables. To conserve tree size and leave space for the uncertainties that distinguish between alternatives, these macroeconomic variables can be combined into one or two nodes. Each branch of the combined node would then represent a scenario in which several macroeconomic variables are set.

For their sensitivities, Broderick and the analyst had three economic variables: inflation, refinance rate, and cap rate. The model was sensitive to all three of these. Because these three variables tended to vary together, Broderick decided to assess economic scenarios in which a value for each variable would be set.

Since ordinarily a few uncertainties really do dominate the problem, we should not be afraid to limit the number of uncertainties in the tree to several with the largest swing in the sensitivity analysis. However, we need to examine our assumptions and results a little more closely to understand how to recognize this dominance. The basic assumptions are listed below.

1. The certain equivalent is the measure that takes into account the uncertainty of a venture. We can therefore determine how important a variable is to the overall uncertainty by determining how important it is to the certain equivalent value.

2. As mentioned in Chapter 5, we can approximate the certain equivalent using the following equation:

$$\text{Certain Equivalent} = \text{Expected Value} - \frac{1}{2} \frac{\text{Variance}}{\text{Risk Tolerance}} \qquad (6\text{--}1)$$

Since the variance accounts for the way uncertainty affects the certain equivalent, the variance is the measure of uncertainty we are looking for.

3. To obtain the variance, we recall the statistical result that, for probabilistically independent variables and for small variations of these variables, the total variance is the sum of the variances for each variable. The variance for each variable is the square of the standard deviation, which is, in turn, proportional to the width of the distribution or swing for each variable. (Recall that the swing is obtained by evaluating the model for the 10 percent and 90 percent points for each variable.)

4. Thus, the square of the swing for a variable determines how important it is to the overall uncertainty.

Accordingly, one easy way to compare the importance of uncertainty in the variables is to square the swing and express it as a percentage of the sum of squares of all the swings. Figure 6–9 displays the results of this calculation for the Modena

Land Company variables. Note that the Broderick Purchase Share variable has been removed (because it is a decision), the discount rate variable has been removed (because it will be determined by the inflation assumption and a time preference), and the individual inflation, refinance rate, and cap rate variables have been removed (because they are included in the joint sensitivity).

─────────────────────────── Figure 6–9 ───────────────────────────

Critical Uncertainties in Broderick's Decision

	Swing	Square of Swing	Percent of Sum of Squares	Running Sum of Percent
Infl./Esc. Difference	186.0	34,596	51.1	51.1
Vacancy Rate	149.0	22,201	32.8	83.9
Infl./Refin./Cap. Rate	103.0	10,609	15.6	99.5
Spread to Refinance	17.8	317	0.5	100.0
Refinance Points	1.4	2	0.0	100.0

Thus, we see that, for this example, the variation in inflation/escalation difference and vacancy rate captures 83.9 percent of the total effect of uncertainty in the problem. In most problems with more variables and more complex models, we find that the top three or four variables capture 80 to 90 percent of the effects of uncertainty.

Remember, though, that for this approximation to be valid, we need to use probabilistically independent variables. With dependent variables, use the joint sensitivity as illustrated above. This joint sensitivity must then be probabilistically independent from the other variables listed.

Probabilistic Evaluation: Building and Pruning the Tree

Even after deterministic sensitivity analysis, it is often difficult to limit the tree to a reasonable size. If there are, for instance, n nodes in a tree and each node has three branches, a symmetric tree will have 3^n paths. For example, for seven nodes, we would have 2,187 paths. If the model takes 10 seconds to calculate an answer (not untypical of a model on a personal computer), the evaluation command will take over five hours to execute. If we add another node or two, change a node from three to four branches, or construct a more elaborate model, we will have a tree that is impractical to evaluate on a personal computer.

How large a tree is reasonable? This depends greatly on the type of problem (and on the opinion of the analyst). However, we feel that for most problems, 50 to 200 paths per alternative is sufficient. This number of paths allows us to include the three generic uncertainties that often affect an alternative: uncertainty about the growth of the market, uncertainty in competitive action or reaction, and uncertainty in how well we will fare. At three branches a node, we have 27 paths per alternative, leaving room for several other nodes if called for. After the full-scale analysis is complete, we will probably find that around 20 paths per alternative are enough to draw all the conclusions. Reducing the tree to this size is often important for clarifying the results and drawing the tree for the final presentation to the decision-maker.

How can you make your tree small enough to evaluate? By reducing the number of branches at each node, by reducing the number of nodes, and by creating asymmetric trees. Simplifying the model can also help by reducing the time required to evaluate the tree. We consider each of these options in turn.

What is a reasonable number of branches at a node? Our experience indicates that chance nodes are usually well approximated by three branches. Going to four or more branches seldom perceptibly affects the overall profit distribution. While we can use two branches for uncertainties that deterministic sensitivity analysis shows to be less important, there is no central branch in a two-branch node to trace the effect of the base case. With decision nodes, we can use the preliminary evaluation to eliminate the inferior alternatives and narrow down to the three or four really distinct and most promising alternatives.

What is a reasonable number of nodes in a tree? A good number to aim for is five or six nodes. Normally, there are too many nodes in the initial version of the tree, and the tree has to be pruned before it can be evaluated. In pruning the tree, four types of nodes compete for a place on the final tree: decision nodes, chance nodes with effects common to all alternatives, chance nodes with effects that distinguish between alternatives, and chance (or decision) nodes that are not really important to the tree but should be included for political reasons.

By using the results of the deterministic sensitivity analysis, we can usually manage to discuss and eliminate the politically important nodes from consideration. Indeed, this may be one of the important insights from the analysis. If necessary, chance nodes with effects common to all alternatives can be combined into one or two nodes whose branches represent scenarios (combinations of events). If there are still too many nodes, we must be creative in combining variables, restructuring the tree, and using further sensitivity analysis to narrow down the number of important uncertainties even more. In cases of real necessity, we may have to run a separate tree for each alternative. If we do this, we will have to do some calculations by hand to reorder the tree (i.e., to obtain value of information), but we can still have Supertree do most of the work for us.

Creating asymmetric trees is another way to reduce tree size. For instance, when uncertainty is important for one alternative but not for another, we can have the chance node for this uncertainty follow only the alternative for which it is important. Similarly, an uncertainty may be important only for certain branches of a chance node, in which case you can have the node follow only those branches.

Finally, we can simplify the model to shorten its running time and, thus, the time required to evaluate the tree. Models can be simplified by eliminating calculations of quantities that were initially of interest but that are not necessary for calculating the net present value of cash flow. Models can similarly be simplified by replacing complicated calculations with simplified ones that produce approximately the same results.

As a practical matter, Supertree on a PC-DOS/MS-DOS personal computer with 640K of RAM can handle trees with up to 8,000 paths, although it may take a long time for some of the operations to execute. Furthermore, while we can evaluate trees this large, we may run out of memory in trying to analyze or reorder. (A more powerful version of Supertree is being developed that can deal with larger trees.)

In general, beginning with a small version of the tree is better. Nothing is as discouraging as starting off by running up against multiple errors from hardware/software limitations—correcting one error, waiting a long time for the tree to reevaluate, and then finding another error.

For Broderick Brokerage, the deterministic sensitivity analysis neatly reduced the problem to three variables: vacancy rate, economic scenario, and the inflation/rent escalation difference (or real rent escalation). Thus, the analyst drew a reduced influence diagram (Figure 6–10).

───────────────────────── **Figure 6–10** ─────────────────────────

Simplified Influence Diagram of Broderick Investment Decision

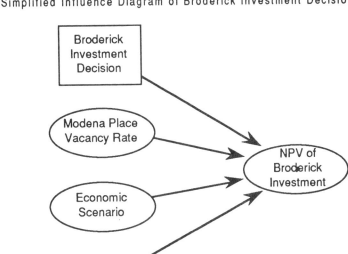

All other variables were set to their base-case values or determined by model calculations.

The decision tree, then, consisted of three uncertainties, a decision, and the spreadsheet model to calculate an NPV for each path through the tree. The analyst drew the tree as shown in Figure 6–11. Because the uncertainties are independent of one another (the dependencies are captured in the economic scenario variable), he could have drawn the uncertainties in any order. He needed to draw all the uncertainties after the decision, because information on the resolution of these uncertainties will not be available until after the decision is made.

—————————————— **Figure 6–11** ——————————————

Decision Tree for the Broderick Investment Decision

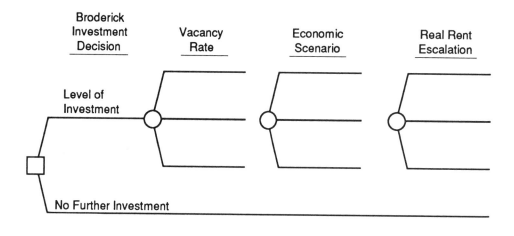

The analyst then went back to Broderick to more carefully examine the uncertainty on the variables in the tree. The previous ranges were fine for sensitivity analysis, but now the analyst wanted to assess complete distributions to obtain better quality information for the tree. (See Chapter 8 for more on this process.) For the Broderick investment decision, he wanted the actual possible levels of investment (including zero for no further investment). He thus obtained the information to fill out the tree (Figure 6–12) and was ready to evaluate it and begin analyzing it.

—————————————— **Figure 6–12** ——————————————

Probability Distributions for Analyzing the Broderick Investment Decision

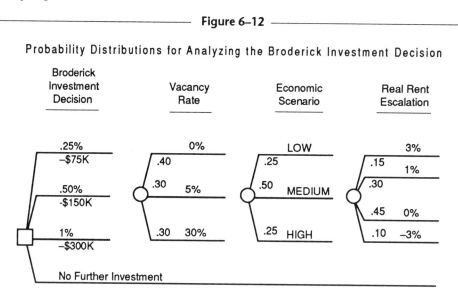

The tree contained a single node for the economic scenario that set three variables at the same time. This is implemented by a lookup table in the spreadsheet, as shown in Figure 6–13. The lookup table is contained in cells B34...D37. The node passes the word LOW, MEDIUM, or HIGH to cell B32, and a lookup function call in the proper data input cell picks up the inflation rate, cap rate, or refinance rate off the proper row of the lookup table: cell B22 contains the formula @HLOOKUP (B32, B34..D37, 1), cell B18 contains @HLOOKUP (B32, B34..D37, 2), and cell B23 contains @HLOOKUP (B32, B34..D37, 3).

Figure 6–13

Scenarios Screen

		A	B	C	D
		A	B	C	D
30	***SCENARIOS SECTION***				
31					
32	Economic Scenario		MEDIUM	scenario	
33					
34			LOW	MEDIUM	HIGH
35	Inflation		2.00%	3.50%	10.00%
36	Interest Rate at Refinance		8.50%	10.00%	15.00%
37	Capitalization Rate		6.50%	8.00%	11.00%

The analyst was surprised to see how much the information from the assessed probability distributions differed from the ranges used in the first pass at the deterministic sensitivity analysis. The data in figures 6–7 and 6–8 are taken from the final pass at the deterministic sensitivity analysis. For instance, the assessment on vacancy rate showed that Broderick felt Modena Place could get up to the prevailing vacancy rate in the area (30 percent). The original range used in the sensitivity analysis went up to only 5 percent! This extraordinarily large change occurred because Broderick's outlook had become more pessimistic as a result of consulting a knowledgeable friend after the sensitivity ranges were encoded. Further, the assessment on real rent escalation after inflation showed just how uncertain Broderick was about whether Modena Place could maintain its commanding market position and pricing. His distribution yielded a .10 chance that Modena Place would have to increase its rates 3 percent below inflation and thus come down to the level of other rates in the area.

The tree information was now ready for input to Supertree. The information from the Supertree Structure Show option is shown in Figure 6–14. Note that for ease of interpretation, range names were assigned to the cells in the spreadsheet. (For example, cell B26 was assigned the range name SHARE.)

--- **Figure 6-14** ---

Data for Decision Tree

Tree name: Modena Land Investment

STRUCTURE	NAMES	OUTCOMES	PROBS	REWARDS
1 D 2 2 2 6	SHARE	.0025 .005 .01 0		-75 -150 -300 0
2 C 3 3 3	VACANCY	0 .05 .30	.40 .30 .30	
3 C 4 4 4	SCENARIO	LOW MEDIUM HIGH	.25 .50 .25	
4 C 5 5 5 5	REALESCALATION	.03 .01 0 -.03	.15 .30 .45 .1	
5 E	L$MODENA$NPV	Depends on 1 2 3 4		
6 E	0			

Basis Appraisal: Obtaining Information from the Tree

The analyst began analyzing the tree by plotting the probability distributions (Figure 6–15). The expected values showed investing the maximum amount for a 1 percent share was preferred, with an expected value of $128,000. The other alternatives had decreasing expected values, with a zero expected value for the no investment alternative. (This assumes that the no investment alternative means putting the money in the bank where it will yield the same rate of return as the discount rate—thus making the net present value always zero.)

However, as illustrated by the width of the distributions, investing the maximum amount for a 1 percent share also had the greatest risk. The potential values for this alternative ranged from –$248,000 to $418,000—illustrating how the joint variation of the uncertainties and the assessed probability distributions produced far more potential variation than was revealed in the sensitivity analysis. On an expected-value basis, Broderick Brokerage should make the maximum additional investment in Modena Place, but there was around a 30 percent chance it would actually lose part of the investment.

Besides getting expected values (certain equivalents) and probability distributions on profit for the alternatives, we can get a wealth of information to help us glean all possible insights from the tree.

Conditional Distributions

First, we can look at the distributions and expected values (certain equivalents) at points other than the first node in the tree and see if these conditional values hold any surprises.

To better understand where the potential risks and profits came from, the analyst decided to look at what the distributions for the preferred (maximum investment) alternative would be, given particular outcomes for each uncertainty. In other words, he wanted the distribution for alternative 3 given a 0 percent vacancy rate, given a 10 percent vacancy rate, and given a 30 percent vacancy rate. To obtain these conditional distributions, he plotted the multiple distributions at node 2 (the vacancy node) and specified branch 3 for node 1 (the maximum investment alternative). The resulting plot (Figure 6–16) showed him that the expected value for this alternative varied from $211,000 to –$94,000 depending on what the vacancy rate was.

––––––––––––––––––––––– **Figure 6–15** –––––––––––––––––––––––

Probability Distributions for Broderick's Investment Alternatives

```
Present Order of Nodes:
  1 2 3 4
New Order of Nodes:
  1 2 3 4
Node at which to plot the probability distribution or distributions? 1
Cumulative or histogram plot? CUMULATIVE
Single or multiple distributions? MULTIPLE
Label for axis? NPV ($000)
Smallest and largest values in distributions are: -247.5 418.0
Enter lower and upper limits for display: -250 450


>> Distribution Plotted     1/1/86  12:00  Modena Land Investment
```

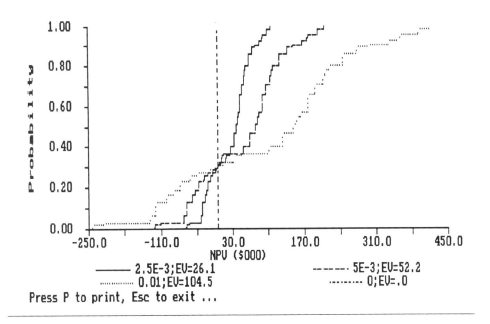

Press P to print, Esc to exit ...

He then plotted the conditional distributions for node 3 (the economic scenario node) by moving it behind node 1 (remember that the relative order of chance nodes does not matter) and then plotting the distributions at node 3. The resulting plot (Figure 6–17) shows little variation in expected value arising from the different economic scenarios. This result surprised the analyst, because the economic variables were sensitive in the initial deterministic sensitivity analysis. However, upon reviewing the tree information, he noted that the tree information reflected the compensating effect that he had seen in the sensitivity analysis from varying all three variables at the same time. Thus, in the tree, the effects of changing inflation, refinance rate, and cap rate nearly canceled each other out.

--- **Figure 6–16** ---

Probability Distribution on NPV Given Maximum Share and Different Vacancy Rates

```
Present Order of Nodes:
  1 2 3 4
New Order of Nodes:
  1 2 3 4
Node at which to plot the probability distribution or distributions? 2
Do you wish the rewards of the initial nodes to be included in the values? YES
Cumulative or histogram plot? CUMULATIVE
Single or multiple distributions? MULTIPLE
Label for axis? NPV ($000)
Branch number for node 1: 3
  SHARE = 0.01
Smallest and largest values in distributions are: -247.5 418.0
Enter lower and upper limits for display: -250 450


>> Distribution Plotted    1/1/86  12:00  Modena Land Investment
```

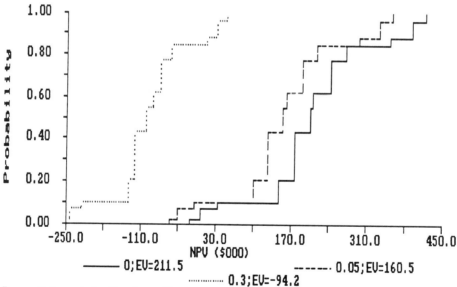

```
Press P to print, Esc to exit ...
```

Finally, the analyst plotted (Figure 6–18) the conditional distributions for node 4 (the real rent escalation node). This uncertainty produced a larger variation in expected value than did the vacancy rate ($350,000 versus a difference of $306,000 for vacancy rate), but it did not have quite as much potential for losses. (The expected loss from vacancy rate is .30 × $94,200 = –$28,260 versus .10 × –$80,500 = –$8,050 for real rent escalation.)

——————————————————— **Figure 6–17** ———————————————————

Probability Distribution on NPV Given Maximum Share and Different Economic Scenarios

```
Present Order of Nodes:
  1 2 3 4
New Order of Nodes:
  1 3 2 4
Node at which to plot the probability distribution or distributions? 3
Do you wish the rewards of the initial nodes to be included in the values? YES
Cumulative or histogram plot? CUMULATIVE
Single or multiple distributions? MULTIPLE
Label for axis? NPV ($000)
Branch number for node 1: 3
   SHARE = 0.01
Smallest and largest values in distributions are: -247.5 418.0
Enter lower and upper limits for display: -250 450
```

>> Distribution Plotted   1/1/86 12:00 Modena Land Investment

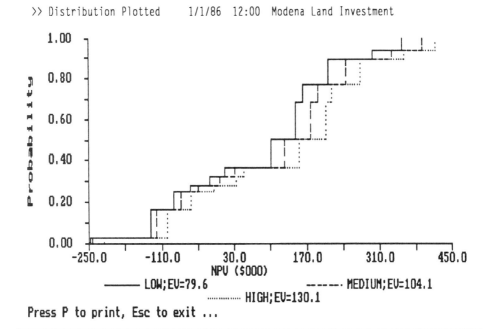

Press P to print, Esc to exit ...

The analyst concluded that while real rent escalation produced the greatest variation in expected value, the vacancy rate had the greatest potential for causing losses.

—————————————————————— **Figure 6–18** ——————————————————————

Probability Distribution on NPV Given Maximum Share and Different Real Rent Escalation Rates

```
Present Order of Nodes:
  1 2 3 4
New Order of Nodes:
  1 4 2 3
Node at which to plot the probability distribution or distributions? 4
Do you wish the rewards of the initial nodes to be included in the values? YES
Cumulative or histogram plot? CUMULATIVE
Single or multiple distributions? MULTIPLE
Label for axis? NPV ($000)
Branch number for node 1: 3
  SHARE = 0.01
Smallest and largest values in distributions are: -247.5 418.0
Enter lower and upper limits for display: -250 450

>> Distribution Plotted     1/1/86  12:00  Modena Land Investment
```

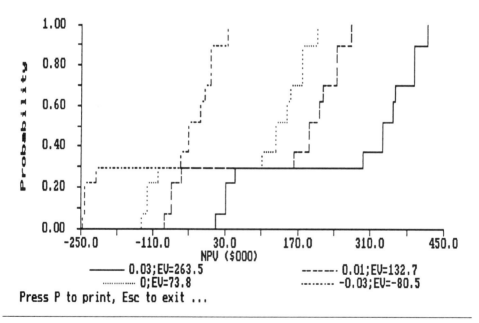

```
Press P to print, Esc to exit ...
```

Value of Perfect Information

Besides looking at conditional distributions, we can calculate the value of perfect information for each uncertainty. If possible information-gathering efforts have costs comparable to these values, we can formulate the decision for gathering imperfect information and see if it is worthwhile.

The analyst rolled back the tree with the chance nodes brought one by one in front of the decision node and then took the difference between the resulting expected value and the original expected value to obtain the values of information (Figure 6–19).

The vacancy rate had the greatest value of information, while the economic scenario had zero value of information. Earlier analysis revealed that changes in the scenario did not change the expected value very much, and now the zero value of information revealed that changes in the scenario would never change the preferred decision. However, the worst outcomes for vacancy and real rent escalation would make the investment not worthwhile (remembering the negative expected values from above for these unfavorable outcomes). The analyst did not research the options for imperfect information because of lack of time.

Value of Perfect Control

Another insight we can glean form the tree is the value of perfect control. If there are feasible control procedures of reasonable cost, we can generate the new alternative of using these control procedures and reevaluate the tree.

To obtain the values with perfect control, the analyst displayed the tree with the uncertain nodes brought to the front of the tree one by one; then he picked the best expected value for that node and took the difference between it and the original expected value (Figure 6–19).

—————————————————— **Figure 6–19** ——————————————————

The Values of Perfect Information and Perfect Control in the Broderick Investment Decision

Uncertainty	Value of Perfect Information ($000)	Value of Perfect Control ($000)
Vacancy rate	28	107
Economic scenario	0	26
Real rent escalation	8	159
All three uncertainties	31	418

The analyst noted that although the vacancy rate had the greatest value of information, which made sense because it also had the greatest potential losses—losses that could be avoided with perfect information—real rent escalation had the greatest value of control, which also made sense because it produced the greatest variation in expected value.

As for controlling these uncertainties, the analyst suggested to Broderick that Modena Place might be able to sign tenants to longer-term leases or might be able to trade off lower rent escalation for lower vacancy rate. Indeed, the analysis had thus far only indirectly addressed the possible interaction of these variables.

Sensitivity Analysis to Probabilities, Risk Attitude, and Value Trade-offs

We can use the tree to perform sensitivity analysis to probability, risk attitude, and value trade-offs (such as the time value of money captured in the discount rate). We can also form new sensitivity displays by picking two values for the axes of a graph, such as the probabilities for two different uncertainties, and by showing which alternative is preferred in which region of the graph.

Sensitivity analysis results like these can suggest areas for refining estimates; show the consequences of using different, conflicting estimates from experts; and avoid potential "Monday morning quarterbacking."

The analyst had already done a form of probabilistic sensitivity by looking at the conditional probability distributions. Now, however, he used the Sensitivity Probability option in Supertree to see if the preferred decision would change with changes in the probabilities for a particular uncertainty. The probability sensitivity for vacancy (Figure 6–20) revealed that when the probability of zero vacancy ranged from 0 to around .3, no investment was preferred, while the highest level of investment was preferred when the probability of zero vacancy was .3 or greater.

As noted earlier from the zero value of information, changes in probabilities for the economic scenario (Figure 6–21) never changed the preferred decision. The analyst concluded that while including the economic scenario was important for capturing the total potential variation in net present value, it was not important for decision-making, because it did not distinguish between the alternatives.

Changes in probabilities for real rent escalation (Figure 6–22) showed no investment to be preferred for low probabilities of 3 percent real rent escalation, while maximum investment became preferred as the probability of 3 percent real rent escalation increased above about 20 percent.

The analyst then performed a sensitivity analysis to risk attitude (Figure 6–23) to see if risk aversion would switch the preferred decision. Indeed, depending on the level of risk aversion, any of the three investment levels might be preferred. From risk neutrality (expected-value decision-making) to a risk tolerance of around $185,000, the maximum additional investment of 1 percent is preferred. From a risk tolerance of $185,000 to around $90,000, the middle-level investment of 0.5 percent is preferred. Then, from $90,000 down to the end of the graph at $50,000, the smallest investment level of 0.25 percent is preferred. Thus, the results showed that increasing risk aversion would make Broderick Brokerage prefer smaller and smaller investments, with their smaller potential gains and losses. However, significantly, the no investment option is never preferred under the range of risk tolerances considered.

To sum up the sensitivity of the decision in one plot, the analyst took the two most decision-sensitive variables (vacancy and real rent escalation) and plotted how changes in their probabilities together changed the preferred decision. To do this, he first set the probabilities for the middle branch of the vacancy node and the two middle branches of the real escalation node to zero. Then he varied the probabilities for the first and last vacancy branches by hand and, for each set of probabilities, ran sensitivity to probability for the real escalation node. He then used these results to produce a plot (Figure 6–24).*

---

*As mentioned in Chapter 4, the S' notation refers to the variations in the underlying state of knowledge S implied by varying the probabilities.

Figure 6-20

Sensitivity of the Broderick Investment Decision to Changes in Probabilities
for Vacancy Rates

Present Order of Nodes:
  1 2 3 4
New Order of Nodes:
  1 2 3 4
For which node do you want the sensitivity to probability? 2
Label for axis? NPV ($000)
Because the sensitivity requires multiple tree evaluations,
       it may take some time to run.
Smallest and largest values encountered are: -94.2 211.5
Lower and upper limits for vertical axis: -100 225
If the first node is a decision, the sensitivity will be shown for all
branches.
The vertical axis is the expected value.
       The horizontal axis is the probability of the first branch of node 2;
       the last branch of node 2 has the remainder of the probability.

>> Probability Sensitivity Plotted   1/1/86 12:00 Modena Land Investment

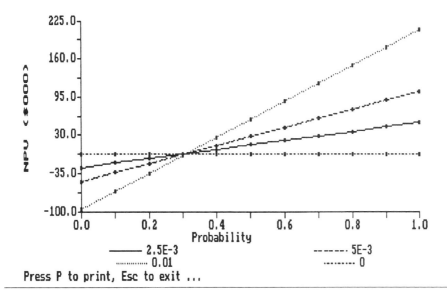

Press P to print, Esc to exit ...

Several interesting conclusions can be drawn from the results developed in
Figure 6–24. First, if Broderick were sure that Modena would experience vacancies
[p(vacancy = 0 | S') = 0], he would require near certainty of high rent escalation [p(real
escalation = .03 | S') ≥ .9] to invest. Conversely, if he were certain that there would be
no vacancies [p(vacancy = 0 | S') = 1], he would invest even if high escalation rates
were very unlikely.

Policy Matrix

If there are decisions at other than the first node in the tree, we can generate a policy matrix to show what they would be. A policy matrix lists all paths through the tree that lead to the final decision node and the alternatives that would be chosen for that path. The policy matrix shows the importance (or lack of importance) of explicitly considering the decision in the analysis and may help in establishing a monitoring program and contingency plans. The simplest way to obtain the policy matrix is to display the tree for all the nodes up to and including the right-most decision node.

For Broderick Brokerage, the only decision node was in the front of the tree. However, if Broderick and the analyst did choose to seek out imperfect information on the uncertainty with the highest value of perfect information (vacancy rate), they might get the policy matrix of Figure 6–25.

At this point, Broderick and the analyst pondered further improvements to the analysis. The most glaring omission was not explicitly considering the other options in the strategy table, such as renting, building, or buying elsewhere. Broderick knew that no amount of sensitivity analysis would reveal the value of an alternative that was not included.

Further, they had not really captured what the no investment alternative would be. If the money was not invested in Modena Place, it would not actually be going into a risk-free investment with the same rate of return as the discount rate. The money either would be going into some sort of bond or certificate of deposit (with uncertainty in interest rates causing uncertainty in the final return) or would be invested in Broderick Brokerage itself (with uncertainty in the firm's performance causing uncertainty in the final return). The preferred decision might be different if investment in Modena Place were evaluated against these similarly uncertain alternatives.

The analyst suggested they might also more carefully model the relationship between vacancy rates and prices in Modena Place and in the market. While Broderick could see how added refinement in this sensitive area might provide more insights into the problem, he was rather more worried about the things left out of the analysis than about refining those things already in the analysis. In any case, the next partners' meeting was fast approaching and the remaining time was needed for digesting and summarizing the results, not expanding them.

———————————— **Figure 6–21** ————————————

Sensitivity of the Broderick Investment Decision to Changes in
Probabilities for Economic Scenarios

```
Present Order of Nodes:
  1 2 3 4
New Order of Nodes:
  1 2 3 4
For which node do you want the sensitivity to probability? 3
Label for axis? NPV ($000)
Because the sensitivity requires multiple tree evaluations,
        it may take some time to run.
Smallest and largest values encountered are: .0 130.1
Lower and upper limits for vertical axis: 0 150
If the first node is a decision, the sensitivity will be shown for all
branches.
The vertical axis is the expected value.
        The horizontal axis is the probability of the first branch of node 3;
        the last branch of node 3 has the remainder of the probability.
```

>> Probability Sensitivity Plotted   1/1/86 12:00 Modena Land Investment

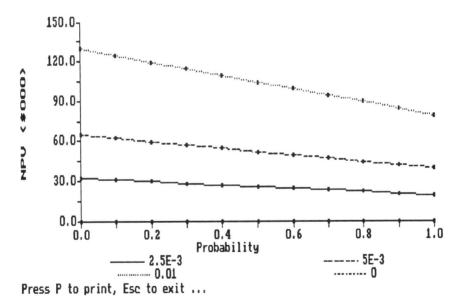

Press P to print, Esc to exit ...

———————————————————— **Figure 6–22** ————————————————————

Sensitivity of the Broderick Investment Decision to Changes in Probabilities for Real Rent Escalation Rates

```
Present Order of Nodes:
  1 2 3 4
New Order of Nodes:
  1 2 3 4
For which node do you want the sensitivity to probability? 4
Label for axis? NPV ($000)
Because the sensitivity requires multiple tree evaluations,
        it may take some time to run.
Smallest and largest values encountered are: -80.5 263.5
Lower and upper limits for vertical axis: -100 300
If the first node is a decision, the sensitivity will be shown for all
branches.
The vertical axis is the expected value.
        The horizontal axis is the probability of the first branch of node 4;
        the last branch of node 4 has the remainder of the probability.


>> Probability Sensitivity Plotted     1/1/86  12:00  Modena Land Investment
```

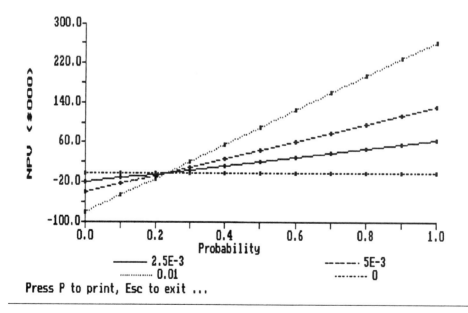

Press P to print, Esc to exit ...

—————————————— **Figure 6–23** ——————————————

Sensitivity of the Broderick Investment Decision to the Value of the Risk Tolerance

```
Present Order of Nodes:
  1 2 3 4
New Order of Nodes:
  1 2 3 4
Vary risk tolerance from infinity down to? 50
Label for axis? NPV ($000)
Because the sensitivity requires multiple tree evaluations,
        the program may take some time to run.
Smallest and largest certain equivalents are: -86.6 104.5
Lower and upper limits to be used for plot: -90 110
If the first node is a decision, the sensitivity is shown for all branches.
The vertical axis is the certain equivalent.
The horizontal axis is the risk tolerance;
    the scale is linear in 1/risk tolerance.


>> Risk Sensitivity Plotted     1/1/86  12:00  Modena Land Investment
```

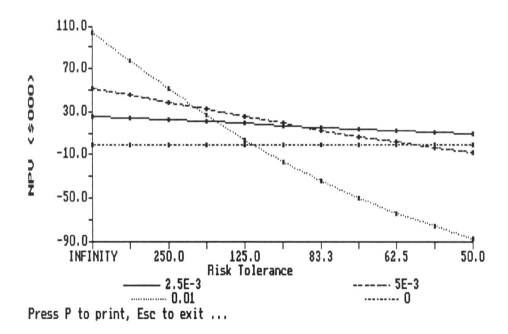

Press P to print, Esc to exit ...

Figure 6–24

Sensitivity of the Broderick Investment Decision to Changes in
Probabilities for Vacancy Rates and for Real Escalation Rates

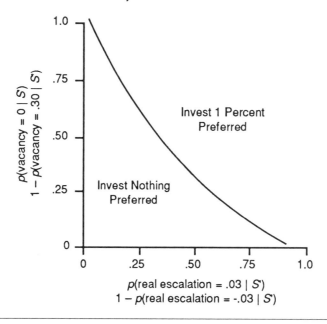

p(real escalation = .03 | S')
1 − p(real escalation = -.03 | S')

Figure 6–25

Policy Matrix for Expanded Version of the Broderick Investment Decision

Seek Imperfect Information on Vacancy	Vacancy Prediction	Invest Further in Modena Place
Yes	0 percent	Yes
	5 percent	Yes
	30 percent	No
No	None	Yes

Time to Prepare and Present

A final, equally important phase of the analysis takes place after the last pass through the cycle and the last tree analysis. The analyst and project team members should set time aside to explore the information contained in the analysis, obtain insight into the real-world problems and questions the analysis was intended to answer, and make sure the analysis addresses all the decision-maker's concerns. The insights and results then need to be packaged for effective communication to the decision-maker. (See Chapter 9 for details.)

An all-too-frequent mistake is to continue the analysis until the last possible moment. There is not sufficient time for the careful preparation necessary for synthesizing, summarizing, and presenting the conclusions. As a result, the report or presentation can be a haphazard one that may omit crucial points, may contain analytical errors, and may (worse yet) be difficult to understand. Such a report may fail to cogently address the decision-maker's concerns and thus fail to provide motivation for action—which relegates the results to a file rather than establishing them as a basis for action.

James Broderick presented his results at the next partners' meeting. Because he knew the partners would want to see some of the nuts and bolts that went into the numbers, he presented a base-case run of the spreadsheet model and then the tree results. The other partners were very impressed with the thoroughness of his analysis and with the way he produced a reasonable but quite different picture from the one painted by the Modena Land Company.

Broderick himself was rather ambivalent at this point about investing further. The other partners agreed with him that while the investment looked good on an expected-value basis, there was considerable risk of losing money. One way or another, increased competition for office space and high vacancy rates would erode Modena Place's current commanding market position. Further, the firm's strategic plan called for opening a second office within two to three years, and, hence, it did not want to tie up capital in the primary office when a second one was on the way. The firm therefore decided not to invest further in Modena Place.

Summary

The decision analysis cycle makes it possible to tackle complex, real-world problems by breaking the decision analysis into four stages: basis development, deterministic structuring, probabilistic evaluation, and basis appraisal.

In the basis development stage, the problem is described, a value measure is chosen, the important decisions and uncertainties are identified, and the relationships between these decisions and uncertainties and the value measure are sketched out.

In the deterministic structuring stage, these decision and chance variables are related together in a deterministic model that calculates a value for any combination of these variables. Deterministic sensitivity analysis is then used to identify the key decisions and uncertainties.

In the probabilistic evaluation stage, these crucial decisions and uncertainties are structured into a decision tree, which is then analyzed.

In the basis appraisal stage, the results of the previous three stages are used to review the analysis for relevance and insight and to formulate recommendations (that may be for action or for further study).

When applied correctly, this cyclical process makes most decision problems tractable. In the case of Broderick Brokerage, the five-day limit allowed only one real pass through the cycle. But the structured approach ensured that at the end of the week, the best possible results were available for decision-making.

Problems and Discussion Topics

6.1   A friend has come to you for help in deciding how to maximize his grade point average. What steps would you go through in developing a basis for the decision? What would you have at the end of the basis development? What are the next steps?

6.2   In the decision analysis cycle, there is a deterministic structuring phase. This phase often includes deterministic sensitivity analysis. In Chapter 3, there is a discussion of probabilistic sensitivity analysis. What are the differences between the two kinds of sensitivity analysis? What effects (or functions) does deterministic sensitivity analysis have in dealing with complex problems? Compare these two sensitivities with the sensitivity to risk tolerance seen in Chapter 5.

6.3   The complexity of a real-world problem is also reflected in its dynamic nature. The process of analyzing a decision problem can create new decision problems and add to the complexity of the original problem. A typical decision faced by the decision-maker (company) after the preliminary or pilot analysis is whether to proceed with the recommendation from the analysis or gather further information. Fortunately, the decision analysis cycle provides a framework with which to make this decision. Frequently, there are even preliminary numerical results available, such as the values of information.

What other complexities can arise in the course of analyzing the decision problem? (Hint: consider the elements of the decision basis.)

6.4   The ways of making decisions can be divided into normative methods and descriptive methods. Normative methods describe what people should do in a given situation. Descriptive methods focus on what people typically do.

For instance, if you face a decision on whether to hold on to a stock or sell it, a decision analysis (normative method) would tell you what you should do. Descriptively, many people make this kind of decision by asking their spouse, broker, or friends to effectively make the decision for them.

Is it possible to reconcile the two methods of decision-making? Provide an argument and example to support your judgment.

6.5   The framing of a decision problem describes how the decision is stated. An example is describing the effects of a new, dangerous, and relatively untested drug in terms of either net lives saved or net lives lost. Decision-makers are often affected by the framing of the problem. For example, the information they provide and preferences they express will vary with the framing of the problem. Many of these framing issues are believed to be psychological in origin. What could you do to avoid these problems?

6.6   Innovative Foods Corporation (IFC) is a wholly owned subsidiary of Universal Foods Corporation (UFC). UFC is a major Fortune 500 company in the food processing industry. IFC is in the market of supplying specialized processed foods for human consumption. In 1979, the total market for specialized processed foods amounted to $600 million and is growing.

IFC's leading products are dehydrated and processed foods targeted at two consumer groups: people on a special diet and people who are recovering after a serious illness. IFC has been using a well-known additive in its food processing, Divit, which is a recognized food additive in the food processing industry.

By carefully researching and testing its products, IFC has established a secure but small market share. IFC has a reputation as a good and reliable company and anticipates a $2 million net yearly cash flow after taxes for the next 20 years.

In the last year, IFC management has become acquainted with some troublesome experiments carried out by its research division. The results of these experiments indicate a high probability that Divit is carcinogenic when applied in very high concentrations to the skin of mice. The carcinogenic properties when Divit is ingested by humans are by no means certain. IFC believes its competitors may be on the same track. If Divit turns out to be carcinogenic, the FDA will surely ban it, thus bringing about a major decrease in IFC's earnings and probably the loss of most of IFC's hard-earned market share.

However, IFC management has also been informed about another option. Its research division has developed another additive, Biovit. The research director believes Biovit is an excellent food additive that will have none of the problems of Divit. At present, the manufacturing costs of Biovit are uncertain. To process its food with Biovit, IFC will have to invest around $150 million. IFC management must make an important decision: should it continue to use Divit and face its potential banning or should it invest in new facilities and start using Biovit?

Assume you are a member of IFC's executive committee. How would you structure your thinking about this problem? Are there ethical considerations?

6.7   Plastic Co. is a fairly large company that manufactures bulk plastics for a large variety of uses. It has an extensive network of customers—companies that turn the bulk plastic into items that are then sold to the end-user.

Tech Co. is a European company that owns a process for formulating a special plastic that is useful for making bearings for high-speed centrifuges. There are several other potential high-tech applications for this special plastic. The same production equipment can also be used for making a common, low-margin type of plastic, which, it turns out, is not a plastic that Plastic Co. currently makes.

Tech Co. does not want to enter the U.S. market and is offering Plastic Co. an exclusive license for the manufacturing technology. The asking price is a $500,000 license fee plus 5 percent of sales for 10 years.

Plastic Co. has determined that the equipment could come in a small size (3 million pounds per year) or a large size (10 million pounds per year). The respective costs for the equipment are $3 million and $7 million. Tech Co.'s experience has been that production costs are $0.20 per pound.

a. Begin to develop the decision basis for this decision. What are the alternatives? What are the uncertainties? What is the value? What information do you have? What information do you still need?

b. Designate someone to be the decision-maker. She will be the president of Plastic Co. Review with her the work you have done so far and finish structuring the decision. Assess any further information you may need.

c. Analyze the decision and produce a recommended course of action. Review the recommendation with the decision-maker. (Does she need to know the details of the analysis?) Is your recommendation useful to her? Does she believe and understand it? Why or why not?

6.8 Form a group to analyze a decision about whether or not to add a salad bar to a pizza parlor. Designate at least one person to be the client and one person to be the analyst. (You may have more than one of each.) Make a pass through the decision analysis cycle as described below.

a. **Background.** Develop an image of the pizza parlor that is as realistic as possible for whoever is playing the client. (This will greatly aid in the assessments.) How large is the place? How old is it? Who owns it? Who runs it? What kind of an area is it located in? What kind of clientele does it have? What is currently on the menu? What is the monthly sales volume? How many customers does it have daily? What are the peak hours? What kind of decor does it have?

b. **Basis Development.** Develop the basis for the decision. If you like, you may use an influence diagram for this step. What decisions must be made? What are the significant uncertainties? How do they relate to one another? What are the values on which the decision will be made? Try to keep the problem description simple.

c. **Deterministic Structuring.** Develop a model to determine the value for any scenario the tree might generate. The model may be assessed values, a Basic endpoint expression in Supertree, or an external spreadsheet model. Use sensitivity analysis, if necessary, to reduce the number of variables in the tree. Focus on modeling to help your understanding of the problem and to distinguish between alternatives.

d. **Probabilistic Evaluation.** Build and analyze the decision tree. For simplicity, try to keep the number of nodes down to four or five. You may start with a larger tree and then eliminate the nodes that do not distinguish between alternatives. Examine profit distributions, expected values, tree drawings, probability sensitivities, etc. Check that the results are consistent with your understanding of the problem.

e. **Basis Appraisal.** What is the preferred decision? How do its expected value and risk compare with those of the other alternatives? Is the preferred decision sensitive to changes in probabilities or risk attitude. What are the values of information and control? Would the client feel comfortable acting at this point, or would further study be advisable?

f. **Action.** Prepare a list of requirements for implementing the recommended alternative. These may include allocating funding, hiring personnel, hiring contractors, etc., or there may be no requirements if the recommendation was to do nothing. Has the analysis shed any light on the steps required for implementation? Is there any value to updating the analysis periodically to provide further guidance?

6.9 Form a small group to perform a decision analysis of a case study you have previously worked on. Assign roles. You will need at least one analyst and one client who can supply structure and probabilities. Complete at least one pass through the cycle, perhaps limiting the exercise to two or three hours. Spend most of the time structuring the problem and preparing a final report.

6.10 Insitu Corp., an energy company, had developed a new technology for oil drilling in cold climates. The technology involved injecting a heated chemical solution into the well field at one location and waiting for the solution to percolate through the oil-bearing formation. Then, the solution was pumped out of the well field at another location and the oil was extracted in a processing plant.

Insitu had proven this technology on a pilot scale and was considering whether to build a full-scale project on its Whalebone property in Alaska. One of the major uncertainties was the capital cost of constructing the complex, consisting of the plant, pipeline, and well field. An engineering and design firm had estimated a base cost of $320 million. To obtain financial backing for the project, Insitu felt it needed to verify this cost.

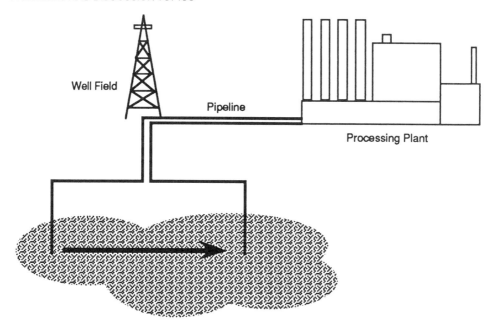

A team assembled in September to review the cost estimate identified two major risks in the estimate. First was the question of the efficiency of the new technology. In the pilot plant, a flow rate of 500 gallons per minute had produced a solution 30 percent saturated with oil. However, if the full-scale process were less efficient and produced, say, only 10 percent saturation at a flow rate of 1,000 gallons per minute, additional equipment would be required for the volume of oil produced to remain constant. Engineering estimates the additional equipment would add 15 percent to the base cost.

The second major risk was the productivity of the union workers. The largest influence on productivity was the unemployment rate in the area. If unemployment were high, then the workers would be less likely to strike and would work harder. Unemployment, in turn, depended on the number of large pipeline and energy projects competing for workers and, ultimately, on energy prices. Changes in energy prices in recent years had been correlated with productivity variations as large as +30 percent. The team decided to include in its estimate a contingency to reflect these risks in the capital cost.

As the team was about to adjourn, someone asked if there were any other reasons the base cost could be exceeded. An inexperienced staffer, Ms. Pessi Mist, asked whether they were sure the construction would be finished on time. Since wage and materials rates were escalating at almost 25 percent a year, she felt a late construction schedule would increase costs. Her question was met with disbelief. The venture manager explained that most of the construction had to be completed before the spring thaw date, because heavy equipment could not be operated on the muskeg once it thawed in June. The EPA was very unlikely to allow summer construction on the fragile muskeg. In addition, a June 1 expected completion date had already been announced publicly by the president of Insitu. No one had to mention the company's unblemished record of completing projects within the allotted time once construction was under way. Because of the cost of interest on funds expended during construction, Insitu had made this its trademark.

Undaunted, Ms. Mist pursued the question of what remained to be done before the three-month construction schedule could begin. A cost engineer explained that the board of directors had taken the position that it would not meet to review the project unless the native claims issues were settled for the pipeline route. Without board approval, a contract could not be let. If the contractor did not arrange for materials delivery to the site by March 1, the start of the project would be delayed. In addition, the board required a minimum of one month for deliberation, and two months each were required to let contracts or deliver materials.

Sparked by the mention of the EPA, another young staffer, Enviro Mann, asked what would happen if the EPA did not allow the spent solution to be pumped back into the mine shaft as planned. The environmental engineer assured him that a waste pond would cost only $5 million to build. The possibility that recycling of the solution would be required was very remote.

a. Draw an influence diagram for the total capital cost of the complex in current dollars.

Slightly unsettled by the questions of Ms. Mist and Mr. Mann, the team assigned them the job of developing a better picture of the risks in the capital cost. Mist and Mann interviewed a number of people in the corporation. From the engineering manager, who knew the most about scaling up chemical processes, they assessed a 75 percent chance that the full-scale plant would work as efficiently as the pilot plant. From the regulatory affairs department, they assessed a 50 percent chance that the spent solution could be put in the mine shaft. There was only a 20 percent chance that recycling would be required. However, if this additional step were required in the process, $120 million of equipment would be added. The manager of regulatory affairs was uncomfortable about whether the EPA would allow summer construction on the muskeg. He could remember only five winter Alaskan projects that had been delayed until summer. Of these, only one had been allowed to proceed before the September 1 freeze date. For the four events necessary to begin construction, the following probabilities were assessed.

Event	Probability
Native claims issues settled for pipeline route by October 1	.70
Board of Directors approval by November 1	.50
Contract let by January 1	.90
Materials on site by March 1	.25

The probability distribution below was assessed for worker productivity. Ms. Mist noted that labor costs were only 35 percent of the total construction costs.

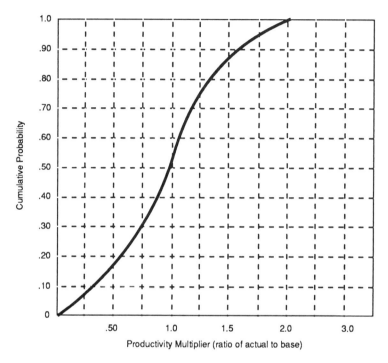

b. Draw a probability tree for the total capital cost of the project in current dollars. Label the branches and put in the probabilities.

c. Write an equation for the cost model to calculate the total capital cost of the project.

d. Calculate a probability distribution on the total capital cost of the project in current dollars. How do you explain its shape?

e. Perform a sensitivity analysis to determine the most important risks in the total cost. Calculate the following quantities.

- The change in total expected cost when each individual variable changes from its lowest to its highest value. This answers the question, "How much difference does this variable make in the expected cost?"

- The expected change in the standard deviation of the total cost if perfect information were available on each variable. This answers the question, "How much does this variable contribute to the risk?" Why can't we do ordinary value of information calculations?

f. What conclusions, insights, and recommendations would you make for risk management and cost control?

7

Corporate Applications of Decision Analysis

In the previous chapters of this book, we used simple examples to illustrate decision analysis techniques. In this chapter, we discuss several of the most important corporate applications of decision analysis—examples that provide some general outlines and points to consider when approaching a problem for the first time.

Because of the tremendous variations encountered in practice, these examples should not be viewed as templates, much less as cookbook formulas for analysis. A decision tree formulation is seldom appropriate for any problem other than the one it was designed for. Thus, the reader should concentrate on the process of understanding and structuring the problem that leads to the tree formulation.

New Product Introduction

One of the classic applications of decision analysis is introducing new products to the marketplace. Such problems have a large amount of uncertainty. Will the market accept the new product? How will the competition respond? How long will the product last? What will the margins be? If the product introduction requires large amounts of investment (such as capital for production equipment, promotion, or advertising), the decision may be a source of substantial risk to the company.

For many products, the model to evaluate the cash flow can be based on a simple product life cycle model (Figure 7–1).

This simple model requires only four parameters (length of introduction phase, maturity phase, decline phase, and market share at maturity) and, given the large uncertainties involved, is usually a sufficiently accurate description.

To complete the calculation of cash flow, we also need the size and growth rate of the market, fixed and variable costs, capital investment, the cost of ongoing research and development, the margin realized, and the value of possible follow-on business.

Figure 7–1

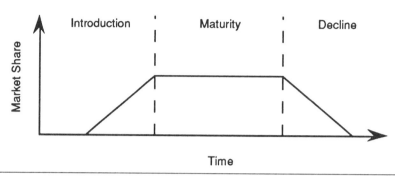

A Simple Product Life Cycle Model for Evaluating Cash Flow

One of the most difficult aspects of analyzing new products is determining precisely how to model revenues and costs. Many products are sold like commodities in that prices are determined by some markup or margin over cost, usually the costs of the highest-cost producer. As a new entry to the market, our costs may be high if we have not moved down the learning curve or low if we have the latest, most efficient means of production. The first possibility can sometimes be handled by including a start-up cost. In the second case, we should consider the possibility that our margins decline over time. Specifically, either the competition strives to match our costs or new competitors enter the market and drive out the old high-cost producers, thus reducing prices.

Other types of products have some differentiation from competing products, at least at the time of introduction. In this case, modeling price over time will be quite difficult. One possibility is to make the absolute price (e.g., $7 each) or relative price (e.g., 20 percent over competition) a decision variable and let market share be an uncertainty, with probabilities depending on the pricing decision. Alternatively, we could make market share a decision (e.g., hold 30 percent of market) and let realized price be an uncertainty, similarly depending on the share decision. In any case, the model should check that margins do not become unreasonably high or low over any extended period.

Two aspects of competition should be considered: (1) What will the competition do over time, perhaps in response to our entry into the market and our pricing? and (2) What is the possibility of some competitive breakthrough that will completely change the market? We might include these considerations by assessing the price necessary to hold a particular market share given different competitor actions or product introductions.

The influence diagram (Figure 7–2a) shows one way of relating all these factors. This influence diagram is a disguised and simplified version of one used in an actual application. We see that the product introduction affects sales volume (because there are no sales if the product is not introduced) and product positioning. Product positioning in turn influences margins, costs, and some aspects of the product life cycle, which, together with market size, share, and sales volume, determine the net present value (NPV) for the product.

Figure 7–2

Critical Uncertainties and Decisions in a New Product Introduction

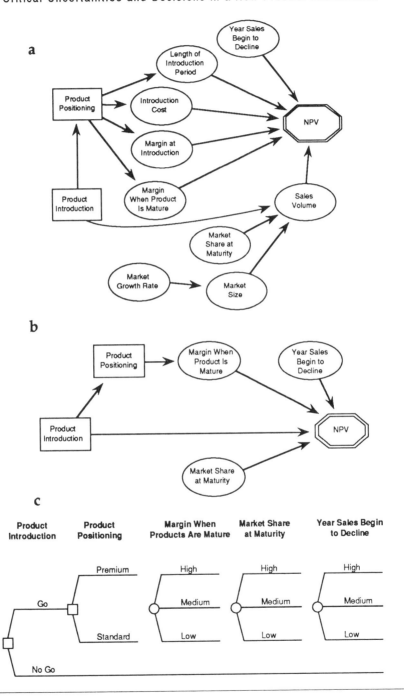

A model was used to capture the relationships in this influence diagram, and sensitivity analysis was then applied to determine the critical uncertainties and decisions. Those uncertainties and decisions are shown in influence diagram form (Figure 7–2b) and in tree form (Figure 7–2c).

The first node is a decision about whether to introduce the product, with the Go option requiring a major capital investment. The second node represents a decision on how the product is positioned relative to existing competitive products, which affects the size of the introduction costs, the length of the growth period, and the initial margins. The third node represents the margins achieved during the maturity period of the life cycle. These margins depend on the product positioning decision. Thus, probabilities for different levels of margin vary according to the product positioning decision; in this case, the company was a market leader, and its initial actions would help set later prices (and margins).

The fourth node represents uncertainty in market share during the maturity phase. The probabilities of this node were independent of the other nodes, since the company and the product were judged important enough that the initial product positioning would not affect the mature market share. The final node is the year the decline phase begins in the product life cycle. The probabilities for this node were also judged probabilistically independent of the previous nodes, implying that in no case is the product so successful (or unsuccessful) as to accelerate (or delay) competitors' introduction of the next generation product.

Research and Development Decisions

Research and development (R&D) is one of the most obvious areas for applying decision analysis in the corporate sector, since R&D decisions usually have large and unavoidable uncertainty. Any evaluation of whether a project justifies its cost must deal with this uncertainty. Though decisions on individual R&D projects usually do not involve large enough costs to pose significant risk to a company, the existence of an adequate portfolio of R&D projects is frequently critically important to the company's continued well-being.

General research without any specific application (also called "blue-sky" research) is difficult to evaluate, no matter what methodology is used. It is usually best to restrict analysis of research to laboratory work with an identified application. One example of research with an identified application is work on a coating to reduce corrosion in chemical plant pipes and to coat nonstick cookware.

In an R&D project where an application has been identified, there are a series of decisions: research, development, scaleup, and commercialization. Luckily, not all these decisions are relevant for every R&D project. For research, we can start or not start the research (or continue or terminate it if it is already in progress). For development, we can abandon development or continue engineering to develop a practical product or process. For scaleup, we can abandon scaleup or build a pilot plant. For commercializing a product, we can abandon commercialization, introduce the product, replace an existing product, or wait until the competition introduces a similar product. For commercializing a process, we can abandon the process, use it ourselves, license it to others, or sell the rights to the process outright.

Besides having very different decision alternatives to evaluate, products and processes also require quite different modeling techniques. Products have a commercial value modeled identically to the new product introductions described above. Processes have value when they replace an existing process and lead to more efficient operations; their value usually disappears when they themselves are replaced.

A difficulty often arises in defining exactly what it means for research to be technically successful. It may be necessary to model several different levels of technical success, with branches in a chance node corresponding to each possible level. Furthermore, it may be desirable to separate into distinct nodes the various technical hurdles that must be surpassed for overall technical success. These nodes might then be collapsed into a single composite node for entry into the tree.

A typical influence diagram for an R&D problem (Figure 7–3a) shows the different decisions that must be made and the uncertainties that must be resolved before an R&D project can be valued. First is the decision of whether or not to conduct the research, followed by an uncertainty on the success or failure of the research. Then follows the decision of whether or not to undertake development of the product, followed by an uncertainty on the success or failure of development. The final decision is of whether or not to commercialize the product, which, in turn, leads to an uncertainty on market success if the product is commercialized. The arrows from each decision to the final net present value show how all the decisions and the market success must be known before the research can be valued.

The influence diagram might have more arrows than shown if, for instance, there were different potential levels of market success depending on the development program chosen (which would mean an arrow from Development Decision to Market Success) or if the level of research affected market success, perhaps because of timing changes in product introduction (which would similarly mean an arrow from Research Decision to Market Success).

In the decision tree for this influence diagram (Figure 7–3b), an initial research decision is followed by a node for the success or failure of the research. (The competitive advances nodes were dropped for simplicity.) Given research success, there is a development (engineering) decision node and a chance node for the outcome of development. Finally, there is a decision on commercialization, followed by the uncertainty on the market value of the product. At each decision point, there is a cost associated with proceeding.

A typical probability distribution from an R&D decision tree has a vertical line corresponding to the probability of research failure, which occurs at a negative value—the cost of performing the unsuccessful research (Figure 7–4). The rest of the distribution corresponds to various outcomes given research success. The distribution shows some probability of outcomes worse than research failure: research success followed by market failure so great that market entry costs are not covered.

Frequently, one of the main benefits of using decision analysis on R&D projects is improved communication between the research and business departments. In particular, research can use the precise language of probability to communicate its hopes and fears about the technical success of different research projects, and the business side can use probability distributions to communicate its knowledge about future markets in a nonthreatening manner. Without this kind of communication,

──────── **Figure 7–3** ────────

Critical Uncertainties and Decisions in an R&D Project

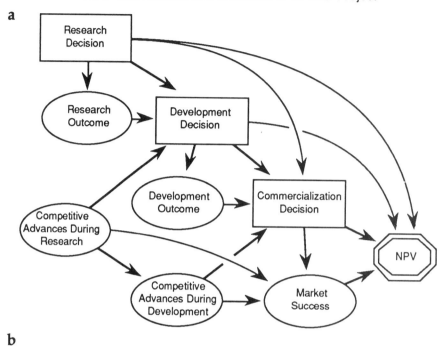

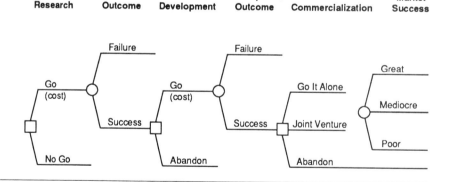

research could work on projects with little commercial potential, and business could have overly optimistic or pessimistic expectations for research results.

Decision analysis can also help the head of research in managing the portfolio of research projects. The two most important numbers used are the probability of research success and the expected value given research success. Of course, the product of these two numbers is the expected value of the research project, which should be greater than the expected cost of beginning or continuing the research. We

Probability Distribution from an R&D Decision Tree

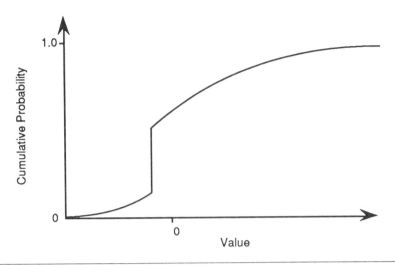

can use a graph to display how each research project fits into the portfolio (Figure 7–5a). The graph shows probability of research success versus expected commercial value given research success; each dot represents an R&D project.

The regions of the graph can be characterized according to the value of the projects that fall within them. The curved lines in Figure 7–5b are lines of equal expected value. (Expected value is the probability of research success × expected commercial value given research success.) The turkeys are low-probability, low-value projects that do not contribute much to the portfolio. Bread-and-butter projects are low-value but high-probability projects; often routine product or process improvements, they are desirable because of their high probability. However, a portfolio unduly weighted in this area can lead to long-term strategic weakness for a company—nothing new and great is on the way. Question marks are the high-value, low-probability projects that typically represent early research into potential product or process breakthroughs. While these projects are desirable, a portfolio unduly weighted in this area tends to perform erratically. Silver bullets (high in value and probability) are the things every research director would love to find. Unfortunately, they are rare.

Litigation Decision Analysis

Litigation is an area in which uncertainty is extremely important and where the stakes may be large enough to pose a serious risk to a company if it loses a suit or provide a significant opportunity if it wins one.

In one common kind of litigation decision, a company is being sued and has the opportunity to settle out of court. Thus, it has to decide on whether to settle the case or to continue in litigation (Figure 7–6). If the company chooses to litigate, there is an uncertainty concerning what the judgment will be and the size of the judgment if the

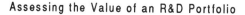

Figure 7–5

Assessing the Value of an R&D Portfolio

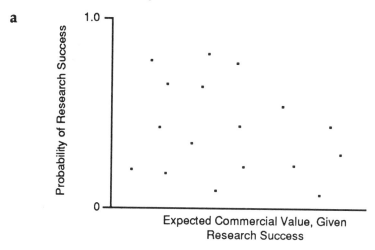

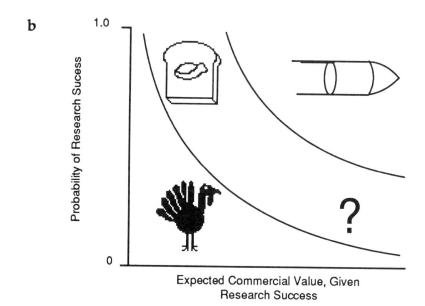

company is found liable. If the company chooses to settle, there is some uncertainty about the final settlement cost. Presumably, however, the plaintiff's counsel has indicated the size of potential settlements. There is a question mark on the arrow between the Settlement Cost node and the Settle/Litigate Decision node to indicate that the arrow should be there if the settlement cost is known and should not be there if it is still an uncertainty.

Figure 7-6

Critical Uncertainties and Decisions in a Litigation Question

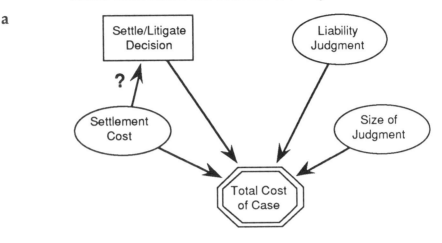

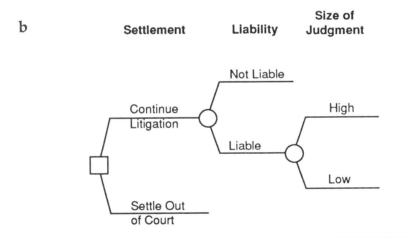

The decision tree formulation for this problem begins with a decision node on whether to litigate or settle. The litigation branch is followed by uncertainties on the verdict and on the size of the judgment if the company is found liable. The Settle Out of Court alternative branch will be followed by an uncertainty in Settlement Cost if the questionable arrow in the influence diagram does not exist.

One implicit assumption in this tree is that this is the company's last opportunity to settle out of court. If this were not the case, there should be another decision about whether to settle out of court later, perhaps after something has been learned to change the probabilities for liability or size of judgment.

Modeling in litigation tends to be simple. However, it is important to discount future values and to include the cost of the proceedings since large cases tend to last a long time. It is also important to include in all the outcome values the cost or value of setting a precedent.

Other litigation decision problems can be examined with decision analysis. For instance, the value of pretrial work and investigation can be analyzed. The value of this work is either value of information (the trial strategy can be chosen better) or value of control (the probability of a favorable outcome can be increased).

Litigation problems can be difficult for the analyst. Lawyers are often highly resistant to the notion that someone (the analyst) is telling them how to do their job. Lawyers, like doctors or polymer chemists or nuclear physicists, are quite right in thinking that their years of training and practice have made them facile with complexities and language to which the ordinary analyst is not privy.

This impression is perhaps reinforced for lawyers by the special legal monopoly accorded their profession and by their traditional independence from clients in all decisions except those decisive to the outcome of a claim (such as whether to accept a particular settlement offer).

Therefore, it is especially important that a legal decision analysis meet two important goals. First, it should reflect the counsel's best judgment about the law and precedent that bear on the client's prospects. Second, it should forcefully direct that judgment to the value measure of importance to the client.

To meet the first goal, analyses will often be very detailed at the influence diagram stage, reflecting alternative legal theories and perhaps even evidentiary issues bearing on what the judge or jury will see.

The second goal of forcefully directing the analysis toward the value measure is accomplished by framing the analysis in terms of what the judge or jury will actually consider and base the decision on.

Decision analysis can dramatically improve the quality of communication about legal questions. Without it, the difficulties in communicating about legal complexities and uncertainties often remove effective control from the hands of the president or CEO of the company—a serious condition since the suit may have major implications for the company's future. In addition, explicitly considering risk attitude through decision analysis can enable management to make litigation decisions in a manner consistent with regular business decisions.

Bidding Strategies

Bidding is another area in which uncertainty plays an important role. The difficulties in bidding problems are twofold. First, we are uncertain about how our competitors will bid and thus about whether we will win the bid or not. Second, as the number of serious competitors increases, competition becomes keener and the likelihood of winning decreases. In these highly competitive bidding situations, the winning bid can yield the winner little profit (and even a net loss).

Figure 7-7

Critical Uncertainties and Decisions in a Bidding Problem

a

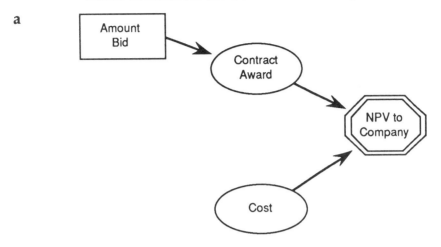

b

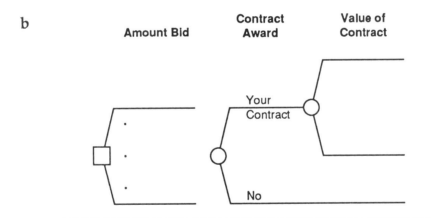

Addressing all the costs and uncertainties associated with losing or winning a particular contract is essential. Assuming there is no cost associated with losing a contract, Figure 7-7 is a good representation of a typical bidding problem. We can look at how some of the quantities described by this tree vary by plotting them (Figure 7-8).

We have superimposed three graphs, with the horizontal axis for each being the size of the bid (the first node in the decision tree). The first line plotted is the probability of winning the contract as a function of the bid size. It obviously decreases as the size of the bid increases. The second line plotted is the expected value of the business, given we win the bid. This line rises, because, as we bid more for the same job, our profit margin increases. The third line is the expected value of the business

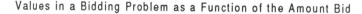

Figure 7–8

Values in a Bidding Problem as a Function of the Amount Bid

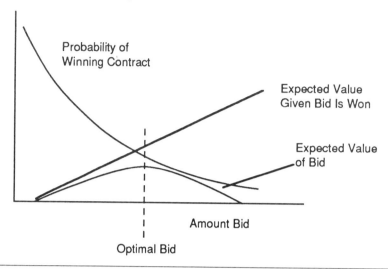

multiplied by the probability of winning the bid, which is the expected value of the bid. The optimal value of the bid for an expected-value decision-maker is the peak of this third line. This optimal bid maximizes the expected value of the bid. (Note that because of differing vertical scales, there is no relation between the position of the "Optimal Bid" and the bid value where the "Probability of Winning Contract" and "Expected Value Given Bid Is Won" lines cross.)

For this type of problem, the bid that maximizes the certain equivalent is frequently somewhat lower than the bid that maximizes the expected value. Risk avoiders prefer to bid lower and increase the probability of getting the business. The higher chances of loss with a lower bid may counteract this tendency, however, and push the risk avoider's bid higher.

(**Note:** For an interesting analysis of oil company bids on leases, see E.C. Capen, R.V. Clapp, and W.M. Campbell, "Competitive Bidding in High-Risk Situations," *Journal of Petroleum Technology* (June 1971): 641-653. Reprinted in *Readings on the Principles and Applications of Decision Analysis*, ed. R.A. Howard and J.E. Matheson, 2 vols. (Menlo Park, California: Strategic Decisions Group, 1984), 2: 805–819.)

Investment and Investment Rollover Decisions

Many investment decisions are extremely difficult to analyze because of the variety and liquidity of available investment instruments and because of the many points when a decision can be made. As a result, attempts to model investment decisions in their most general form can produce an unmanageable decision tree. However, once the choice of investments and the time frame have been restricted, decision analysis formulations can be applied.

Figure 7–9

Critical Uncertainties and Decisions in an Investment Question

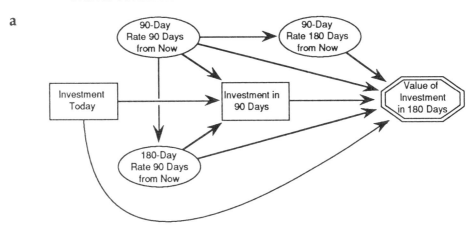

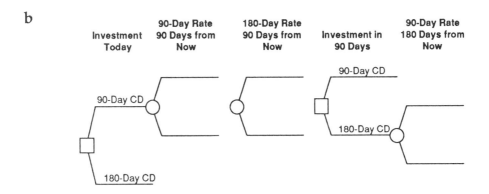

For instance, banks frequently sell 90- or 180-day certificates of deposit (CDs) to maintain some of their funds in relatively short-term, liquid form. In the CD investment decision, the first decision is whether to buy 90- or 180-day CDs. If we choose 180-day CDs, that decision will take us to the end of the time period considered (Figure 7–9).

However, if 90-day CDs are chosen, we have to decide what to do with the money in 90 days when the CD matures. At that time, we will know what the 90- and 180-day CD rates have gone to, though this is an uncertainty now.

Finally, we need to be able to value the investment decisions made in each scenario. For the initial choice of a 180-day CD and for any choice of a 90-day CD, the value is simply the face value at maturity. However, if we choose 180-day CDs 90 days from now, they will only be halfway to maturity at the end of the 180-day time horizon. At that point, the 180-day CDs will have 90 days to go and, therefore, will be valued as if they were 90-day CDs. Thus, to value the 180-day CDs bought 90 days from now, we need to know what the 90-day CD rates will be 180 days from now (Figure 7–9).

Corporate Strategies and Portfolios

Large businesses must often evaluate strategic options that affect many or all of their component businesses or business units. Since these strategies commonly involve decisions for the company as a whole, decisions in the individual business units, uncertainties that affect all the business units, and uncertainties that affect only certain business units, the problem formulation may be very large. As we noted in the preceding chapter, while decision analysis tools and concepts are exceedingly valuable in evaluating the strategies, the resulting influence diagram may be very large and the actual decision tree may be unmanageable.

To construct a decision tree for evaluating strategies for multiple businesses, we put the decision node for the different strategies first and then the chance nodes for the uncertainties that affect all businesses—uncertainties that are usually economic or environmental factors, such as energy prices or interest rates (Figure 7–10). Then we have the uncertainties specific to each of the business units. All business-unit uncertainties must appear on each path through the tree so that a model at the end of the tree can calculate the value of each business unit and combine these values to obtain the value of the whole company for each scenario.

--- Figure 7–10 ---

Critical Uncertainties in Deciding on Business Strategies

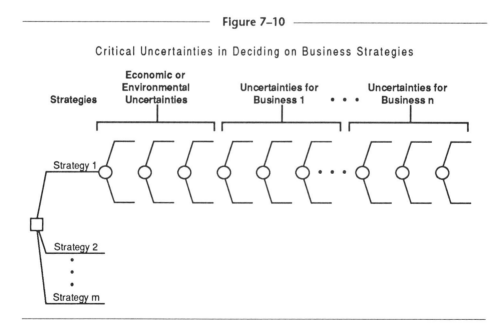

Figure 7–11

Examining Uncertainties by Business Unit

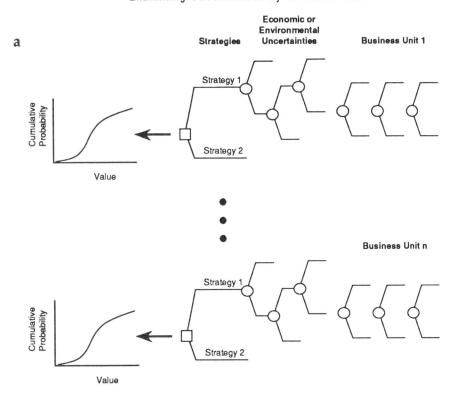

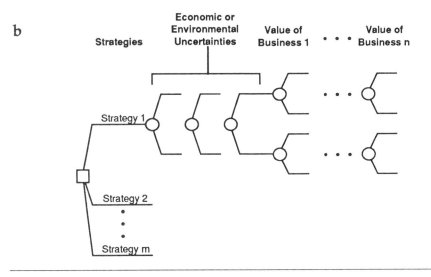

As we can see, this tree is impossibly large. However, by using a two-step process, we can reduce the tree to a manageable size. First, we construct a tree for each business unit that has the uncertainties particular to that unit. This tree allows us to calculate the probability distribution for each business unit given a particular strategy and set of economic uncertainties (Figure 7–11a). We can then calculate the probability distribution for each business unit for each combination of environmental factors and strategies. By discretizing these distributions into the form of chance nodes, we can restructure the tree (Figure 7–11b).

While this tree is significantly smaller than the original tree, it is still probably too large to evaluate. Therefore, we will reduce the tree again by combining the distributions for the business units for each strategy/environmental scenario to produce a combined distribution for the business uncertainty for each scenario (Figure 7–12). We can do this by tree evaluation. Another way to do this is to recognize that the business-unit distributions are independent of each other because we formulated the problem that way; we can therefore combine them by adding their cumulants together and then constructing a single distribution that duplicates those cumulants.

The cumulants can be obtained from the moments of the distribution.* For example, the first three cumulants are the mean (expected value), the variance, and the third central moment.

This tree is now small enough to evaluate and analyze. Though it is cumbersome to evaluate a portfolio of businesses this way, few other options exist for problems this large. While we could simply truncate the tree to a manageable size, we would lose much of the accuracy, believability, and insight necessary for handling decisions this large and this important. We could also use a Monte Carlo simulation to estimate the value of the full tree, but again at the cost of some lost insight.

Fortunately, strategic portfolio evaluations do not need to be done often and can be updated fairly easily once they have been done the first time. Considering that the direction of a multibillion-dollar business may be at stake, the effort is well worth it.

--- Figure 7–12 ---

Examining Combined Business Uncertainties

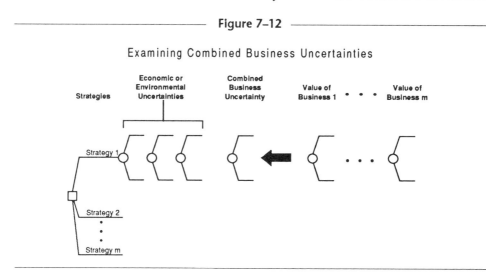

---

* Harold Cramer, *Mathematical Methods of Statistics* (Princeton, New Jersey: Princeton University Press, 1946), Section 15.10.

Summary

In this chapter, we discussed several of the most common applications of decision analysis to business problems. These examples are not intended as models for other problems, but rather to illustrate the considerations and process that go into structuring an influence diagram and decision tree. Most problems should be individually structured and analyzed to ensure that the analysis is relevant, useful, and insightful.

Problems and Discussion Topics

7.1 Huntenpeck Company manufactures typewriters, and Huge company has requested a bid on a contract for 10,000 new typewriters, which cost $1,000 to manufacture. Huntenpeck would very much like the contract, especially since the publicity would lead to additional sales to Huge's subsidiaries. On the other side of the coin, losing this large contract would introduce a competitor with the potential to cut into Huntenpeck's sales of dictaphones to Huge Company. The secondary impact of winning or losing the contract would be felt for about five years.

a. Begin structuring the problem and decide what information you need. Make sure you draw an influence diagram.

Huntenpeck decided to make its decision on purely economic factors and to be an expected-value decision-maker.

After heated discussion, Huntenpeck estimated that if it won the contract, it would sell between 1,000 and 1,400 extra typewriters a year to Huge's subsidiaries over the next five years, with equal probabilities of the high and low figures. These typewriters would be sold at $2,000 (in 1986 dollars). If it lost the contract, it would lose about $1 million profit a year in dictaphone sales over the next five years. After even more heated discussion, Huntenpeck decided to use a discount rate (time value of money) of 10 percent for constant dollar analysis.

Concerning the contract itself, there seemed to be two principal competitors: Carboncopy and Misprint. No one was sure what their bids would be. However, their typewriters were similar enough to Huntenpeck's that it was certain that Huge would accept the lowest bid. Probability distributions were encoded for both competitors' bids.

Bid Level ($ per typewriter)	Probability of Competitor Bidding Lower	
	Carboncopy	Misprint
1,200	.01	.00
1,300	.05	.00
1,400	.20	.05
1,500	.50	.45
1,600	.80	1.00
1,700	1.00	1.00

b. Finish structuring the problem and draw the decision tree for it.

c. What is Huntenpeck's optimal bid ($ per typewriter)?

d. What are the values of information for the crucial uncertainties? Are there circumstances under which the optimal bid would be different given perfect information?

e. If Huntenpeck had a risk tolerance of $10 million, what would its optimal bid be?

7.2   The ABC Construction Corporation is being sued for damages as a result of an accident in which the plaintiff fell from a second-floor balcony. The open side of the balcony had been closed off only by a pair of chains held in place by hooks at each end. The plaintiff was leaning against the chains when one of the hooks snapped. He incurred serious injuries in the subsequent fall. In his complaint, the plaintiff charges ABC Construction Corporation with negligence in designing the balcony and the Wisconsin Hook Company with negligence in manufacturing the hooks and asks for $2 million in damages, including pain and suffering.

ABC has a $3 million policy covering this kind of claim with United Insurance Company. United's attorneys have told the claims supervisor that a jury might find ABC negligent in this case. Furthermore, they have said that independent of the jury's finding about ABC's negligence, the hook manufacturer could be found negligent. If both defendants are found negligent, each would have to pay 50 percent of the total damages awarded to the plaintiff. If only one is found negligent, that defendant would have to pay the full award. It is believed that the jury would probably award only $500,000 or $1 million, but there is some chance of the full $2 million award.

United Insurance Company has been approached by the plaintiff's counsel and been given the opportunity to settle out of court for $500,000. Should the offer be accepted?

a. Structure the litigate/settle problem as an influence diagram and then draw the decision tree.

b. Assign dollar outcomes to all endpoints of the tree.

Noticing that litigation could produce losses substantially in excess of the $500,000 settlement offer, the claims supervisor realized that he should quantify the likelihood of the various outcomes. After a long, rigorous discussion of the legal and damage issues, the lawyers provided the claims supervisor with the following probabilities.

There is a 50 percent chance of a jury finding ABC negligent, but only a 30 percent chance of it finding the hook manufacturer negligent. If both defendants are found negligent, there is 1 chance in 5 the full $2 million will be awarded. The $500,000 and $1 million awards are equally likely. If only one defendant is found negligent, on the other hand, the probability of the full $2 million award is cut in half, and there is a 60 percent chance of the $500,000 award and a 30 percent chance of the $1 million award.

c. Find the expected value of each of United Insurance Company's alternatives.

d. Draw the profit distributions for United Insurance Company's alternatives.

The attorneys were surprised to hear that the claims supervisor was going to reject the settlement offer. Because they felt that a little more pretrial discovery could greatly reduce their uncertainty about whether the hook manufacturer would be found negligent, they urged the claims supervisor to briefly delay his decision until they could complete some additional pretrial work.

e. Determine the expected value of perfect information about whether the hook manufacturer will be found negligent.

7.3 Hony Pharmaceutics is a manufacturer engaged in developing and marketing new drugs. The chief research chemist at Hony, Dr. Bing, has informed the president, Mr. Hony, that recent research results have indicated a possible breakthrough to a new drug with wide medical use. Dr. Bing urged an extensive research program to develop the new drug. He estimated that with expenditures of $100,000 the new drug could be developed at the end of a year's work. When queried by Mr. Hony, Dr. Bing stated that he thought the chances were excellent, "about 8 to 2 odds," that the research group could in fact develop the drug.

Dr. Bing further stated that he had found out that High Drugs, Hony's only competitor for the type of product in question, had recently started developing essentially the same drug. He felt that working independently, there was a 7 out of 10 chance that High would succeed. Mr. Hony was concerned about the possibility that High would be able to develop the drug faster, thus obtaining an advantage in the market, but Dr. Bing assured him that Hony's superior research capability made it certain that by starting development immediately, Hony would succeed in developing the drug before High. However, Dr. Bing pointed out that if Hony launched its development, succeeded, and marketed the drug, then High, by copying, would get its drug on the market at least as fast as if it had succeeded in an independent development.

Worried about the sales prospects of a drug so costly to develop, Mr. Hony talked to his marketing manager, Mr. Margin, who said the market for the potential new drug depended on the acceptance of the drug by the medical profession and the share of the market Hony could capture. Mr. Hony asked Margin to make future market estimates for different situations, including estimates of future profits (assuming High entered the market shortly after Hony). Margin made the estimates shown below.

Market Condition	Probability	Present Value of Profits ($)
Large market potential	.1	500,000
Moderate market potential	.6	250,000
Low market potential	.3	80,000

Mr. Hony was somewhat concerned about spending the $100,000 to develop the drug given such an uncertain market. He returned to Dr. Bing and asked if there was some way to develop the drug more cheaply or to postpone development until the market position was clearer. Dr. Bing said he would prefer his previous suggestion—an orderly research program costing $100,000—but that an alternative was indeed possible. The alternative plan called for a two-phase research program: an eight-month "low-level" phase costing $40,000, followed by a four-month "crash" phase costing $80,000. Dr. Bing did not think this program would change the chances of a successful product development. One advantage of this approach, Dr. Bing added, was that the company would know whether the drug could be developed successfully at the end of the eight-month period. The decision would then be made whether to undertake the crash program. In either case, the cost of introduction and marketing would be $50,000.

Mr. Hony further consulted Mr. Margin about the possibility that more market information would be available before making the decision to introduce the drug or to complete the crash development program if that strategy were adopted. Mr. Margin stated that without a very expensive market research program, he would have no new information until well after the drug was introduced.

Mr. Hony inquired about the possibility of waiting until High's drug was on the market and then developing a drug based on a chemical analysis of it. Dr. Bing said this was indeed possible and that such a drug could be developed for $50,000. However, Mr. Margin was dubious of the value of such an approach, noting that the first drugs out usually got the greater share of the market. He estimated the returns would only be about 50 percent of those given in the table, but that the cost of introducing the drug would be only $20,000. Mr. Hony thought briefly about the possibility of going ahead with development after High had failed, but quickly realized that the chance of Hony's success under such circumstances would be much too low to make the investment worthwhile. The chances of a successful development by High after Hony had failed in its development attempt were considered so remote (1 percent) that the "imitate-and-market" strategy was not considered once Hony had failed.

a. Draw the influence diagram for this case.

b. Draw the decision tree for this case.

c. Determine the best decision, assuming risk indifference.

d. Draw the profit distribution for each alternative.

e. Determine the best decision, assuming the payoff on each terminal node is certain and that Mr. Hony's risk tolerance is $100,000.

Consider a clairvoyant so specialized that he could perfectly predict market outcomes but not development or competitive outcomes. Distinguish this case of partial perfect information (perfect information on only one of the uncertain variables) from the case of imperfect information.

f. Determine the value of market clairvoyance for a risk-indifferent (expected-value) decision-maker.

g. Determine the value of market clairvoyance for a risk-averse decision-maker using Mr. Hony's utility. Assume that the cost of information is zero.

7.4 Mr. Able is the president of Blackgold, a petroleum distribution and marketing company that supplies refined products to a number of customers under long-term contracts at guaranteed prices. Recently, the price Blackgold must pay for petroleum has risen sharply. As a result, Blackgold is faced with a loss of $480,000 this year because of its long-term contract with a particular customer.

Able has consulted his legal advisers to see if this supply contract might be relaxed in any way, and they have advised him that it contains a clause stating that Blackgold may refuse to supply up to 10 percent of the promised amount because of circumstances beyond its control (a force majeure clause). Able's marketing staff estimates that invoking the clause and selling the contested 10 percent at prevailing market prices would turn a loss of $480,000 into a net profit of $900,000.

However, the lawyers caution that the customer's response to Blackgold's invoking the clause is far from certain. The marketing staff claims there is a small chance that the customer will accept the invocation and agree to pay the higher price for the 10 percent. If the client does not agree to pay the higher price, the lawyers feel it might sue for damages or it might simply decline to press the issue. In either case, Blackgold could then immediately sell the 10 percent on the open market at prevailing prices. A lawsuit would result in one of three possible outcomes: Blackgold loses and pays normal damages of $1.8 million, Blackgold loses and pays double damages of $3.6 million, and Blackgold wins. If it loses, it must also pay court costs of $100,000, but it need not deliver the oil.

a. Draw the influence diagram for Mr. Able's problem.

b. Structure the decision tree for Mr. Able's problem.

c. Assign dollar outcomes to all endpoints of the tree.

Noting that invoking the clause could lead to a profitable outcome, Able has asked his staff to assess the likelihood of the various outcomes. After a great deal of discussion, they report that their best judgment indicates 1 chance in 5 the customer will agree to pay the market price for the contested 10 percent and, if it does not agree, a 50/50 chance it will sue Blackgold for damages. Based on past experience with cases of this type, the lawyers believe there is only a 10 percent chance of Blackgold's winning the lawsuit, an 80 percent chance of losing normal damages, and a 10 percent chance of losing double damages.

d. Find the expected value of each of Blackgold's alternatives.

e. Draw the profit distribution for each of Blackgold's alternatives.

Distressed by Mr. Able's persistence in pursuing what they regard was an extremely risky course, the legal and marketing people propose two investigations with the hope of delaying any "reckless" actions. These include $2,000 for wining and dining the customer's executives to sound out whether they might accept a revocation and $10,000 to have an objective outside survey team gather information on the possibilities of a lawsuit.

f. Determine the expected value of perfect information about whether Blackgold's customers would agree to a price increase under the 10 percent clause and about whether they would sue if they did not agree to the increase. In each of these determinations, assume that only one of these two uncertainties can be resolved. How would you advise Able about the proposed studies?

One further investigation that could be conducted is a $15,000 study by an outside legal firm on the likelihood of the possible outcomes of the lawsuit.

g. Determine the expected value of perfect information about the outcome of a lawsuit (assuming this is the only uncertainty that can be resolved). How would you advise Able about the above study?

h. Determine the expected value of perfect information (simultaneously) about all three uncertainties facing Blackgold.

8

Encoding a Probability Distribution

Although most analysts are familiar with data-gathering methods and problems, decision analysis uses two types of data that require quite different methods to gather and pose quite different sorts of problems. One type of data is the utility curve. (The methods and conditions for encoding utility curves are discussed in Chapter 5.) The other type of data is the probability distribution, which is used throughout decision analysis. Encoding a probability distribution can be one of the most difficult tasks to perform well in decision analysis. This chapter provides a review of some of the problems encountered in encoding a probability distribution and an outline of the encoding process.

Problems in Encoding Probability Distributions

In Chapter 2, we stated that since probability is used to represent a person's state of knowledge about something, there are no correct or incorrect probabilities. However, two major questions arise in encoding and using probability distributions.

The first question concerns choosing a person to furnish the probability distribution. Does that person have an adequate state of relevant knowledge? Are sufficient and correct experience and data available; does the person have the training and intelligence to assimilate this experience and data? These questions are familiar to everyone who wonders whom to believe or rely on.

Decision analysis does not offer a new solution to this problem; it simply ensures that the decision-maker considers the person chosen to be knowledgeable or expert in the relevant area. Usually, the analyst and decision-maker can agree easily on who the appropriate experts are. If there are several possible experts, the analyst can encode probability distributions from each of them and compare the effect the distributions have on the problem. Different probability distributions may or may not lead to different decisions.

The second question is whether the encoded probability distributions really represent the state of knowledge of the persons involved. A surprising number of biases can sneak in (often at an unconscious level) and make carelessly encoded probability distributions inadequate representations of the subject's state of knowledge. Decision analysis handles this problem by devising methods to deal with the biases that inevitably arise.

Motivational Biases

Motivational biases arise when the encoded probabilities do not reflect the expert's conscious beliefs. The cause of this behavior is usually desire for a reward or fear of punishment, which can be economic, psychological, or physical. An example of this type of bias can occur when a salesman is asked for an estimate of future sales. Sales personnel are often conditioned to respond artificially high (possibly to obtain the rights to sell the product) or artificially low (perhaps to appear good when they exceed their estimates). Another example of motivational bias occurs when people give estimates based on "real, objective data" (which may have limited relevance), rather than take the responsibility to express their own judgment and intuition.

The long-term cure for motivational biases is to align the reward structure to encourage truthful responses. In the short term, however, the analyst can show the expert the importance to the company of his responses and emphasize that he is recording a state of knowledge—not asking for a prediction or commitment. If the expert has a personal stake in having a particular course of action chosen, the analyst can divide the quantity being assessed into several subfactors, which brings the assessment down to a level of detail where the expert does not know how to give answers that serve his self-interest. As a last resort, if the above cures do not appear to be working, we can disqualify the expert.

Three forms of behavior can be loosely classified as motivational biases: the manager's bias, the expert's bias, and the analyst's bias.

The manager's bias is typified by the statement: "If that's what the boss wants, I'll get it done!" In this case, the encoded uncertainty may be very small, while the manager has shifted all the uncertainty to some other unsuspected factor, such as the cost of getting it done.

The expert's bias is typified by the attitude that experts are expected to be certain of things rather than uncertain. Given this attitude, an expert will give a narrow distribution. The obvious errors associated with this sort of reasoning should be discussed with the expert.

The analyst's bias results from not wanting to appear in disagreement with official company information. It often occurs in an organization with an official in-house forecast. This forecast, which may merely be the result of the latest computer run, is intended primarily to impose consistency on company analyses. Except at top-management levels, it is rare to find anyone who is willing to disagree publicly with this forecast. The encoder must show the expert the origins, limitations, and purpose of the forecast and encourage candid responses. (The in-house forecast can also create a powerful anchor, as discussed below.)

Cognitive Biases

How do people assess the probability of an uncertain event? It turns out there are a limited number of heuristic methods used in this process. (A heuristic involves or serves as an aid to learning, discovery, or problem-solving by experimental, and especially, trial-and-error methods.) In general, these heuristics are quite useful, but sometimes they lead to severe and systematic errors.* Improperly using the cognitive heuristics causes biases and leads to incorrect conclusions.

An example of a heuristic is the use of visual clarity to judge the distance of objects: hazy objects are thought to be distant. An example of an incorrect use of this heuristic occurs in the clear air of deserts where distant objects appear to be quite near. Although biases tend to occur at an unconscious level, they are correctable. For example, in a desert, one learns to say "Objects are farther away than they seem!"

One type of common bias in probability encoding is called the availability bias. In this case, the heuristic is to think of occurrences of an event (or of similar events); the easier it is to think of occurrences, the more likely the event is judged to be. For instance, if eight out of ten small businesses you can think of failed within their first year, you may judge it quite likely that a new small business will fail. This heuristic is quite useful and generally works well. However, a problem occurs because of quirks in the way we store and retrieve information in our minds. For instance, information that is ordered, redundant, dramatic, recent, imaginable, certified, or consistent with our world view is much more likely to be stored and recalled than information that does not have these qualities. As a result, probabilities tend to be unduly weighted by the more available information.

We can counteract this bias in several ways. First, we can check to find out if there are reasons some information is more readily available than other information. If there are, we can discuss and research the less available information. Another cure (which is a powerful cure for other biases as well) is to postulate extreme outcomes and request the expert to give some scenarios that would lead to these outcomes. This technique forces the expert to search his or her mind for little-used information. A final cure (also valuable in confronting other biases) is to have the expert pretend to consider the situation retrospectively from the future. A change of perspective often opens the mind up to new possibilities.

A second type of bias is called the representativeness bias. The heuristic in force here is to look at some evidence and then assign a high probability to the event that makes the evidence most likely. What can go wrong? Studies show that when faced with specific evidence, people often tend to discard (or undervalue) previous experience and general information. For instance, a sharp decrease in a company's net income might lead someone to assign a relatively high probability that the company is in financial trouble. However, mature reflection might reveal that the particular industry has net incomes that tend to vary wildly from year to year and that the latest change has little significance.

---

* There is much literature on the subject. A seminal paper in this area is the excellent and readable article: A. Tversky and D. Kahneman, "Judgment Under Uncertainty: Heuristics and Biases," *Science* 185 (September 27, 1974): 1124-1131. This article is reprinted in *Readings on the Principles and Applications of Decision Analysis*, ed. R.A. Howard and J.E. Matheson, 2 vols. (Menlo Park, California: Strategic Decisions Group, 1984) 2: 903-910.

Another example of the representativeness bias is the common error of stereotyping: "All people who do X are Y. Therefore, anyone who is Y is very likely to do X." Very few people stop to consider the possibility that there may be many people who are Y and only a few cases of people who do X.

Besides being very common, this bias can be quite subtle and complex, both in its manifestations and in its causes. (For more discussion of this bias, see the article by Tversky and Kahneman.) The cure for this bias is to separate prior or general information from new evidence and to update prior information explicitly using probability theory. (See the treatment of Nature's tree in Chapter 4.)

Adjustment and anchoring give rise to a third common bias. The heuristic is to start from some initial estimate and then adjust the estimate until it seems reasonable. This heuristic is the basis of many engineering or other quantitative estimates. Unfortunately, the adjustment is rarely adequate, and the final estimate tends to be anchored near the initial estimate—no matter how arbitrary the initial estimate was. We see this bias a great deal when encoding probability distributions. For example, people sometimes start by making a best estimate and then attempt to estimate how uncertain the best estimate is, thus arriving at the width of the distribution. What happens is that they get anchored by the best estimate and almost always wind up with too narrow a probability distribution. Other examples of this bias are anchoring on the corporate plan and corporate forecasts—it is difficult to think of futures that are too different. The cure for this bias is to start by discussing extreme outcomes and asking the expert for explanatory scenarios. If the analyst must start with an initial best estimate, he or she should try to do so in a way that does not commit the expert.

A special case of the anchoring and adjustment bias arises because of conjunctive distortions. We tend to overestimate the probability of success for conjunctive events (where all the individual events must happen for success), because we anchor on the probability of each individual event happening. This bias is particularly important in R&D, where a number of hurdles must be cleared before success is achieved. The obvious cure for this bias is to obtain the probabilities for each event happening and then to multiply them to obtain the probability of success. This type of distortion also occurs when we underestimate the probability of success for disjunctive events (any individual event happening gives success). This bias occurs in research and development when we tend to underestimate the probability of technical success in following parallel but independent research paths.

Finally, there is the implicit conditioning bias. One form of the heuristic is to tell a story; the more coherent and plausible the story, the more likely we judge the outcome we are trying to explain. The bias is that we can forget to examine the likelihood of the enabling events needed to start the story. Another form of the heuristic occurs when we make certain assumptions to make the assessment process easier. The bias arises when we subsequently forget these assumptions exist. The cures for this type of bias are, first, to postulate extreme outcomes and request explanatory scenarios and, second, to examine probabilities of any enabling events for the scenarios. It also helps to have a checklist of some common assumptions (no fire, strikes, lawsuits, war, competitive breakthrough, etc.). You can also identify hidden assumptions by asking the expert what he or she would like to insure against. One way to verify that the results are now accurate is to ask the expert if he or she would invest personal funds using the probability distribution just encoded.

Probability Encoding Process

After the preceding discussion, it may seem virtually impossible to get a reliable probability distribution. However, the process described below incorporates cures for the common biases. The process has a strong effect—experts usually adjust their answers considerably when it is used and usually in the "right" direction of broader probability distributions. Moreover, we can obtain a high degree of consistency in encoded distributions: points tend to lie along smooth curves, and the degree of repeatability in responses is high. Finally, experts have considerable confidence in the results generated through the process compared with those obtained through other methods. As a result, they typically become strong supporters of the analysis.

The process related here (originally described in the 1972 joint ORSA-TIMS-AIEE national meeting in Atlantic City*† is typically conducted in five stages. While the process may seem long and very detailed, many of the steps take only a few seconds, and the process is natural enough that the details are not obvious.

It is usually best to conduct the encoding in private, so that group pressures do not bias the results. After the initial encoding, however, a group review frequently proves useful in resolving differences and sharing information.

Stage 1: Motivating

The motivating stage establishes the necessary rapport with the subject and explores whether a serious potential for motivational biases exists. After explaining his delegated authority to conduct the interview, the encoder explains the decision problem, describes the decision model that has been constructed, and shows how all the uncertain factors will be accounted for in the analysis. This ensures that the subject can clearly focus on the task at hand.

Next, the encoder explains the importance of accurately assessing uncertainty on the quantity and emphasizes that the intent is to measure the expert's knowledge and best judgment—not to predict the value. The importance of emphasizing this distinction depends on how much the encoder detects the possibility of the manager or expert having the biases mentioned above.

Finally, the encoder discusses the expert's personal involvement with the decision and with the variable being encoded to identify any asymmetries in the payoff structure that might encourage the expert to bias his or her estimates high or low. Note-taking by the encoder is useful because it encourages a more balanced presentation of issues.

---

* Carl S. Spetzler and Carl–Axel S. Staël von Holstein, "Probability Encoding in Decision Analysis," *Management Science*, Vol. 22, No. 3 (November 1975): 340-358. A slightly different version of this article is reprinted in *Readings on the Principles and Applications of Decision Analysis*, ed. R.A. Howard and J.E. Matheson, 2 vols. (Menlo Park, California: Strategic Decisions Group, 1984) 2: 601-625.

† Much of the material in this section is drawn from work done with M.W. Merkhofer, "Quantifying Judgmental Uncertainty: Methodology, Experiences, and Insight," *IEEE Transactions on Systems, Man, and Cybernetics*, Vol. SMC–17 (Sept.–Oct. 1987): 741-752.

Stage 2: Structuring

The structuring stage has two purposes: to structure the variable clearly and to explore how the subject thinks about it. The first step is to precisely define the variable whose uncertainty is to be assessed, using, for example, the clairvoyance test described in Chapter 2. The next step is to explore the possibility of decomposing the variable into more elemental quantities and then to assess those elemental quantities individually. The third step is to elicit and list all assumptions the subject is making in thinking about the variable. To identify hidden assumptions, it is useful to ask the subject what he or she would like to insure against. Finally, the encoder selects an appropriate measuring scale—most importantly one that uses the units most familiar to the expert. (One unit to avoid is a growth rate. Encoding the uncertainty on compound growth rates is difficult, because few people adequately appreciate the effects of compounding over long periods of time. It is better to encode the uncertainty on the actual value of the quantity at the end of the growth period and then calculate the implied growth rate.)

Stage 3: Conditioning

In the conditioning stage, the expert draws out the expert's relevant knowledge about the uncertain variable. Often, discussion will indicate that the expert is basing his or her judgment on both specific information and general information. Given the problems of the representativeness bias, it may be appropriate to encode probabilities from prior information and to update this prior information with the specific information. (See Chapter 4.) Fortunately, it is usually adequate to educate the expert about the representativeness bias.

The next step is to counteract the anchoring and availability biases, something the encoder can do by eliciting extreme values of the variable from the expert and then asking for scenarios that would explain these outcomes. (At this point, hidden assumptions are often uncovered.) The encoder should also explore for the presence of anchors, such as corporate plans or forecasts.

This step is very important. Working with the subject to explore how extreme scenarios may occur (and perhaps even writing down the reasons why) broadens and unlocks (unbiases) people's thinking in an almost magical way.

Another useful method is to explain or demonstrate what we call the 2/50 rule. In many seminars, we have asked attendees to assign probability distributions to the answers to questions drawn from an almanac. Usually, the specific question is to give a range such that the correct answer has only a 2 percent chance of falling outside that range. In other words, if people correctly perceived their uncertainty about the answer, 2 percent of the time the answers would be expected to fall outside the 1 percent and 99 percent fractiles they defined. Over the 15 years we have been giving this demonstration, we have found that over 50 percent of the answers fall outside this range. People tend to think they know things better than they actually do, and probability distributions tend to be far too narrow.[*]

---

[*] Similar experiences are reported in E.C. Capen, "The Difficulty of Assessing Uncertainty," *Journal of Petroleum Technology* (August 1976): 843-850. This article is reprinted in *Readings on the Principles and Applications of Decision Analysis*, ed. R.A. Howard and J.E. Matheson, 2 vols. (Menlo Park, California: Strategic Decisions Group, 1984) 2: 591-600.

Stage 4: Encoding

Having defined the variable, structured it, and established and clarified the information useful for assessing its uncertainty in the first three stages, the encoder quantifies that uncertainty in this stage.

Of the various encoding methods available, we have found a reference method using a probability wheel (Figure 8–1) to be the most effective.

——————————————— **Figure 8–1** ———————————————

Probability Wheel

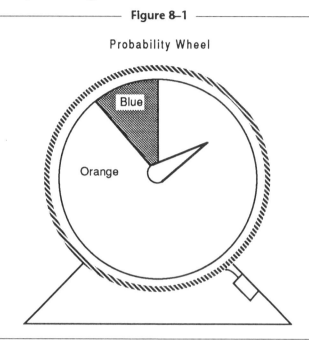

The probability wheel is divided into a blue and an orange sector, the relative sizes of which can be adjusted. To use the wheel, the encoder selects a value for the variable the expert thinks is not too extreme—but not the most likely or central value. The encoder then asks the expert, "Would you rather bet that the variable will be less than this value or that when I spin this wheel the pointer lands in the blue region?" The relative sizes of the blue and orange regions are then adjusted and the question repeated until a setting is found for which the subject is just indifferent. In other words, the encoder finds the point where the expert believes the probability of the two events (variable less than stated value or pointer landing in blue) are identical. The quick check of reversing the question—"Would you rather bet that the variable would be greater than this value or that the pointer lands in the orange?"—frequently makes the expert rethink the question and adjust the answer. A scale on the back of the wheel gives the probability of the event. This value is then plotted as one point on a cumulative distribution. Repeating this process for different values of the variable leads to a collection of points that may be connected by a smooth curve (Figure 8–2).

Figure 8–2

Cumulative Distribution of Values from Encoding

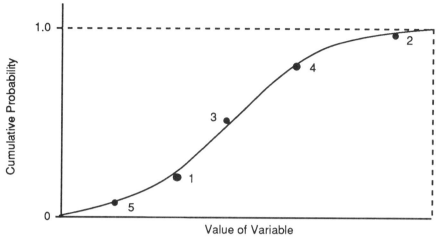

In using the probability wheel, the encoder should follow two important rules. First, the encoder must carefully avoid leading the expert to a value the analyst thinks makes sense or is consistent. A wiser approach is to strive to confound the expert's possible attempts to mislead or impose false consistency in responses by, for example, varying the form of the questions and by skipping back and forth from high to low values so that the expert really has to think about each individual question.

Second, the encoder should plot and number the encoded points out of the expert's view and then look for inconsistencies and odd discontinuities. The encoder should note any changes in the expert's thinking that might be indicated by shifts in the points plotted. Often, he or she will see the curve along which the points lie shift because the subject has suddenly thought of some new piece of information. When this happens, the encoder should discuss the new thought and be prepared to discard all the earlier points if the perspective has been improved.

Stage 5: Verification

The last stage of the encoding process is to test the judgments obtained in the encoding stage by explaining the encoded distribution to the subject. It is often useful to convert the cumulative distribution into histogram form and to discuss bimodal shapes or sharp extremes with the expert. To verify the distribution, the encoder can ask whether the expert would willingly invest his or her own money based on the encoded results. The encoder can also form equally likely intervals based on the distribution and see if the expert would have a difficult time choosing which interval to bet on.

Experiences and Insights from Practice

One obvious question is how long the encoding process normally takes. If the encoding session goes smoothly, the process may be completed in as little as half an hour, but that is unusual. Typically, it requires one to three hours. Incidentally, if resources permit, having a second analyst present at the interview to record the data and to observe will expedite the interview and help in the subsequent review of results.

One point that new analysts are often skeptical about is whether the probability wheel really works. Furthermore, they worry that the executive or expert will not take seriously questions based on the probability wheel and will not tolerate the exercise for the length of time involved. Our experience is that assuring experts that their superiors have approved and requested their participation in the encoding usually leads to a positive response. In virtually all cases, the expert readily accepts the wheel and adapts quickly to its use.

Probability encoding is gaining considerable use by practicing decision analysts. The process yields results, and experts and analysts seem to like it.* As with quantitative analysis in general, the real value of probability encoding is determined not so much by whether it does or does not produce the correct bottom line as by the insights and improved clarity it provides decision-makers. And regardless of whether quantitative methods like probability encoding are perfectly accurate, decision-makers must continue to make decisions based on incomplete knowledge. Methods like probability encoding have proven too valuable to be dismissed lightly.

Summary

Obtaining high-quality probability distributions for crucial uncertainties is a vitally important step in every decision analysis. Although common motivational and cognitive biases tend to reduce the quality of a probability assessment, careful attention to the five steps of the assessment process can greatly improve the quality of the assessment.

---

* Encoded probabilities have been tracked in the business area. The reported results show that carefully encoded probabilities correspond quite well to the frequencies with which the outcomes actually occur. See the following articles: H.U. Balthasar, R.A.A. Boschi, and M.M. Menke, "Calling the Shots in R&D," *Harvard Business Review* (May–June 1978): 151–160; Irwin Kabus, "You Can Bank on Uncertainty," *Harvard Business Review* (May–June 1976): 95–105; and W.E. Sander, "The Validity of Subjective Forecasts by R&D Project Managers," *IEEE Transactions on Engineering Management* (February 1969): 35–43.

Problems and Discussion Topics _____

8.1   Discuss the differences in the processes by which motivational and cognitive biases arise. What implications do these differences have for the methods to overcome them?

8.2   List a bias that commonly arises in an area other than probability assessment. How is the bias recognized and overcome? If it is not overcome, is it because it is not possible to do so or not important enough to do so? Or is it because it is not even recognized?

8.3   You are about to assess the probability distribution on the average growth rate over the next year for the entire energy industry. The expert is a market analyst who closely follows the stocks of the large oil companies. What biases might you expect to encounter?

8.4   One technique for overcoming several kinds of biases is called the "Rip Van Winkle Technique." To apply it, you would discuss with the subject the highest and lowest possible outcomes of an uncertain variable. You would then say that it is a number of years after the actual outcome of the variable was discovered. The two of you run into each other again. You inform him that the variable turned out to be 10 percent higher than his highest possible estimate years before. You ask him to explain how it turned out higher than either of you had thought possible.

Why does this technique work?

8.5   Find a friend to serve as a subject in the following subjective probability experiment. Alternatively, try the experiment on yourself.

a. Tell the subject that a fair coin [p(head | S) = .5; p(tail | S) = .5] will be flipped six times. Assess the subject's cumulative probability distribution on the number of heads that occur in the six flips. Discourage your subject from trying to make any mathematical calculations of the odds. If you ask the questions in the right way, it will be very difficult for him or her to make any such calculations.

b. Now tell your friend that you have three coins (two of which are unfair) with different probability distributions.

1. p(head | S) = .25, p(tail | S) = .75
2. p(head | S) = .50, p(tail | S) = .50
3. p(head | S) = .75, p(tail | S) = .25

Then tell the subject that one of those coins will be randomly selected and flipped six times. Assess his or her subjective cumulative distribution on the total number of heads that result.

c. Calculate the actual distributions for a and b under the given assumptions. Compare these distributions with the assessments from your subject. Also note any difference between the subject's distributions in a and b. What might explain the differences, if any, between the various distributions?

8.6 Break into groups of two or three and encode probability distributions. Role playing by the "expert" and the "analyst" can help make the exercise more realistic, especially if assumed motivational biases are written down beforehand (but not revealed to the analyst). The quantity encoded should be a continuous variable for which the uncertainty will be resolved some time after the encoding session. Be sure to spend time describing and structuring the variable and exploring the possibility of biases. You may find it useful to structure a simple influence diagram with the subject before assessing the probability.

Some possible topics for assessment are (make sure the definitions pass the clairvoyance test):

a. The price of a stock two weeks from now

b. The difference in temperature between Stockholm and Rio de Janeiro on a particular day

c. The number of people attending a large undergraduate class on a given day.

8.7 Slippery Company produces, among other things, special types of lubricants for specific mechanical applications. There is one type of lubricant it does not produce. This lubricant is currently produced by several large companies from a feedstock of ethylene. Since ethylene prices are rising along with petroleum prices, the cost to produce this lubricant is rising. (This case is a disguised version of an analysis done in the late 1970s.) Slippery knows that the lubricant can be made from the oil of the "oily bean" at a cost that appears competitive today with the ethylene-based process. Since oily bean oil prices are not rising, Slippery is considering constructing a facility to produce the lubricant from oily bean oil. However, two factors worry Slippery. First, there is a rumor that several other companies are considering the same move, which would saturate the market with cheap lubricant. Second, although oily bean oil prices are fairly constant, droughts make the price jump temporarily every couple of years.

a. Structure the problem and determine your information needs. Be sure to draw an influence diagram.

b. For one of the necessary items of information, designate an expert, motivate the expert, and assess a probability distribution on the item.

9

Presenting and Institutionalizing Decision Analysis

We have seen some of the techniques, considerations, and philosophy necessary to conduct an insightful and successful decision analysis of a business problem. However, two more elements are necessary to successfully apply decision analysis in a corporate environment: (1) effectively presenting the results of a decision analysis and (2) providing effective in-house decision analysis support.

Presenting a Decision Analysis

One of the most important tasks in conducting a decision analysis is simply and convincingly presenting the analysis results. After all, since decision analysis is supposed to help the decision-making process, the findings are of little use unless they are well communicated. Unfortunately, in most cases, not enough effort is spent preparing the presentation.

The first consideration in preparing a presentation is determining its purpose. Is it solely intended for the decision-maker(s)? Or is it intended as a communication tool and consensus builder—perhaps serving to make others appreciate the rationale behind the decision and build their enthusiasm for a course of action that they might not originally have championed? In the first case, the presentation should emphasize the conclusions and qualitative insights that came out of the analysis and discuss the next steps. In the second case, emphasis should be placed on how information derived from many different sources within the company comes together in the conclusions.

A second consideration is determining the appropriate level of detail. A good rule of thumb is that the higher in the organization the audience, the less the audience's interest in how the analysis was done. Rather, senior managers need to be convinced the work was well done, dealt with their major concerns, and has intuitively reasonable recommendations.

In preparing the actual report or presentation, avoid concentrating on the methodology of the probabilistic or deterministic analysis. Generally, the decision-maker is interested only in the overall flow from believable input to reasonable conclusions. Presentations should not contain (unless particularly relevant or necessary) explanations of risk attitude, value of information and control, the techniques of tree evaluation, and the like.

Nor should the analyst talk too much about the model or deterministic sensitivity analysis. In many companies, those attending the presentation will tend to concentrate on what is familiar from most other presentations within the company: deterministic detail. The presenter must be skillful in leading the discussion smoothly but reasonably quickly through the deterministic phase and into the probabilistic phase. Again, the speaker should avoid (unless relevant or necessary) discussions of the discount rate, details of depreciation and tax treatment, undue concentration on the early years of the cash flow, and similar details.

A short presentation might have the following set of slides as a backbone:

- Introduction

- Principal alternatives

- Deterministic model, chart of principal submodels

- Deterministic model, base-case results. (Often, a table of financial and performance results for the first five or ten years is an efficient way to present model logic and input data.)

- Deterministic model, net present value of cash flow for the base case and for principal alternatives

- Deterministic sensitivity analysis results

- An abbreviated form of the tree with no probabilities

- Key probability assessments

- The tree with probabilities added

- Probability distribution for the alternatives (cumulative preferred, but histogram if necessary)

- Conclusions

- Value of information or control, probabilistic or risk sensitivity analysis, and the like, only if relevant.

Decision analysis results lend themselves well to graphic rather than tabular presentation—e.g., sensitivity analysis plots, trees, and probability distribution plots. Graphics have been shown to be the most effective way of ensuring both immediate comprehension and subsequent retention of the material presented.

Graphs should be presented as smooth, continuous curves. For instance, the staircase cumulative probability curves should be smoothed out, because the variable plotted (such as net present value) is usually a continuous variable. The process to smooth these graphs is the reverse of the discretization process discussed in Chapter 2.

Implementing Decision Analysis in a Company

Although decision analysis techniques have been used for several decades to treat difficult corporate problems, the analysis itself has often been done on an *ad hoc* basis, often by outside consultants. To an increasing extent, however, the use of these techniques has become part of the problem-solving apparatus in many companies. While it is difficult to generalize, several traits are characteristic of successful decision analysis implementations within these companies.

- Decision analysis must be accepted, understood, and required by upper level management within the company. More important, decision analysis must have a strong sponsor at this level to thrive. This does not necessarily mean that upper management must understand the techniques; rather, it means the managers accept as a fact of life that uncertainty can and must be addressed in important decisions.

- Middle management also must be aware of, and sympathetic to, the decision analysis process. After all, these are the managers who commission the analyses and support their execution.

- There must be a talented, experienced technical champion of decision analysis. Since he or she will have to deal with often reluctant "clients" within the company, the individual needs skills in managing people, time, and budgets. A viable and attractive career path for this type of person must be created. More than once, a budding decision analysis effort has failed when the key technical person was promoted or left the company.

- A fairly large number of people must have the technical capability to perform the decision analyses. This provides not only stability and continuity in the decision analysis effort, but also contributes to corporate commitment and enthusiasm.

- There must be a mechanism for training new analysts within the company or for obtaining them from outside the company. A good analyst requires some form of internship or apprenticeship—not just an academic background in the subject.

- The decision analyst should be positioned in the company so he or she has access to the decision-maker, is authorized to obtain whatever information is necessary, and is not identified with any particular party or faction within the company.

- Many decision analysts (and decision analysis groups) have a strong engineering or physical science background or philosophy. Decision analysis uses mathematical tools only insofar as they contribute toward an end. The personality of the analyst (and group) must be comfortable with this limitation; otherwise, analyses tend to become overly complicated and miss the decision-maker's real needs.

- The first decision analyses within the company should be chosen with care, being neither too simple ("Why spend all this effort on the obvious?") nor too complex. When problems are too complex, there is the danger of spending an inordinate amount of effort on the analysis and frustrating everyone involved.

Decision analysis may seem to be an expensive and time-consuming process. However, time and experience will show this is not so. When the philosophy, framework, process, and methodology have become established, decisions will be made efficiently and economically.

Once the initial effort has been made, most companies have found the investment in decision analysis capability justified. The variety of options considered, the quality of the knowledge employed, and the clear logic used lead to a decision process of high quality.

Summary

For long-term, effective utilization of decision analysis in corporate environments, the insights of the analysis must be well-communicated and the analysts themselves must be appropriately positioned and supported. Presentations are the most important in-house means of communicating the results of a decision analysis. Properly positioning and supporting the analysts includes personnel selection and training, management understanding and support, and appropriate analysis project selection.

Problems and Discussion Topics

9.1 In presenting a decision analysis, you often need to clearly and credibly present results to people who may not be familiar with or understand the methodology used to arrive at the results. In what other kinds of business situations is this also the case?

9.2 List some of the considerations in deciding what level of detail to include in a decision analysis presentation.

9.3 How might you prepare a presentation differently if you were presenting to the operations research staff group as opposed to the vice president of marketing?

9.4 What kinds of changes in procedures for making decisions might occur as a company adopts decision analysis? How would the number and function of people involved in decision-making change?

9.5 Why might decision analysis have been adopted more rapidly in some industries than in others? Can all industries benefit from decision analysis?

9.6 The Lone Star Drilling Company has several prospects in Oklahoma, Texas, and Louisiana. One of these prospects, in the state of Oklahoma, is called Moose Hill. A promising region for natural gas underlies the Moose Hill area at 20,000 feet. Gas discovered at this depth qualifies as "deep gas" and is allowed to sell at a free market price under current regulations. (This is a disguised version of an analysis performed in the late 1970s.) There is little chance of finding oil under Moose Hill.

For gas to be found, there must be a structural trap. Currently available seismic studies indicate 7 chances in 10 there will be a structural trap. Even with a trap, there is a good chance that the water saturation will be too high for a producing gas well. A producing well could yield between 2 and 25 MCF/day the first year (MCF = million cubic feet); yields over 30 MCF/day are unlikely. Over the 10-year life of the well, annual production is expected to decline by 20 to 25 percent per year.

Lone Star is currently drilling a well on the Moosejaw 1 section at Moose Hill. While that well is not expected to reach 20,000 feet for another year, it appears that the cost of drilling a 20,000-foot well will be $6 million to $10 million, plus about $2 million for completing the well if sufficient gas potential is found. Annual operating costs for similar wells run between $15,000 and $25,000.

Property in the area is divided into sections of one square mile. Operators with mineral leases within a given section usually pool together and drill one well per section. However, under Oklahoma's forced-pooling statutes, any mineral leaseholder in a given section can decide to drill and invoke "forced pooling." Holders of the remaining leases in the section must then either join in a drilling operation within 90 days, sharing proportionally in drilling costs and potential gas yield, or offer to sell their rights to the first leaseholder at a price set by the state. The purpose of the statute is to encourage drilling in Oklahoma.

Lone Star holds 99 percent of the mineral rights to Moosejaw 2, a section adjacent to Moosejaw 1. The holder of the other 1 percent of the mineral rights has invoked forced pooling. The state is in the process of setting a "fair" price.

If Lone Star decides to pool and drill on Moosejaw 2, it has the option of negotiating with another exploration company, Delta Resources, for a joint venture—proportional sharing of all future costs and revenues from the property. Delta Resources has expressed an interest in this joint venture opportunity.

Your group is to recommend the best courses of action for the Lone Star Drilling Company. As part of your presentation, include the following.

- What is the minimum amount of compensation Lone Star should accept to sell its current 99 percent share to the owner of the remaining 1 percent, assuming Lone Star must otherwise bear 99 percent of the costs of drilling (no joint venture with Delta Resources)?

- Assuming Lone Star decides to go ahead and drill, what joint venture share should it offer to Delta Resources?

- Assume the state sets $500,000 as the "fair" price for Lone Star's interests in the lease. Calculate the expected value of perfect information on a few crucial uncertainties.

Make sure the presentation will be acceptable to, and understood by, the president of Lone Star, an old-time driller who never graduated from high school, but who has acquired considerable wealth, experience, and expertise over the years.

9.7 Air Wars, Inc., a U.S. manufacturer of fighter planes, is aggressively marketing its popular Galaxy-MX and Scoop-UMi models to several emerging countries of the world. Sales discussions with two such countries, the Democratic Republic of Azultan (which has a reasonably stable government) and Byasfora's new government (which is an uneasy coalition between the Leninist-Marxist wing and the rightist Christian Democrats), are in the final stages in early 1985. Both of these governments are also concurrently negotiating their air force armament needs with Le Mon Corporation, a European manufacturer. The discussions between the Le Mon Corporation and the governments of Azultan and Byasfora are of serious concern to the management of Air Wars, Inc.

Dr. Ian Winthrop, the CEO of Air Wars, Inc., has called an urgent meeting on the coming Saturday to assess Air Wars' position and to develop a clear strategy to make these sales. Dr. Winthrop, in his memo to senior management, reaffirmed the urgency of the situation and called for their input during the weekend meeting. Dr. Winthrop stressed Air Wars' commitment to growth during the coming years. He also brought senior management up to date on the key items in connection with the potential sale of the planes to Azultan and Byasfora.

- Air Wars' Washington representative thought the U.S. government favorably regarded the plane sales to both the Azultan and Byasfora governments. However, the future stability of the new government in Byasfora was in question. A change in Byasfora's government was likely to result in a much more extreme left-wing government supported by neo-communists, creating concern about a reversal of the U.S. government's current support of the sale.

  Probability of change of government in Byasfora by 1990: .45

  The Washington representative also stressed the importance of the 1988 presidential election in relation to the sales to Byasfora. The most likely contender for president, if elected, is expected to consider the seriousness of the reported human rights violations in Byasfora and oppose the sale.

  Probability of administration change in 1988: .80

  Probability of opposition by new administration to Byasfora sale: .90

- The negotiations with the U.S. government on Air Wars' cost structure for the sale of the Galaxy-MX and Scoop-UMi planes are nearing completion. Air Wars' Finance Department projects the following prices in 1985 dollars (contingent upon three possible U.S. government positions on cost structure).

Unit Price ($ million)

	$p = .30$	$p = .60$	$p = .10$
Galaxy-MX	$3.9	$4.6	$5.2
Scoop-UMi	$2.65	$2.8	$3.15

- Last week, Dr. Winthrop met with the Secretary of State and the National Security Advisor. He was briefed on the current U.S. position with regard to the regional strategic balance of power in the Azultan and Byasfora area. As a result, Dr. Winthrop feels that the current administration is unlikely to approve the sales to both the Azultan and Byasfora governments.

  Probability of approving sales to both Azultan and Byasfora during 1987–1988: .01

- Recent discussions between Dr. Winthrop and both the Minister of Air Defense of Azultan and the General of Strategic Air Forces of Byasfora resulted in satisfactory agreement on the numbers of planes needed and a shipment schedule for each country:

Shipment Schedule

	1989 Galaxy	1989 Scoop	1990 Galaxy	1990 Scoop	1991 Galaxy	1991 Scoop	1992 Galaxy	1992 Scoop
Azultan	22	9	21	12	8	4	—	—
Byasfora	—	—	18	13	22	8	11	8

In addition, the Azultan agreement calls for a five-year technology assistance contract at the rate of $185 million per year beginning in 1989; the Byasfora agreement calls for a six-year $205 million per year technology assistance contract beginning in 1990. These technology assistance contracts would be terminated if the employees or assets of Air Wars were threatened by any future catastrophic sociopolitical change in these countries.

Probability of Catastrophic Sociopolitical Situation in Early 1990s

Azultan   .10
Byasfora   .45

- The Finance Department of Air Wars has completed reports on the credit worthiness of Azultan and Byasfora. The credit worthiness was found to be closely tied to the economic condition of these countries. These countries were also dependent on world economic conditions for a portion of their natural resource base revenues. Based on an analysis of world and domestic economic outlook, the probability of their being unable to finance the necessary portion of the sales amount and honoring the technical assistance contracts is as follows:

Probability of Defaulting on Payments After 1990

Azultan   .30
Byasfora   .25

The option of insuring the credit risk is being considered, and Air Wars is making confidential inquiries to determine the fees for such protection.

- Dr. Winthrop wants senior management to come up with a clear strategy for Air Wars and explain why it is the best strategy. In addition, Dr. Winthrop is also interested in trade-offs between price and risks. In view of the Le Mon competition, Dr. Winthrop believes that price flexibility to achieve a competitive price is extremely important for closing the sale. Therefore, an analysis comparing Air Wars' risks in relation to potential sales to Azultan and Byasfora is of significant value to Dr. Winthrop.

Your group is to prepare a presentation for Dr. Winthrop that addresses these concerns and clearly lays out the risks and possibilities inherent in this situation. The information given to you above may be redundant, incomplete, inconsistent, or unbelievable. Your group has to make the best of the situation and present a report. Your report should include:

a. A clear structuring of the uncertainties and their relation to one another and to Air Wars ultimate sales revenues

b. An analysis of the overall risk and the relative risk imposed by the individual uncertainties

c. Values of information for the most crucial uncertainties

d. Recommendations for further study or for possible actions to manage the most serious risks.

A

Probability Theory

Theory Overview

In both business and personal life, we must confront the reality of uncertainty in the world and be able to describe it. As we have emphasized throughout this book, the natural language to describe uncertainty is the language of probability.

The words "probability theory" can induce feelings of apprehension in people who have little experience (or desire to acquire experience) in mathematics. Yet virtually everyone has some familiarity with probability. For example, almost everyone agrees that you win only half the time when calling the outcome of the flip of a fair coin, and most people are even comfortable with more sophisticated statements, such as "There is a 70 percent chance that it will rain today" or "There is only one chance in four that my alma mater will win the football game tomorrow."

The probability theory used in this book does not involve any abstruse concepts or difficult mathematical formalism. The development is as intuitive and simple as possible. This appendix reviews those elements of probability theory that are important for decision analysis. The text of the book does not depend explicitly on the material in this appendix, and, thus, readers already familiar with probability theory can use this as a refresher.

Definition of Events

What is an event? An event is something about which you can say "It happened" or "It did not happen"—if you have sufficient information. This intuitive definition links the "real world" and the formulation of probability theory. The following examples may help to clarify the definition.

- "The spot price of oil was less than $20/barrel at some time during 1986." This is a statement about an event about which you can say "It happened." Note that an event does not necessarily imply some dramatic change in conditions.

- "Our company's net income in 1997 will be greater than $2 million." This statement describes an event which, in 1998, you will be able to characterize as having happened or not. Today, all you can say is that the event may or may not happen.

- "Company Q has developed a new product that will directly compete with our product." You may have heard a rumor to this effect. People at Company Q know whether this event has happened or not. However, your information is insufficient to tell you whether the event has happened or not.

The Venn diagram furnishes a convenient way of representing events. In the Venn diagram, each point represents a different possible world. For instance, one point in the square might represent a world in which the price of oil in 1998 is greater than $300 per barrel, in which the great-great-granddaughter of John F. Kennedy becomes president of the United States, in which Company Q does not come out with its rumored new product, and in which many other events, trivial or important, happen or do not happen. However, only one point in the square represents the world that will be realized as time unfolds.

This rather abstract construct is useful for representing a real problem when the points are arranged into areas in which specific events do or do not happen.

Throughout this appendix, we use the fictitious case of Medequip as a simple example. All Medequip discussions are set in italics.

Medequip manufactures a complete line of medical diagnostic equipment. Medequip's planning department is studying one of the products in this line. The product in question has been a good performer, but competitive pressures have caused unit revenues to decline steadily over the past five years. There is some concern that, even given Medequip's experience in the area, the unit costs will not decline enough over the coming years to keep the product profitable. The planning department has chosen 1997 as a good year to represent the end of the long-term trends. It has defined the following three events in terms of unit costs in that year:

- *C_1—Unit Cost less than $1,000*

- *C_2—Unit Cost between $1,000 and $1,500*

- *C_3—Unit Cost more than $1,500.*

These three events are graphically represented in the Venn diagram (Figure A–1). The area labeled C_1, for instance, includes all possible worlds in which event C_1 happens.

—————————— **Figure A–1** ——————————

Venn Diagram Divided into Regions with Different Unit Costs

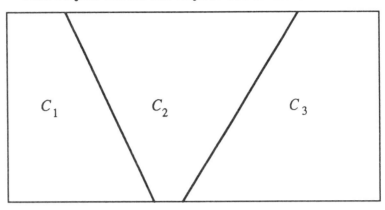

Algebra of Events

The Algebra of Events is a powerful formalism developed to deal with events and whether they happen or not. We present only a very small portion of this formalism.

Three important operations are used to combine or modify events. If A and B are any two events, then the effect of these operations can be seen graphically in Figure A–2.

It is convenient to define two special subsets of the possible worlds that can occur. These are the universal set (I) and the null set ($\emptyset$), as defined below.

- I: All possible worlds. Graphically, this is the whole area of the diagram.

- $\emptyset$: No possible worlds. Graphically, this is none of the diagram.

The definition of events and the operations defined above appear in a number of quite different disciplines. Four of these are Algebra of Events, Formal Logic, Boolean Algebra, and Set Theory.

Mutually Exclusive and Collectively Exhaustive Events

Probability analysis (and decision analysis) often moves in the direction of dividing up all the possible worlds into finer and finer subsets. This process allows better discrimination among the quantities of interest and better use of the data available. The set of events used to characterize the decomposition or subdivision should be mutually exclusive and collectively exhaustive.

───────────────── **Figure A–2** ─────────────────

Representation of the Operations "And," "Or," and "Not"

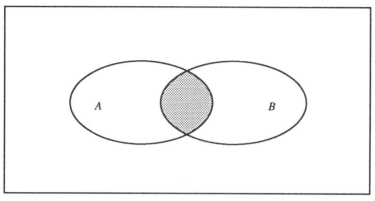

A and *B*: This operation gives the shaded region, where region *A* and region *B* overlap—worlds in which both *A* and *B* happen.

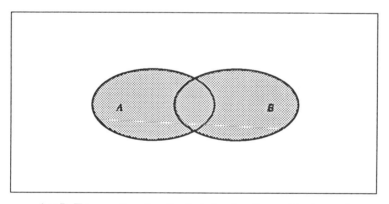

A or *B*: This operation gives the shaded region, the combined area of region *A* and region *B*—worlds in which either *A* or *B* (or both) happen.

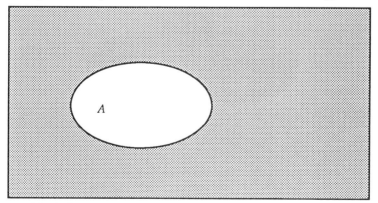

Not *A*: This operation gives the shaded region, the area outside region *A*—worlds in which *A* does not happen.

Mutually Exclusive

Let us imagine that we have a set of m events, X_i, with $i = 1, 2, ..., m$. This set of events is mutually exclusive if

$$X_i \text{ and } X_j = \emptyset \qquad (A\text{--}1)$$

for all values of i and j except those values for which $i = j$. In graphical terms, there is no overlap of the regions associated with events X_i.

Collectively Exhaustive

The second property desired of a list of events is that it include all possibilities. A set of m events, X_i, with $i = 1, 2, ..., m$ is collectively exhaustive if

$$X_1 \text{ or } X_2 \text{ or } ... \text{ or } X_m = I \qquad (A\text{--}2)$$

If the set of events is collectively exhaustive, then any point in the Venn diagram is in at least one of the regions X_i. If the set is also mutually exclusive, then any point will be in one (and only one) of the regions X_i.

An example of a set of events that is *neither* mutually exclusive *nor* collectively exhaustive is the set K_1 and K_2 defined below.

- K_1: Company Q introduces an inexpensive new product (priced less than \$2,000)

- K_2: Company Q introduces an expensive new product (priced greater than \$1,500)

--- **Figure A–3** ---

Set of Events (K_1 and K_2) That Is Neither Mutually Exclusive nor Collectively Exhaustive

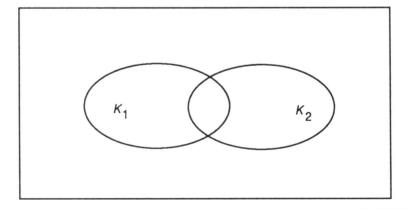

The set in Figure A–3 is not mutually exclusive because there is some overlap of the regions K_1 and K_2; a price of $1,750 falls in both K_1 and K_2. The set is not collectively exhaustive since there is an area outside the regions K_1 and K_2; the event that Company Q does not come out with its new product falls outside the regions K_1 and K_2.

Medequip was satisfied that its set of events—C_1, C_2, and C_3—was mutually exclusive. However, the planning department found that it is difficult to verify that a list of events is collectively exhaustive. Even in this simple case, there were some problems. For instance, where do the values $1,000/unit and $1,500/unit fall? In event C_2? What of the possibility that the product is not even produced in 1997? Is this represented in event C_3? The planning department refined its definitions as follows:

- C_1—Unit Cost $\leq$ $1,000

- C_2—$1,000 < Unit Cost $\leq$ $1,500

- C_3—$1500 < Unit Cost

The possibility of not manufacturing the product was judged so remote that it could be effectively included in the high-cost scenario, C_3.

In cases of real difficulty, it is possible to define an "all other" event.

$$X_{m+1} = \text{not } (X_1 \text{ or } X_2 \text{ or } \dots \text{ or } X_m) \qquad (A\text{–}3)$$

This will make the set of events X_i ($i = 1, 2, \dots, m, m+1$) collectively exhaustive. However, this event is useful only as a reminder to keep looking for the (as yet) unknown events needed to completely describe all the possible worlds.

Joint Events

As mentioned above, probability analysis (and decision analysis) often moves in the direction of dividing up all possible worlds into finer and finer subsets. This process is frequently accomplished by combining two different sets of events to give a joint set of events. If A and B are any two events, a joint event is defined as

$$A \text{ and } B \qquad (A\text{–}4)$$

In addition to being concerned about unit costs, Medequip's planning department was also concerned about unit revenues. For the initial phase of the analysis, they were content to define the following very simple set of mutually exclusive and collectively exhaustive events in terms of unit revenue in 1997 for the product:

- R_1—Unit Revenue $\leq$ $1,750

- R_2—$1,750 < Unit Revenue

Graphically, this second set could be represented as in Figure A–4.

Venn Diagram Separated into Regions of Different Unit Revenue

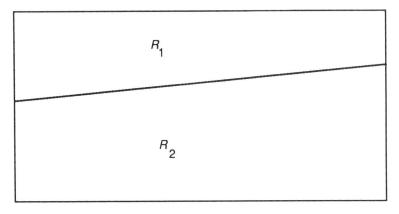

These two sets of events combine to give six joint events, M_i, which describe the margin in 1997 (margin equals unit revenue minus unit cost). These six joint events can be represented in the Venn diagram (Figure A–5).

- M_1—R_1 and C_1
- M_2—R_1 and C_2
- M_3—R_1 and C_3

- M_4—R_2 and C_1
- M_5—R_2 and C_2
- M_6—R_2 and C_3

Note that the operation "and" is often denoted by a comma, as in Figure A–5.

——————————— Figure A–5 ———————————

Venn Diagram Separated into Regions of Different Joint Events

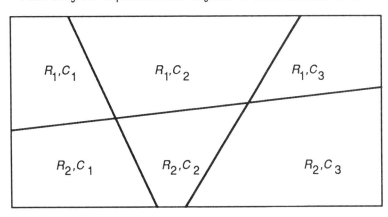

Tree Representation of Events

Because the tabular definitions and the Venn diagram representations used above become cumbersome for all but the simplest problems, we use tree forms as a simple way to represent even complicated problems. Each set of events is represented by a "node" or branching point in the tree. Each branch emanating from a node represents an event. Each path through the tree (moving from left to right) describes one joint event composed of all the events on the path. By convention, the sets of events used at a node are always mutually exclusive and collectively exhaustive.

Figure A–6 is the tree for the margin for Medequip's product.

──────────────────────── **Figure A–6** ────────────────────────

Tree Representation for Different Unit Cost and Revenue Combinations

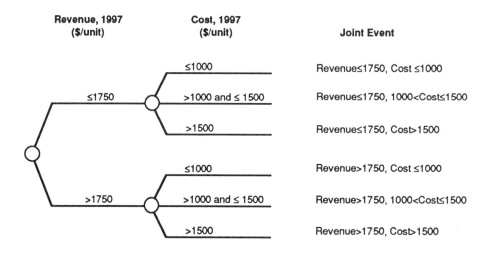

Probability and States of Information _____

There are some events for which we have sufficient information to say "It happened" or "It did not happen." For instance, most people would agree that the event "Thomas Jefferson became the first president of the United States" did not happen. However, there are other events about which we do not possess enough information to say whether they did or did not happen. We may simply not know what happened in the past. For instance, we may not know whether our competitor had a successful R&D outcome or not. More typically, the event in question is a possible future event. We do not know if our unit cost in 1997 will be less than $1,000. The answer to that question cannot be given until 1998.

While we may not have sufficient information to give a definitive answer to "Did it or will it happen?," we can assign some probability (or likelihood) to whether an event did or will happen. This is something we do informally in everyday business and personal situations.

Let us define

$$p(A \mid S) \tag{A-5}$$

to be the probability we assign that event A did or will happen, given our present state of information, S. While the S is commonly dropped from the notation, if it is dropped there will often be confusion about just what state of information underlies a probability. For instance, someone may judge the probability that event C_1 (unit costs in 1997 less than $1,000) will occur is 1 in 10:

$$p(C_1 \mid S) = .1 \tag{A-6}$$

However, some days later, after learning that a large deposit of a rare and critical raw material has recently been discovered, the person may revise his probability assessment, given the new state of information, S', to 1 in 4:

$$p(C_1 \mid S') = .25 \tag{A-7}$$

If we define the event

D: Large deposit of raw material discovered,

then

$$S' = D \text{ and } S \tag{A-8}$$

As mentioned above, the "and" operation is frequently denoted by a comma in probability notation. We can then write

$$p(C_1 \mid S') = p(C_1 \mid D, S) \tag{A-9}$$

In performing decision analyses, it is often necessary to combine or compare probabilities obtained from different people or from the same person at different times. Explicit reference to the underlying state of information is essential to keeping the calculations consistent and meaningful.

Probability Theory

The theoretical underpinnings of probability theory are really quite simple. There are only three axioms necessary, given our understanding of the events above. If A and B are any two events, then we can state the axioms as follows:

$$p(A \mid S) \geq 0 \qquad (A\text{–}10)$$

$$p(I \mid S) = 1 \qquad (A\text{–}11)$$

If A and $B = \emptyset$, then

$$p(A \text{ or } B \mid S) = p(A \mid S) + p(B \mid S) \qquad (A\text{–}12)$$

If we take the Venn diagram and rearrange and stretch its surface so the areas of each region are proportional to the probability that the event that defines the region happens, then the axioms have the following graphical interpretation:

1. There are no regions of negative area.

2. The area of the total square is unity. This is the definition of the unit of area.

3. If two regions are nonoverlapping (A and $B = \emptyset$) as in Figure A–7, then the combined region (A or B) as represented by the shaded region has area equal to the sum of the areas of the two component regions.

––––––––––––––––––––––––––– **Figure A–7** –––––––––––––––––––––––––––

Venn Diagram with A and B Not Overlapping

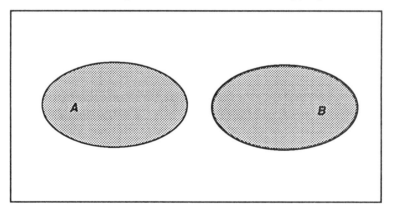

Given these three axioms, we can easily deduce properties commonly associated with probabilities. The following four properties are frequently used. The proof of these properties is left to the problems at the end of this appendix.

1. Probabilities are numbers between zero and one.

$$0 \le p(A \mid S) \le 1 \tag{A–13}$$

2. Probabilities sum to one. More precisely, if X_i with $i = 1, 2, ..., m$ is a set of mutually exclusive and collectively exhaustive events, then

$$\sum_{i=1}^{m} p(X_i \mid S) = 1 \tag{A–14}$$

3. For A (any event) and X_i with $i = 1, 2, ..., m$ a set of mutually exclusive and collectively exhaustive events,

$$p(A \mid S) = \sum_{i=1}^{m} p(A, X_i \mid S) \tag{A–15}$$

This property is often called the Expansion Theorem.

4. For A and B (any two events), then
$$p(A \text{ or } B \mid S) = p(A \mid S) + p(B \mid S) - p(A, B \mid S) \tag{A–16}$$

The last term on the right in the above expression compensates for the double counting (if the events are not mutually exclusive) of the overlapping (double shaded) region in Figure A–8.

───────────────────────── **Figure A–8** ─────────────────────────

Venn Diagram with *A* and *B* Overlapping

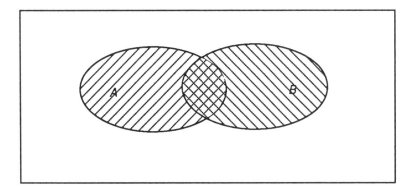

Joint, Marginal, and Conditional Probabilities

Rarely is the uncertainty of a problem well described in terms of a single set of mutually exclusive and collectively exhaustive events. More frequent is a description in terms of a set of joint events—several sets of mutually exclusive and collectively exhaustive events are used to subdivide the possible worlds into fine enough detail for the work at hand. The probability of the joint events occurring is called the joint probability. If A and B are any two events, the joint probability for the two events occurring is

$$p(A,B\,|\,S) \tag{A–17}$$

Medequip's planning department used all the information it possessed to estimate the joint probabilities for unit revenue and unit cost. It gathered all the information it could on the principal competitor's process and on his pricing policy. The department studied historical trends on raw material cost and used the judgment of the managers of the production process to estimate future cost trends. All this information was used to estimate the joint probabilities shown in the table below.

$$p(R_i C_j\,|\,S)$$

	C_1	C_2	C_3
R_1	.10	.25	.03
R_2	.22	.26	.14

This set of joint probabilities is also displayed in the tree in Figure A–9.

—————————————— **Figure A–9** ——————————————

Display of Joint Probabilities in Tree Form

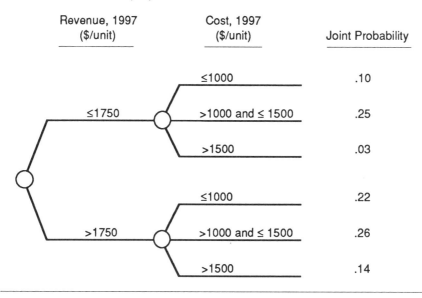

Revenue, 1997 ($/unit)	Cost, 1997 ($/unit)	Joint Probability
≤1750	≤1000	.10
	>1000 and ≤ 1500	.25
	>1500	.03
>1750	≤1000	.22
	>1000 and ≤ 1500	.26
	>1500	.14

The marginal probabilities are those placed at the right or bottom edges (margins) of the table of joint probabilities and are obtained by summing probabilities across rows or down columns. This process uses the Expansion Theorem:

$$p(A \mid S) = \sum_{i=1}^{m} p(A, X_i \mid S) \qquad \text{(A–18)}$$

In the above expression, A is any event and X_i $(i = 1, 2, ..., m)$ is a set of mutually exclusive and collectively exhaustive events.

In the Medequip case, the marginal probabilities are easily obtained from the table above. For instance,

$$p(C_1 \mid S) = p(R_1, C_1 \mid S) + p(R_2, C_1 \mid S)$$

$$p(C_1 \mid S) = .10 + .22 = .32 \qquad \text{(A–19)}$$

The full set of marginal probabilities is presented in the following table.

	$p(R_i, C_j \mid S)$			$p(R_i \mid S)$
	C_1	C_2	C_3	
R_1	.10	.25	.03	.38
R_2	.22	.26	.14	.62
$p(C_j \mid S)$	.32	.51	.17	

Conditional probabilities are defined from the joint and marginal probabilities. If A and B are any two events, then

$$p(A \mid B, S) \qquad \text{(A–20)}$$

is the conditional probability—the probability that A occurs, given that B occurs and given the state of information S. This conditional probability is obtained from the joint and marginal probabilities by the following definition:

$$p(A \mid B, S) = \frac{p(A, B \mid S)}{p(B \mid S)} \qquad \text{(A–21)}$$

For the Medequip case, the conditional probabilities are easily obtained from the table above. For instance, the probability of C_1 occurring, given that R_1 occurs is

$$p(C_1 \mid R_1, S) = \frac{p(R_1, C_1 \mid S)}{p(R_1 \mid S)} = \frac{.10}{.38} \qquad \text{(A–22)}$$

Tables of the values of the conditional probabilities $p(C_j \mid R_i, S)$ and $p(R_i \mid C_j, S)$ are given below.

$$p(C_j \mid R_i, S)$$

	C_1	C_2	C_3
R_1	10/38	25/38	3/38
R_2	22/62	26/62	14/62

$$p(R_i \mid C_j, S)$$

	C_1	C_2	C_3
R_1	10/32	25/51	3/17
R_1	22/32	26/51	14/17

These probabilities show, for instance, that high unit costs are much more likely when unit revenues are high than when unit revenues are low.

In tree form, the probabilities written at the nodes of the tree are, by definition, the probabilities conditional on all the nodes to the left of the node in question. The probabilities of the leftmost node are its marginal probabilities.

For the Medequip case, the tree can be written with the unit revenue node on the left. In the display in Figure A–10, the values and symbols for the probabilities are both written. The symbols are usually omitted.

––––––––––––––––––––––––––– **Figure A–10** –––––––––––––––––––––––––––

Tree Representation with Probabilities Displayed at the Nodes

Revenue, 1997 ($/unit)	Cost, 1997 ($/unit)	Joint Probability
	≤1000 $10/38 = p(C_1 \mid R_1, S)$	.10
≤1750 $.38 = p(R_1 \mid S)$	>1000 and ≤ 1500 $25/38 = p(C_2 \mid R_1, S)$	.25
	>1500 $3/38 = p(C_3 \mid R_1, S)$	.03
	≤1000 $22/62 = p(C_1 \mid R_2, S)$	.22
>1750 $.62 = p(R_2 \mid S)$	>1000 and ≤ 1500 $26/62 = p(C_2 \mid R_2, S)$	.26
	>1500 $14/62 = p(C_3 \mid R_2, S)$	.14

Bayes' Rule

Bayes' Rule is a simple rule that relates conditional and marginal probabilities. It is of central importance to decision analysis.

Bayes' Rule solves the following problem: Let X_i $(i = 1, 2, ..., m)$ and Y_j $(j = 1, 2, ..., n)$ be two sets of mutually exclusive and collectively exhaustive events. Given the following marginal and conditional probabilities,

$$p(Y_j|S) \tag{A-23}$$

$$p(X_i|Y_j,S) \tag{A-24}$$

how do we calculate the other marginal and conditional probabilities? This operation is called for when we reverse the order of nodes in a tree. We can write the joint probability in terms of the given probabilities as follows:

$$p(X_i,Y_j|S) = p(X_i|Y_j,S)\, p(Y_j|S) \tag{A-25}$$

We can just as well write the joint probability in the reversed order, as follows:

$$p(X_i,Y_j|S) = p(Y_j|X_i,S)\, p(X_i|S) \tag{A-26}$$

Equating the right-hand sides of the two equations above enables us to solve for the conditional probability term, as shown below.

$$p(Y_j|X_i,S) = \frac{p(X_i|Y_j,S)\, p(Y_j|S)}{p(X_i|S)} \tag{A-27}$$

The only unknown in the right-hand side of this equation is $p(X_i | S)$. This can be obtained by using the Expansion Theorem (Equation A–15) to write this probability in known terms, as illustrated below.

$$p(X_i|S) = \sum_{j=1}^{n} p(X_i,Y_j|S) \tag{A-28}$$

The joint probability on the right-hand side of the above equation can then be written in terms of the known conditional and marginal probabilities. The probabilities we are seeking are then written in terms of known quantities, as follows:

$$p(X_i|S) = \sum_{j=1}^{n} p(X_i|Y_j,S)\, p(Y_j|S) \tag{A-29}$$

$$p(Y_j|X_i,S) = \frac{p(X_i|Y_j,S)\, p(Y_j|S)}{\sum_{k=1}^{n} p(X_i|Y_k,S)\, p(Y_k|S)} \tag{A-30}$$

In the Medequip example, assume we know the marginals $p(R_i | S)$ and the conditionals, $p(C_j | R_i,S)$. This is the information given on the tree at the end of the previous section (Figure A–10). Then, for example, we could calculate the following probabilities from those given.

$$p(C_2|S) = [p(C_2|R_1,S)p(R_1|S)] + [p(C_2|R_2,S)p(R_2|S)]$$

$$p(C_2|S) = [(25/38)\times.38] + [(26/62)\times.62] = .51 \qquad (A–31)$$

$$p(R_2|C_1,S) = \frac{p(C_1|R_2,S)p(R_2|S)}{p(C_1|R_1,S)p(R_1|S) + p(C_2|R_2,S)p(R_2|S)}$$

$$p(R_2|C_1,S) = \frac{(22/62)\times.62}{(10/38)\times.38 + (22/62)\times.62} = 22/32 \qquad (A–32)$$

Figure A–11

Reversing the Tree in Figure A–10

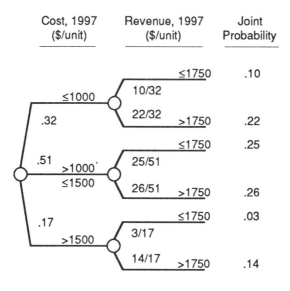

| Cost, 1997 ($/unit) | Revenue, 1997 ($/unit) | Joint Probability |

For Medequip, the tree when reversed is as shown in Figure A–11.

In this tree, we can see an easy, graphical way of performing the calculations to reverse the order of nodes. First, the joint probabilities are taken from the tree in Figure A–10 and put at the end of the appropriate branches in the tree in Figure A–11. The probability for each Cost branch is then obtained by summing the joint probabilities for the Revenue branches following that Cost branch. The individual Revenue probabilities, then, are simply the joint probability divided by the Cost probability (so that the Cost and Revenue probabilities give the right joint probability when multiplied together).

Probabilistic Independence

Sometimes conditional probabilities turn out to be the same regardless of which conditioning event occurs. For instance, prices could be set by a competitor using a process quite different from our own. In this case, the probabilities for prices and for costs might be independent of each other. If there is no correlation among the probabilities, they are said to be probabilistically independent. If A and B are two events, they are probabilistically independent if

$$p(A \mid B,S) = p(A \mid S) \qquad (A\text{--}33)$$

Multiply or Add Probabilities?

Inevitably, the question arises "When should I multiply probabilities and when should I add them?" For joint ("and") events, conditional probabilities for the component events are multiplied together. For combined ("or") events, probabilities are added (if the events are mutually exclusive).

This is illustrated in terms of the Medequip example. A joint ("and") probability is

$$p(R_2,C_3 \mid S) = p(R_2 \mid S)\, p(C_3 \mid R_2,S) = .62 \times (14/62) = .14 \qquad (A\text{--}34)$$

A combined ("or") probability is (since the set C_i is mutually exclusive)

$$p(C_1 \text{ or } C_2 \mid S) = p(C_1 \mid S) + p(C_2 \mid S) = .32 + .51 = .83 \qquad (A\text{--}35)$$

Events, Variables, and Values

Many events can be defined by a qualitative description. For instance, "The president of the United States in 1997 will be a Democrat" is a description of a possible event.

In many quantitative situations, however, the event is defined by a variable or parameter taking on a specific value or having a value within a specified range. For instance, in the Medequip example, events have definitions such as "Unit Cost less than or equal to $1,000."

In quantitative situations of this sort, it is convenient to define events by the value the variable takes on—rather than by defining the event by a range of values. Values can be discrete (the variable can take on any one of a finite number of different values) or continuous (the variable can take on any value out of a continuum). Some variables have discrete possible values, such as the marginal income tax rate. Most variables, however, have a continuum of possible values, such as unit cost. Unfortunately, continuous values are difficult to work with, and we will always approximate a continuous set of values by a few discrete values. A good process for making this approximation is discussed in Chapter 2.

To make it clear that an event is defined by a value, we will write the value as a lowercase letter rather than the uppercase letters we have been using for general definitions.

Probabilities and the values associated with them are often referred to as a probability distribution for the variable in question.

Medequip's planning department proceeded to assign a value to represent each of the ranges in the definitions of the events. For unit cost in 1997, they defined the following values:

- c_1—$800

- c_2—$1,250

- c_3—$1,700

For unit revenue in 1997, they defined the following values:

- r_1—$1,500

- r_2—$2,000

This yielded the following set of values for the margin in 1997:

- m_1—$700   = $1,500 – $800

- m_2—$250   = $1,500 – $1,250

- m_3—-$200   = $1,500 – $1,700

- m_4—$1,200 = $2,000 – $800

- m_5—$750   = $2,000 – $1,250

- m_6—$300   = $2,000 – $1,700

Representations of Probabilities for Discrete Values

There are a number of ways to represent the probabilities for a set of discrete values. These representations include tabular form, tree form, mass distribution plot, cumulative probability plot, and histogram. We will illustrate each of these representations using the example of the margins from the Medequip case.

Tabular Form

The values and their probabilities are presented in the following simple tabular form:

i	m_i	$p(m_i \mid S)$
1	$700	.10
2	$250	.25
3	–$200	.03
4	$1,200	.22
5	$750	.26
6	$300	.14

———————————————— Figure A–12 ————————————————

Representation of Probabilities and Values in Tree Form

Margin, 1997
($/unit)

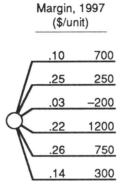

Tree Form

These values can be presented in the tree form displayed in Figure A–12.

Mass Density Plot

Probabilities can be graphed directly against values in what is called, for discrete values, the mass density plot. The plot in Figure A–13 graphs the probability distribution on margin.

———————————————— Figure A–13 ————————————————

Representation of Probabilities and Values in a Mass Density Plot

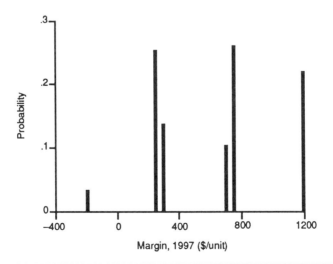

Cumulative Probability Graph

Another graphical representation frequently used is the cumulative probability graph. This graph plots the probability that the value is less than or equal to the value shown on the horizontal axis. Formally, the cumulative probability is defined as

$$P_\leq(x\,|\,S) = \sum_i p(x_i\,|\,S) \qquad\qquad (A\text{--}36)$$

where the sum is over all values of i for which $x_i \leq x$. In practice, the outcomes are placed in a table ordered from lowest to highest value; the cumulative probability at each value is calculated as the running sum of the probabilities down to each row. For the margin example, we have the following table:

m_i	$p(m_i\,|\,S)$	$P_\leq(m_i\,|\,S)$
−$200	.03	.03
$250	.25	.28
$300	.14	.42
$700	.10	.52
$750	.26	.78
$1,200	.22	1.00

——————————— **Figure A–14** ———————————

Representation of Probabilities and Values in a Cumulative Probability Plot

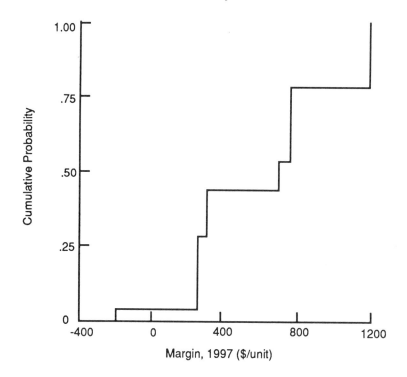

The cumulative probability is then plotted (Figure A–14). Note that the curve is flat except at points where the value on the horizontal axis is equal to one of the values in the table.

Histogram

A final representation is by histogram form. Although this plot is an approximation, it takes the mass density plot and converts it into a form that is more readily interpreted by the eye. The horizontal axis is divided into bins of equal width, and a bar for each bin shows the sum of the probabilities for all the events in that bin. In Figure A–15, bins of a width of $400 were chosen, with bin edges falling at values that are integer multiples of $400.

─────────────────────── Figure A–15 ───────────────────────

Representation of Probabilities and Values in a Histogram

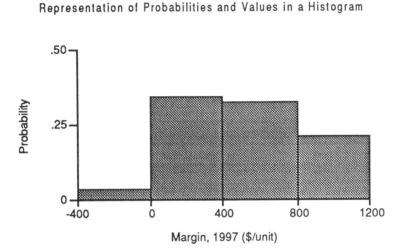

───

Mean, Median, Mode, Variance, Standard Deviation, and Moments _____

Another way to represent a set of probabilities is to use a few values to characterize the whole set. A common measure is the mean (or average) of the distribution. In decision analysis, the mean is usually called the expected value. If x_i for $i = 1, 2, ..., m$ is a set of values that define a set of mutually exclusive and collectively exhaustive events, the mean is calculated using the following formula:

$$\text{mean} = \sum_{i=1}^{m} x_i p(x_i | S) \qquad (A\text{--}37)$$

The median is the value at which it is just as probable to be below that value as above it. The mode is the most probable value in the set. The mean, mode, and median are measures that identify the center or most important values in the distribution. Of these measures, though, the mean is most sensitive to the shape of the distribution. The median is often the easiest measure to understand (it is the 50/50 probability point). The mode often works well for describing highly asymmetric distributions (such as the cost). Neither the mode nor the median is very important in applications of probability theory to decision analysis, though they may be important in helping people relate to and understand a probability distribution.

The mean of the probability distribution on Medequip's margin in 1997 is calculated as follows:

$$\text{mean} = (700 \times .10) + (250 \times .25) + (-200 \times .03) + (1200 \times .22) + (750 \times .26) + (300 \times .14)$$

$$\text{mean} = \$628 \tag{A-38}$$

The median is somewhere around $700, since there is a 42 percent chance that the value is less than $700 and a 48 percent chance that the value is greater than $700. (In a set of values this small, there will seldom be a value that is exactly the median.) Finally, the mode of the distribution is $750, since it has the largest probability of any of the values (26 percent).

The variance is a more complicated measure. If the mean measures the average value of the distribution, the variance is a measure of how far off the value might be from this average; it is a measure of how "wide" the distribution is.

$$\text{variance} = \sum_{i=1}^{m} (x_i - \text{mean})^2 p(x_i | S) \tag{A-39}$$

The standard deviation (written as σ) is the square root of the variance and is a direct measure of the spread or width of the distribution.

The planning department at Medequip calculated the variance in the probability distribution on margin in 1997 as follows. Note that the units of variance here are ($)^2.

$$\text{variance} = .10(700-628)^2 + .25(250-628)^2 + .03(-200-628)^2 + .22(1,200-628)^2$$

$$+ .26(850-628)^2 + .14(300-628)^2$$

$$\text{variance} = 147,719 \tag{A-40}$$

The standard deviation is the square root of the variance.

$$\sigma = (147,719)^{1/2} = \$384 \tag{A-41}$$

A more complete and systematic set of parameters to represent a probability distribution is provided by the set of moments. If x_i for $i = 1, 2, ..., m$ is a set of values that define a mutually exclusive and collectively exhaustive set of events, then the moments are defined by the following equation:

$$\mu_n = \sum_{i=1}^{m} x_i^n p(x_i | S) \tag{A-42}$$

The zeroth moment, μ_0, is 1; this is just the normalization condition that probabilities sum to one. The first moment, μ_1, is the mean of the distribution. There is a second set of moments that can also be used to describe the distribution—the central moments. For the same values, x_i, the central moments are defined by the following equation:

$$v_n = \sum_{i=1}^{m} (x_i - \mu_1)^n \, p(x_i | S) \qquad \text{(A–43)}$$

The zeroth central moment, v_0, is just 1; again, this is just the normalization condition for probabilities. The first central moment, v_1, is identically zero. The second central moment, v_2, is the variance.

Representations of Probabilities for Continuous Variables

Throughout this book, we use discrete approximations instead of continuous values. In the interest of completeness, however, we discuss a few properties and definitions for probability distributions on continuous variables. Continuous probability distributions are usually defined by graphs or by a functional form rather than using an infinite tabular form. For instance, the normal or Gaussian probability distribution is defined by the following equation:

$$p(x | \mu_1, v_2, \text{normal}) = \frac{e^{(x-\mu_1)^2/2v_2}}{\sqrt{2\pi v_2}} \qquad \text{(A–44)}$$

The state of knowledge is completely specified in this case by the value of the mean, μ_1, the value of the variance, v_2, and the knowledge that it is a normal distribution. The value of the function $p(x | S)$ is the probability that the value falls in the range between x and $x + dx$. In the graph of the normal probability distribution (Figure A–16), σ is the standard deviation, the square root of the variance.

The shaded area equals the probability that x lies within one standard deviation, σ, of the mean, μ_1. For the normal or Gaussian distribution in Figure A–16, this probability is 68 percent.

The cumulative probability graph is smooth (instead of the staircase found with discrete distributions) and is defined by the following integral:

$$P_\leq(x | S) = \int_{-\infty}^{x} p(x' | S) \, dx' \qquad \text{(A–45)}$$

For the normal or Gaussian distribution, the cumulative probability distribution is as shown in Figure A–17.

Note that for a normal or Gaussian distribution, $84 - 16 = 68$ percent of the probability lies within one standard deviation of the mean and $98 - 2 = 96$ percent of the probability lies within two standard deviations of the mean.

Figure A-16

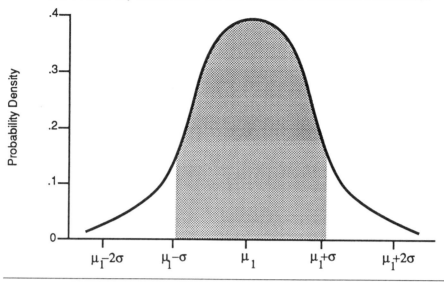

The Probability Distribution for the Normal or Gaussian Distribution

Figure A-17

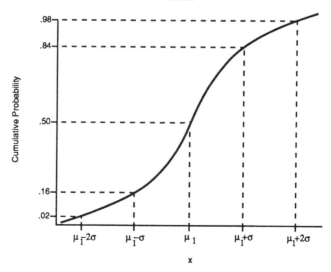

Cumulative Probability Graph for the Normal or Gaussian Probability
Distribution

The moments of a probability distribution for a continuous variable are calculated by the equations below.

$$\mu_n = \int_{-\infty}^{\infty} x^n p(x \mid S) \, dx \qquad \text{(A-46)}$$

$$v_n = \int_{-\infty}^{\infty} (x - \mu_1)^n p(x \mid S) \, dx \qquad \text{(A-47)}$$

As you can imagine from the equations above, the use of continuous distributions almost always leads to problems of overwhelming analytical complexity for real situations. For this reason, discrete approximations are almost always used in actual decision analysis applications.

Problems and Discussion Topics

A.1   State whether each of the following statements is or is not an event and if not, why not.

a. The temperature will be greater than 53 °F in Bombay tomorrow.

b. General Motors stock sold for more than $55 per share on the New York Stock Exchange.

c. The weather is nice today.

d. The final version of the first printing of this book contains 1,034,246 characters.

e. Elm trees are taller than oak trees.

A.2   Draw the Venn diagram for the following events: $1,000 \le$ Units Sold $< 5,000$; Profit Margin per Unit $< \$2$; Profit Margin per Unit $\ge \$2$. In which region(s) of the Venn diagram do the following events occur? (Profit = Units Sold × Profit Margin.)

a.   Margin = $2 and Profit = $4,000
b.   Margin = $1.50 and Profit = $2,000
c.   Profit < $2,000 and Sales = 500 units
d.   Profit = $15,000

A.3   The New England Patriots and the Cincinnati Bengals both have one game left in the season. They are not playing each other, and each game will go into overtime if necessary to produce a winner.

a. Draw the Venn diagram for this situation.

If the Patriots win and the Bengals lose, then the Patriots go to the play-offs. If the Patriots lose and the Bengals win, then the Bengals go to the play-offs. Otherwise, you are not sure who goes to the play-offs.

b. Show the region on the Venn diagram where you know the Patriots go to the play-offs for certain.

The Miami Dolphins also have one game left in the season and are playing neither the Patriots nor the Bengals. If Miami wins and both the Patriots and the Bengals lose, then the Patriots go to the play-offs. If Miami loses and both the Patriots and Bengals win, then the Patriots also go to the play-offs. Otherwise, the Miami game is not relevant.

c. Redraw the Venn diagram and show the regions where the Bengals go to the play-offs for sure.

A.4   For each of the following events or list of events, complete the list to make it mutually exclusive and collectively exhaustive.

a. The number of passenger automobiles assembled in the United States in 1985 was at least 20 million and less than 22 million.

b. The average length of all great white sharks reported caught off the coast of Australia is less than 15 feet.

c. The variable unit cost for producing the product is $1.75.

d. The market demand for adipic acid is at least 100 pounds per year and less than 150 million pounds per year. The market demand for adipic acid is greater than 400 million pounds per year.

e. A competitive product is introduced before our product is introduced.

f. Our market share is twice that of our nearest competitor.

A.5   A soldier is taking a test in which he is allowed three shots at a target (unmanned) airplane. The probability of his first shot hitting the plane is .4, that of his second shot is .5, and that of his third shot is .7. The probability of the plane's crashing after one shot is .2; after two shots, the probability of crashing is .6; the plane will crash for sure if hit three times. The test is over when the soldier has fired all three shots or when the plane crashes.

a. Define a set of collectively exhaustive events.

b. Define a set of mutually exclusive events.

c. Define a set of mutually exclusive and collectively exhaustive events.

d. What is the probability of the soldiers shooting down the plane?

e. What is the mean number of shots required to shoot down the plane?

A.6 Define the joint events for the following two sets of events.

m_1—Market Share < 5 percent

m_2—5 percent ≤ Market Share < 10 percent

m_3—10 percent ≤ Market Share

d_1—Development Cost ≤ $2 million

d_2—$2 million < Development Cost ≤ $5 million

d_3—$5 million < Development Cost

A.7 For the data in the preceding problem, assume that the events have been approximated by discrete values as follows.

m_1—Market Share = 3 percent

m_2—Market Share = 7 percent

m_3—Market Share = 13 percent

d_1—Development Cost = $1.5 million

d_2—Development Cost = $3 million

d_3—Development Cost = $7 million

a. Define the joint set of events.

b. If Market Size = $100 million and Revenue = (Market Size × Market Share) – Development Cost, calculate the Revenue for each joint event.

c. Calculate the Revenue for each joint event given a Market Size of $60 million.

A.8 On the air route between Chicago and Los Angeles, there is either a head wind or tail wind. Depending on which way the wind is blowing and how fast, flights from Chicago to Los Angeles may be early, on time, or late. We define the following events:

w_1—Head Wind

w_2—Tail Wind

a_1—Arrive Early

a_2—Arrive on Time

a_3—Arrive Late

The joint probabilities are as follows:

w_1 and a_1— .06

w_1 and a_2— .12

w_1 and a_3— .22

w_2 and a_1— .39

w_2 and a_2— .18

w_2 and a_3— .03

a. What is the marginal probability of a head wind?

b. What are the conditional probabilities for arriving early, on time, or late given a tail wind?

c. Given you arrive on time, what is the probability you had a tail wind? If you arrive early? If you arrive late?

A.9   The Surprise Dog man at Fenway Park sells all his hotdogs for the same price, but he does not tell you in advance what you are getting. You could receive a regular dog or foot-long dog, either of which could be a cheese or chili dog. We define the following events:

l_1—You get a foot-long dog

l_2—You get a regular dog

c_1—You get a cheese dog

c_2—You get a chili dog

The marginal probability of getting a foot-long dog is .25. The probability of getting a foot-long chili dog is .225, and the probability of getting a regular cheese dog is .45.

a.   What is the marginal probability of getting a cheese dog?

b.   What is the probability of getting a regular chili dog?

A.10   A weather forecaster said that San Francisco and Los Angeles have probabilities of .7 and .4, respectively, of having rain during Christmas day. She also said that the probability of their both having rain is .28.

a.   Find the probability of rain in San Francisco on Christmas day given rain in Los Angeles on Christmas day.

b.   Find the probability of rain in Los Angeles on Christmas day given rain in San Francisco on Christmas day.

c.   Find the probability of rain in San Francisco or Los Angeles (or both) on Christmas day.

A.11   Your resident expert on Soviet deployments, Katyusha Caddell, has just given you his opinion on recent Soviet missile developments. The Soviets are building silos that may be of type 1 or type 2 (it is too early to tell), and Katyusha is unsure about which of two possible missile types the Soviets will be deploying in them. He describes the following events:

s_1—Silo of type 1 built

s_2—Silo of type 2 built

m_1—Type 1 missile deployed

m_2—Type 2 missile deployed

Katyusha puts the probability of the silos being type 2 at .6 and figures that type 2 silos mean a .7 probability of type 1 missiles, while type 1 silos mean a .8 probability of type 2 missiles. He further puts the marginal probability of type 2 missile deployment at .6. Do the marginal probabilities agree?

A.12 You and a friend are pondering buying tortilla chips and salsa at a baseball game. Your friend tells you he has made a systematic study of the different varieties of salsa and says the possible types are salsa tomatillo, salsa fresca, and traditional salsa. (The workers at the snack bar do not know what kind it is.) Furthermore, the salsa could be hot (spicy) or not hot. Your friend makes the following predictions:

> The chance of hot salsa tomatillo is .08.
>
> The chance of hot salsa fresca is .15.
>
> The chance of not-hot traditional salsa is .18.
>
> The chance of getting salsa fresca is .3 and of getting traditional salsa is .6.

a. What is the probability of getting not-hot salsa tomatillo?

b. What is the conditional probability that the salsa is hot, given that it is salsa tomatillo?

c. What is the marginal probability that the salsa is hot?

d. What is the conditional probability of getting traditional salsa, given that it is not hot?

A.13 Frequently, people use tests to infer knowledge about something. A current (controversial) example is the use of a blood test to see if a person has the AIDS virus or not.* The test results reflect current knowledge of the virus' characteristics, and test accuracy may be a matter of concern. How should the information represented by the blood test result be used to update knowledge of the test subject's condition? Bayes' Rule gives the answer to this question.

Suppose a number of people have taken an XYZ virus test with the result shown below. (The numbers are purely illustrative and are not intended to reflect current understanding of the AIDS blood test.)

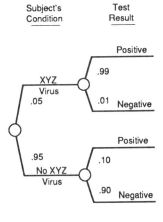

---

*Testing for the AIDS virus also involves serious issues of rights to privacy and due process. This problem addresses only the information gained by using a test where the outcome of the test is not a perfect indicator of the underlying condition.

If a person has taken this test and the result turns out to be positive, what is the probability that he or she does not have the XYZ virus?

A.14 Your professor tells you that only 50 percent of the students in her class will do the homework and pass the class; 25 percent will not do the homework and will still pass the class; 8.3 percent will do the homework and study too much (missing sleep) and still pass. The professor figures 30 percent will not do the homework, 60 percent will do the homework, and 10 percent will work too much.

According to the professor, are doing the homework and passing the class probabilistically dependent or independent?

A.15 You suspect that your corns hurt when your mother is about to call you. However, you think that the chance of getting a call from your mother and your corns not hurting is about .5. Your corns hurt about 10 percent of the time.

What is the marginal probability of your mother calling if her calling and your corns hurting are probabilistically independent?

A.16 Use the information from problem A.7 to perform the following calculations:

a. Formulate the joint events and calculate the probabilities and revenues for them. Assume probabilities .25, .50, and .25 for m_1, m_2, and m_3 and for d_1, d_2, and d_3, respectively.

b. Plot the cumulative probability distribution for revenue.

c. Plot the histogram for revenue. (Choose the bin size to give a good representation of the data.)

d. Calculate the mean, variance, and standard deviation of the distribution.

A.17 The annual revenues from a new gasoline additive depend on annual U.S. gas consumption and on the average price of gasoline over the next year. It is estimated that 1 bottle of additive will be sold for every 1,000 gallons of gasoline consumed. The price will be set at twice the price for a gallon of gas. Discretized estimates of U.S. gas consumption next year put a .3 chance on consumption being 1 billion gallons, a .6 chance on consumption being 1.5 billion gallons, and a .1 chance on consumption being 2 billion gallons. Similarly, average gas prices have a .25 chance of being $0.50, a .5 chance of being $1.00, and a .25 chance of being $1.25.

a. Formulate a probability tree for revenue.

b. Calculate the probabilities and revenues for the joint events.

c. Plot the cumulative probability distribution for revenue.

d. Plot the histogram for revenue.

e. Calculate the mean, variance, and standard deviation of the distribution.

A.18 You are offered an opportunity to engage in a series of three coin flips (.5 probability of winning or losing). For the first flip, you would bet $1 and either double your money or lose it. For the second flip (if you had won the first flip), you would reinvest your $2 and either double your money or lose it; if you had lost the first flip, you would bet another $1 and double or lose it. The process is repeated for the third coin flip, with having either the money you won on the second flip or a new $1 investment if you lost the second flip.

a. Draw the probability tree for the three coin flips.

b. Calculate your winnings or losses for each joint event and the associated probabilities.

c. Plot the cumulative probability distribution for your proceeds from the flips (wins or losses).

d. Plot the histogram for your proceeds from the flips.

e. Calculate the mean, variance, and standard deviation for your proceeds from the flips.

A.19 Explain graphically why the following relationships are true for the events I and $\varnothing$:

$$I \text{ and } \varnothing = \varnothing$$
$$I \text{ or } \varnothing = I$$

Use these relationships and the probability axioms to prove the following probability:

$$p(\varnothing \mid S) = 0$$

A.20 Let A and B be any two events and let $A' = \text{not } A$. Explain graphically why the following relations are true:

$$A \text{ or } B = A \text{ or } (A' \text{ and } B)$$
$$B = (A \text{ and } B) \text{ or } (A' \text{ and } B)$$
$$A \text{ and } (A' \text{ and } B) = \varnothing$$

Use these relationships, the results of problem A.19, and the probability axioms to prove the following relationship among probabilities:

$$p(A \text{ or } B \mid S) = p(A \mid S) + p(B \mid S) - p(A \text{ and } B \mid S)$$

A.21 Let A and B be any two events and let $B' = \text{not } B$. Explain graphically why the following relationships are true:

$$A = (A \text{ and } B) \text{ or } (A \text{ and } B')$$
$$\varnothing = (A \text{ and } B) \text{ and } (A \text{ and } B')$$

Use these relationships and the probability axioms to prove the following simple application of the Expansion Theorem:

$$p(A \mid S) = p(A,B \mid S) + p(A,B' \mid S)$$

A.22 Let A and B be any two events. Assume that A is probabilistically independent of B:

$$p(A \mid B,S) = p(A \mid S)$$

Prove that B is probabilistically independent of A.

$$p(B \mid A,S) = p(B \mid S)$$

A.23   Conditional probability is defined as:

$$p(A \mid B,S) = \frac{p(A,B \mid S)}{p(B \mid S)}$$

Show that the definition of conditional probability satisfies the three axioms of probability introduced in Equations A–10, A–11, and A–12.

B

Influence Diagram Theory

Theory Overview

The decision analyst learns early that decision trees grow with amazing rapidity. Add a three-branch node, and the tree becomes three times larger. Add a few more nodes, and you need a wall-size piece of paper to represent the tree. And yet you are discussing only a relatively small number of uncertainties.

Influence diagrams are a means of representing the same decision problem much more compactly. For each chance and decision variable in the tree, there is a single object in the graph. Arrows connecting these objects represent probabilistic and informational relationships.

Influence diagrams are growing in popularity and importance in the practice of decision analysis for three reasons.

- The influence diagram is compact enough that even the most complex problems can be developed and discussed on a single large sheet of paper. This is a tremendous advantage when structuring the problem, organizing analytical tasks, monitoring problem analysis, and presenting an overview of the problem.

- Influence diagrams appear to be the easiest way to introduce and work with probabilistic dependence, an unfamiliar and difficult concept for many decision-makers.

- An influence diagram is a theoretical construct and an evaluation device with all the power of a decision tree.

In this book, we use the influence diagram for the first and second reasons. Although software that makes influence diagrams practical calculational tools is being developed, it is not yet ready for use at the level appropriate for this text.

Elements of Influence Diagrams _____

Six basic elements are used in an influence diagram (Figure B–1).

_____ **Figure B–1** _____

Elements of the Influence Diagram

To define each of these elements, we will use the fictitious Medequip example introduced in Appendix A.

Medequip's planning department continued its study of the product's declining revenues. The planners were considering changing the long-term pricing strategy for the product. Two alternatives suggested themselves. Medequip could choose a Premium Pricing strategy: promote the special characteristics of the product, target specific segments of the market, and set a price 20 percent above the principal competitor's price. Or it could choose a Market Pricing strategy: set price at the competitor's price and compete in all segments of the market.

Critical to the competitive position of Medequip's product was the availability of an essential raw material. It was suggested that a raw material survey could be initiated that could help predict future availability and cost of the raw material. Information like this could help Medequip enter into advantageous long-term supply contracts.

Medequip brought together a number of people from management and planning and created an influence diagram (Figure B–2) that represented their perception of the problem.

Uncertainty

Uncertainties are represented by ovals. Within the oval is a label that indicates the mutually exclusive and collectively exhaustive set of events among which the node distinguishes. The most desirable label is a variable name, where the value of the variable defines the events. An oval represents a set of possible events and the probabilities assigned to these events.

The planning department was uncertain about how rapidly the market for the product would grow. The oval labeled Market Growth Rate in the influence diagram represented the uncertainty on the average annual market growth rate during the period until 1997. After the influence diagram had been completed, several of those most knowledgeable about the market

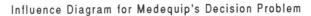

Figure B–2

Influence Diagram for Medequip's Decision Problem

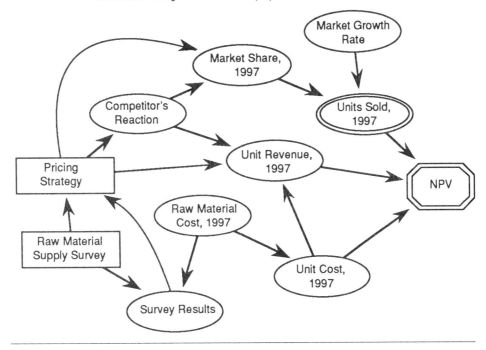

assessed the probability distribution represented by the oval. The information contained "inside" the oval is shown in Figure B–3. This tree representation for the data at a node is called a distribution tree and represents a probability distribution on a single set of events.

Figure B–3

Distribution Tree for the Data Contained in the Market Growth Rate Node

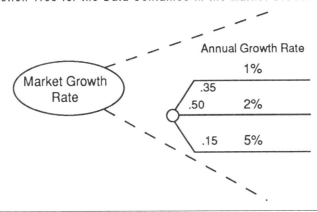

Decision

Decisions are represented by rectangles. Written in the rectangle is a label for the set of significantly different alternatives being considered.

Representatives from manufacturing were concerned about the cost of the critical raw material used in making the product. It was suggested that a raw material survey would help predict availability and cost of the raw material, and this in turn would have an impact on product unit cost. The rectangle labeled Raw Material Supply Survey represents the decision on whether to perform this survey (Figure B–4).

Figure B–4

Alternatives Represented by the Raw Material Supply Survey Node

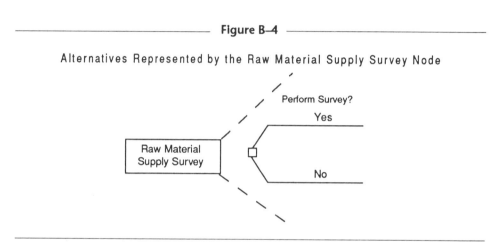

Influence

Influences are indicated by arrows and represent a flow of information and, with decision nodes, a time sequence. As discussed in Appendix A, all probability assignments are based on the state of knowledge of a particular person at a particular time. Decisions are also made based on a state of knowledge. It is essential that all the probability assignments and decision nodes in an influence diagram share a common state of information, S. The arrow indicates that, in addition to this common state of information, S, there is information concerning the node at the base of the arrow available at the node at the head of the arrow. This concept is made more explicit in the four cases presented below.

Arrow from Uncertainty Node to Uncertainty Node

If the arrow is between two uncertainty nodes, the probability distribution for the node at the head of the arrow is probabilistically dependent (conditional) on the node at the base of the arrow. If there is an arrow from node A to node B, the diagram is read as "A influences B."* The information flow in this case does not necessarily imply a causal link or a time sequence

Representatives of manufacturing felt much more comfortable assigning probabilities to Unit Cost, 1997 conditional on the cost of raw material around that time. Accordingly, they

---

* If there are arrows from several nodes to node B, it is this set of nodes (rather than each individual node) that influences node B.

drew an arrow between the Raw Material Cost, 1997 node and the Unit Cost, 1997 node. If A_i and C_j are a set of mutually exclusive and collectively exhaustive events describing Raw Material Cost and Unit Cost, respectively, and if S is the state of knowledge common to all the nodes in the influence diagram, then the probability distribution represented by the node Unit Cost, 1997 is

$$p(C_j|A_i,S)$$

At a later meeting, the probability assignments (Figure B–5) were assessed by the representatives of manufacturing.

--------------------------------- **Figure B–5** ---------------------------------

Distribution Tree Representing the Data Contained in the
Unit Cost, 1997 Node

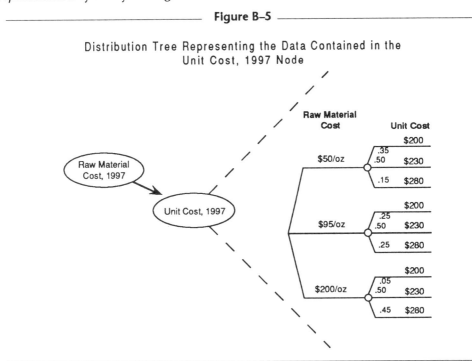

The tree representation for the conditional probability distribution above is a more complex form of distribution tree than the one shown in Figure B–4. The difference between a distribution tree and a decision tree is that the nodes on the left side of a distribution tree are there only to specify the state of knowledge used in assessing the probabilities for the node on the right. They can be arranged in whatever order helps the assessor assign probabilities. The order of nodes in a distribution tree is not necessarily related to the order of nodes in the decision tree.

Arrow from Decision Node to Uncertainty Node

If the arrow is from a decision node to an uncertainty node, the probability distribution for the node at the head of the arrow is probabilistically dependent (conditional) on the alternative chosen at the node at the base of the arrow. This implies that the decision is made before the uncertainty is resolved and that there is some sort of causal link between the decision and the resolution of the uncertainty.

The representatives of the marketing department were uncertain just how their principal competitor would react to either of the pricing strategy alternatives, but they were sure that the probabilities they assigned would depend on the pricing strategy chosen. For this reason, an arrow was drawn from the Pricing Strategy node to the Competitor's Reaction node. The assessed probability distribution is shown in Figure B–6.

--------------------------------- **Figure B–6** ---------------------------------

Distribution Tree for Data Contained in Competitor's Reaction Node

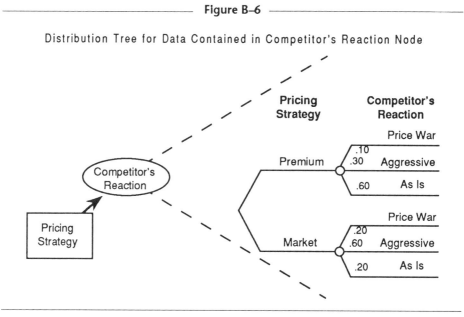

Arrow from Decision Node to Decision Node

An arrow between two decision nodes means that the decision-maker remembers which alternative was chosen at the node at the base of the arrow when he or she comes to make the decision at the node at the head of the arrow. There is a strong chronological assertion here: the decision represented by the node at the base of the arrow will be made before the decision represented by the node at the head of the arrow.

Arrow from Uncertainty Node to Decision Node

If the arrow is from an uncertainty node to a decision node, the uncertainty is resolved before the decision is made and the decision-maker learns what happened before making the decision. Note that, in this case, there is a strong assertion about chronology: the uncertainty is resolved and the information received by the decision-maker before the decision is made.

The Medequip team decided that a decision on whether to perform the raw material supply survey would be made before the pricing strategy decision. Furthermore, it was decided that if a raw material supply survey were decided on, the pricing strategy decision would not be made before the results of the survey were available. The decision-maker would know the survey results when he or she made the decision. An arrow was drawn from the Raw Material Supply Survey node to the Pricing Strategy node and from the Survey Results node to the Pricing Strategy node (Figure B–7).

———————————————— **Figure B–7** ————————————————

Tree Representing the Alternatives in the Pricing Strategy Node

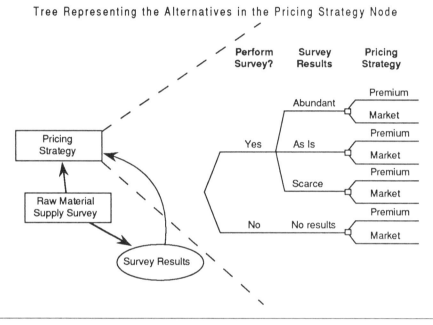

The last example shows one way to represent an asymmetry in an influence diagram. The set of events represented by the node may differ, depending on the event occurring at a node that influences it. In this case, the events represented by the Survey Results node include a single event (no results), which occurs if the survey is not performed.

Determined Uncertainty

As an influence diagram grows and influences (arrows) are added, the uncertainty at a node frequently disappears: once the outcomes are known at all the influencing uncertainty and decision nodes, there is no more uncertainty about the actual event at the influenced node. The node can be left in the diagram, denoted by a double oval. This type of node is usually called a "deterministic node." (The node can also be removed from the diagram, provided you assure the proper information flow by connecting all incoming arrows to all outgoing arrows.)

A deterministic node usually represents either a formula or calculation for which the influencing nodes supply input. Often this calculation is complicated enough that it is made by a computer spreadsheet or other computer program. Occasionally, the deterministic node represents a table of values, one entry for each combination of the events of the nodes that influence it.

One of the first uncertainties the Medequip team identified was the uncertainty represented by the node Units Sold, 1997. As the influence diagram grew, two nodes were created (Market Growth Rate and Market Share, 1997), both of which influenced the node Units Sold, 1997. At this point, there is no uncertainty left at the node Units Sold, 1997: once you know what happened at the influencing nodes, all that remains is a simple calculation (Figure B–8).

Figure B–8

Equation Used at Deterministic Node Units Sold, 1997

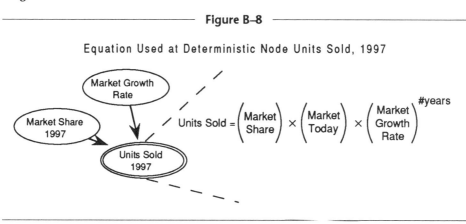

$$\text{Units Sold} = \left(\begin{array}{c}\text{Market}\\\text{Share}\end{array}\right) \times \left(\begin{array}{c}\text{Market}\\\text{Today}\end{array}\right) \times \left(\begin{array}{c}\text{Market}\\\text{Growth}\\\text{Rate}\end{array}\right)^{\#years}$$

The node Units Sold, 1997 could be removed from the diagram if the arrows coming into it are rerouted to the node that it influences—that is, if arrows are drawn from the Market Growth Rate node to the NPV node and from the Market Share, 1997 node to the NPV node—thus assuring that information flows are maintained.

Value and Determined Value

Implicit in an influence diagram is a rule by which decisions are made. As discussed earlier in the text, decisions are made by choosing the alternative that maximizes the certain equivalent of the value measure. In simpler terms, we choose the alternative that gives us the most of what we want.

If there are decision nodes in an influence diagram, there must be one (and only one) node in the influence diagram that represents the value measure used in making the decisions. This value node is always an uncertainty node or a deterministic (determined uncertainty) node. To identify its role, an octagon (double octagon if it is deterministic) is used rather than an oval.

Very early, the Medequip team had chosen NPV of cash flow as the value measure used in making decisions. Given the outcomes of the influencing nodes (Units Sold, 1997; Unit Revenue, 1997; and Unit Cost, 1997), it was felt that most of the uncertainty in NPV would be resolved. For this reason, the node representing NPV was represented by a double octagon (Figure B–9).

--- Figure B–9 ---

Model Used at Deterministic Node NPV

Spreadsheet model using Units Sold, 1997; Unit Revenue, 1997; and Unit Cost, 1997 as input

Rules for Constructing Influence Diagrams

The following four rules must be obeyed to create meaningful influence diagrams for the type of decision problems dealt with in this book:

1. *No Loops*—If you follow the arrows from node to node, there must be no path that leads you back to where you started. This is most readily understood in terms of the information flow indicated by the arrows.

2. *Single Decision-Maker*—There should be just one value measure (octagon), and all decisions should be made to maximize the same function (expected value or certain equivalent) of this value.

3. *No Forgetting Previous Decisions*—There should be an arrow between all pairs of decisions in the diagram. This will establish the order in which the decisions are made and also indicate that the decision-maker remembers all his or her previous choices.

4. *No Forgetting Previously Known Information*—If there is an arrow from an uncertainty node to a decision node, there should be an arrow from that uncertainty node to all subsequent decision nodes.

Procedures for Manipulating Influence Diagrams

There are two useful procedures for manipulating influence diagrams without changing the information in the diagram. These procedures are necessary when solving an influence diagram directly, but may be useful in restructuring a diagram to facilitate drawing a decision tree.

1. *Adding an Arrow*—An arrow can be added between two uncertainty nodes in an influence diagram, provided it does not create a loop. The lack of an arrow between two nodes is a statement that information from one node is not needed to assess the probabilities at the other. Adding an arrow can be thought of as making this information available, even though it does not affect the probabilities assessed.

2. *Reversing an Arrow*—An arrow between two uncertainty nodes can be reversed if the state of knowledge available at both nodes is the same. Therefore, to reverse an arrow between two nodes, all the arrows into both nodes must be the same (except, of course, the arrow between the two). Once the state of information is the same, the operation of reversing an arrow in an influence diagram is the same operation as applying Bayes' Rule to a probability distribution and "flipping" a probability tree.

The Medequip team had recognized that the easiest and most reliable means of assessment was first to have procurement personnel provide probabilities for raw material cost, then to have manufacturing estimate unit cost (conditional on raw material cost), and finally to have sales and marketing provide probabilities for unit revenue conditional on unit cost (Figure B–10a).

There was a desire to see whether assessing the probabilities in a different order made a difference. First, sales and marketing would estimate unit revenues, and then manufacturing would estimate unit cost conditional on unit revenues. (There was some feeling that perhaps cost rose when revenue was high and was squeezed down when revenue was low.) This assessment entails reversing the arrow between Unit Cost, 1997 and Unit Revenue, 1997. Before this can be done, an arrow from the Raw Material Cost node to the Unit Revenue node must be added (Figure B–10b) so that both the Unit Revenue and Unit Cost nodes share the same state of knowledge. (For this exercise, the arrows from Pricing Strategy and Competitor's Reaction to Unit Revenue, 1997 were dropped from the diagram.)

Now the arrow between the Unit Revenue and Unit Cost nodes can be reversed (Figure B–10c). At this point, the team realized that the job of the sales and marketing representatives was harder than they had thought. Unit Revenue probabilities had to be assessed conditional on Raw Material Cost!

Turning an Influence Diagram into a Decision Tree

The procedure for turning an influence diagram into a decision tree is quite simple.

1. Arrange the decision nodes such that all arrows with a decision node at their base or head point to the right-hand side of the page. Arrows pointing to or emanating from decision nodes imply a chronology that must be followed in decision trees. By convention, the chronology of decisions in a decision tree flows from left to right, and therefore these arrows must point from left to right.

2. Arrange the uncertainty nodes so that no uncertainty node is to the left of a decision node unless there is an arrow from that node to the decision node. In a decision tree, the outcome of a node to the left of

---
Figure B–10

Manipulating Influence Diagrams

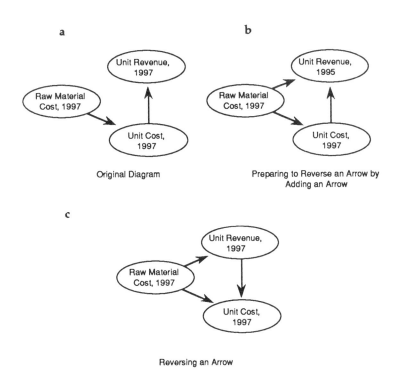

a

Original Diagram

b

Preparing to Reverse an Arrow by
Adding an Arrow

c

Reversing an Arrow

---

a decision node is known to the decision-maker when he or she makes the decision; in an influence diagram, this means there is an arrow from the uncertainty node to the decision node.

3. Arrange, insofar as possible, the uncertainty nodes so that all arrows point to the right. This will cause conditional probabilities to be displayed simply on the tree.

The rules for manipulating influence diagrams can be used to reverse arrows between nodes and make all arrows point to the right. However, Supertree can accept input in which probabilities at a node depend on nodes that follow it in the tree—that is, for which the arrow to the node points left—and so this last step of arrow reversal is not necessary.

4. Make the deterministic value node a tree endpoint node. This will usually involve calculations to find the value associated with each combination of events at the nodes that influence the value node.

5. Number the nodes, give each node a node name, and input the structure and data into Supertree.

The Medequip analysts decided to put the influence diagram into tree form. First, they eliminated the Units Sold, 1997 determined uncertainty node, rerouting the two arrows coming into it to the node it influenced, the NPV node. Following the rules given above, they rearranged the diagram and formed the tree shown in Figure B–11. Since the tree would be entered in Supertree, they did not need to reverse the arrow from the Raw Material Cost, 1997 node to the Survey Results node because Supertree does this automatically.

The tree is ready for input to Supertree. All the information necessary for inputting the nodes is shown except for the probabilities. The probabilistic dependence is shown by the arrows in the influence diagram. For instance, the probabilities of node 9 depend on nodes 3 and 4, and the probabilities for node 2 depend on node 7. The endpoint, node 10, depends on nodes 5, 6, 8, and 9 and will probably be calculated by a spreadsheet. Note the difference in orientation between "influences" and "depends on": if node 3 influences node 9 in the influence diagram, then in the language of Supertree, the probabilities at node 9 depend on node 3.

Particular care should be taken to distinguish the use of the word "successor" between influence diagrams and decision trees. In influence diagrams, it is quite natural to say that a node at the head of an arrow is the successor to the node at the base of the arrow. Thus, in Figure B–11, the node Survey Results is the successor (direct successor, to be precise) of the node Raw Material Cost, 1997. In decision trees, successor refers only to the order in the decision tree and does not imply any information flow or dependence between the nodes. Thus, in the tree in Figure B–11, Market Growth Rate is the successor to Market Share, 1997.

Summary

This example illustrates the power of the influence diagram to represent a problem compactly and to lead people naturally through the complexities of probabilistic dependence. There are 3,888 paths through this tree; at 66 lines per page, the printout of the full tree would be 59 pages long. The dependent probabilities weave a complex pattern through the tree. On the other hand, for the influence diagram we need only one page to draw the diagram and several other pages on which to list the events and probabilities represented by the nodes.

In practice, influence diagrams are currently used mostly in the initial phases of a decision analysis. The process of model construction, data gathering, and sensitivity analysis normally leads to insight and simplification of the structure of the problem and to the natural construction of a simple tree. However, given the rapid evolution of software tools and consulting practice, we can expect to see the unification of these two representations of the problem in a single system.

Figure B-11

Turning the Medequip Influence Diagram into a Decision Tree

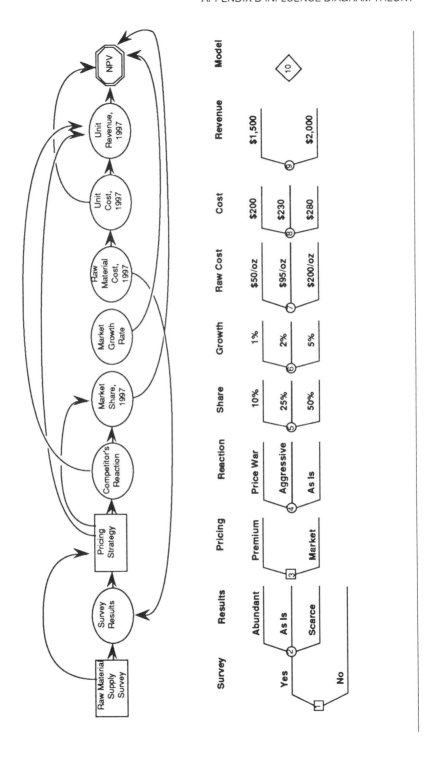

Problems and Discussion Topics _____

B.1 How does an influence diagram contribute to making good decisions? (Refer to the elements of a good decision.) What elements of a good decision does an influence diagram not help with and why?

B.2 Describe at least one way that using influence diagrams helps you draw better decision trees and one way that being familiar with decision trees helps you draw better influence diagrams.

B.3 How do you know when an influence diagram has become complicated enough? Relate your answer to the problem of assessing probabilities and to the clairvoyance test.

B.4 Think of a significant decision you have made. Draw the influence diagram for that decision. Were there significant uncertainties? How did you identify and deal with them at the time? Do you have any new insights into the decision? (Relate this last answer to the good decision/good outcome distinction.)

B.5 Draw the influence diagram for the date and time when a specific close relative walks through your front door. Make sure the uncertainty passes the clairvoyance test and try to summon all your information and experience on the factors influencing the uncertainty. Has the exercise changed your understanding of the uncertainty at all? Could you now draw a decision tree and do a meaningful probability assessment? Draw the tree and explain what (if anything) would prevent you from assessing probabilities and calculating the expected date and time that the relative walks through your door.

B.6 Draw an influence diagram for the probability of a major war within the next ten years. Make sure your uncertainties pass the clairvoyance test. How is this problem different from the previous one? Is there anything preventing you from drawing a tree and calculating a probability distribution for this problem?

B.7 Draw the influence diagram for the number of times you eat pizza within the next month. Again, make sure the uncertainty passes the clairvoyance test. Are there any difficulties in completing this problem and, if so, what are they?

B.8 In the influence diagram used to construct the tree in Figure B–11, there is an arrow pointing to the left.

  a. Reverse this arrow to make the diagram a "decision tree network," one in which the nodes can be arranged so that all the arrows point to the right.

  b. Why is it necessary to reverse this diagram to create a tree? (Hint: How would you display the probabilities at node 2 in the tree?)

B.9 Adding an arrow between an uncertainty and a decision node is related to the value of information calculation described in chapters 2 and 4.

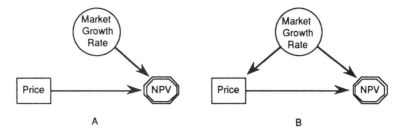

a. Draw the trees represented by influence diagrams A and B above.

b. How are influence diagrams A and B related to the value of perfect information on Market Growth Rate?

B.10 In the Howard canonical form of an influence diagram, there are no arrows from a decision node to any uncertainty node aside from the value node. For the purposes of this definition, groups of uncertainty nodes can be amalgamated into a larger uncertainty node (the value node) provided no loops are created.

A company has several different routes it could pursue in developing a new product. The influence diagram representing its problem is shown below.

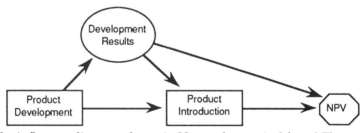

a. Is the influence diagram above in Howard canonical form? The one below?

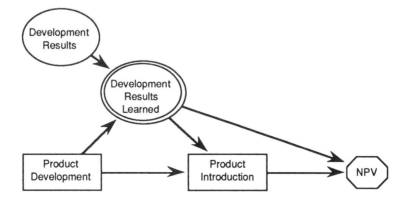

b. Suppose some preliminary work could predict the results of the product development effort before all the necessary development work was done. Which influence diagram could be used to calculate the value of information about development results?

c. Which influence diagram is in Howard canonical form? Draw a tree showing the logic contained in the deterministic node that would make the second diagram equivalent to the one that preceded it.

d. Can the second influence diagram be manipulated to a form from which the value of information about development results can be calculated?

B.11 It is possible to use deterministic nodes to represent asymmetries in the problem in a straightforward way.

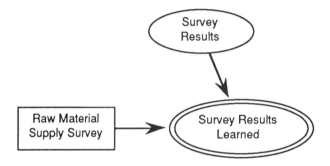

a. Redraw the influence diagram in Figure B–11 using the deterministic node defined above. What arrows should be drawn from these nodes to the remainder of the diagram?

b. What is the logic contained in the deterministic node Survey Results Learned?

c. Is the tree drawn from the new diagram different from the tree in Figure B–11?

d. Make this diagram into a decision tree network. (See problem B.8 for the definition of a decision tree network.)

e. Is the influence diagram in Figure B–11 in Howard canonical form? (See problem B.10.)

f. Is the influence diagram drawn as part of this problem in Howard canonical form?

B.12 In Appendix A, a joint probability distribution was given for the two sets of mutually exclusive and collectively exhaustive events, R_i and C_j.

$$p(R_i, C_j \mid S)$$

	C_1	C_2	C_3
R_1	.10	.25	.03
R_2	.22	.26	.14

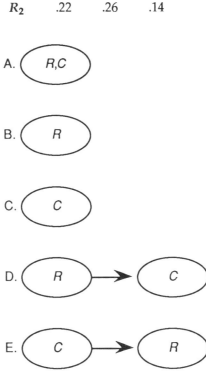

A. R,C

B. R

C. C

D. R → C

E. C → R

Draw the distribution trees for the nodes in the five influence diagrams above.

B.13 In Figure B–1, there is no arrow going to the Market Growth Rate node. The lack of arrows is of great significance to the analyst, since the absence of arrows makes modeling and probability assessment relatively simple.

a. There is no arrow between the nodes Pricing Strategy and Market Growth Rate. What does this indicate about the nature of the market and Medequip's place in the market? Under what circumstances should an arrow be drawn between these two nodes?

b. There is no arrow between the nodes Competitor's Reaction and Market Growth Rate. What does this indicate about the nature of the market and the companies that supply products in this marketplace? Under what circumstances should an arrow be drawn between these two nodes?

c. Under what circumstances should there be an arrow from both the Pricing Strategy and Competitor's Reaction nodes to the Market Growth Rate node?

d. We are not allowed to draw an arrow from Pricing Strategy to Competitor's Reaction, from Competitor's Reaction to Market Growth Rate, and from Market Growth Rate to Pricing Strategy (perhaps to represent a pricing adjustment to changes in market dynamics). Why is this not allowed? How might you represent an adjustment of pricing strategy to market dynamics?

C

Supertree

The student version of Supertree packaged with this text is for teachers' and students' use only. It is not suitable for a business environment because we have restricted its capability to run problems of the size generally found in the corporate world. Furthermore, the software license that covers this student version legally restricts its use to schools, colleges, universities, and other academic institutions.

This appendix describes the implementation of Supertree on PC-DOS/MS-DOS personal computers. Implementations of Supertree on the Macintosh and other systems are similar.

Computer Setup

Supertree is best run from the computer's hard disk. The program is not copy protected so it can be copied to the hard disk from the floppy disks provided with this book. The exact procedure will vary slightly depending on the size and capacity of the floppy disks provided and on the type of computer being used. Instructions for installation and start-up are included with the floppy disks.

The 640K RAM limit on PC-DOS/MS-DOS personal computers frequently imposes memory limitations on Supertree. If your computer has expanded memory, Supertree can use 64K of this expanded memory, thus freeing a surprisingly important amount of RAM. To use expanded memory, use Edlin or a text editor to change the batch file supertree.bat from rts8 k=u w=supert to rts8 k=u w=supert e=8192. Note, however, that this option is not compatible with Lotus 1-2-3, version 2.2, called from inside Supertree.

To check the amount of available RAM, type chkdsk after booting the PC. The total bytes of memory and the bytes free will be listed. The first number (total bytes) should be around 655,000 for a 640K machine, and the second number (bytes free) should be 570,000 to 590,000. If the second number is much less than this, check the files \autoexec.bat and \config.sys; there may be memory-resident programs such as mail, menus, and networks using valuable RAM space. To use Supertree efficiently, these memory-resident programs should be temporarily disabled.

Color monitors will occasionally have a noisy ("snowy") display. You can minimize the noise by modifying the option that calls the program. Use Edlin or a text editor to change the batch file supertree.bat from rts8 k=u w=supert to rts8 k=u w=supert e=64. To combine this option with the use of expanded memory (explained above), change the number at the end of the batch file from e=8192 to e=8256.

Running Supertree

Supertree is run from a main option menu that leads to submenus (Figure C–1). The options in the main menu and their functions are as follows:

- Structure inputs, modifies, and displays the tree structure.

- Evaluate assigns a value to each path through the tree.

- Analyze obtains results from the evaluated tree.

- Utility enables you to do "housekeeping" tasks.

- Programs suspends Supertree and calls a modeling program.

- Files stores and retrieves previous work.

- Quit permits you to leave Supertree.

Menu selections can be made by pressing the Enter key when the entry is highlighted; move the highlight by using the cursor (arrow) keys. Selections can also be made by typing the first letter of the desired option. The ESC (escape) key can be used to move from a submenu to the next higher menu level.

Once you have selected a menu option, Supertree displays a screen showing the information it needs to complete the action, with default actions displayed. Use the arrow/cursor keys to move around the screen. The F1 key enters the data. Pressing the Escape key aborts the option and cancels the data input. If you are uncertain about what to enter, type ? and press the Enter key for messages or instructions. Error messages or instructions will be displayed just below the main menu line.

Use the up and down arrow/cursor keys or the PgUp (page up) and PgDn (page down) keys to review screens above and below the current screen.

Press Shft PrtSc to print the current screen of information, or press Ctrl PrtSc to print a copy of everything that appears on the screen; press Ctrl PrtSc again to turn printing off. Some printers print the lines in Supertree displays as a capital D. If this happens, go to the Configuration option in the Utility menu and answer No when asked about the use of line graphics.

The Structure menu consists of six selections that input, modify, or display the structure and input data of the tree.

- Input, one of the most important and complex Supertree options, is used to enter or change the data that define the tree.

- The Show option displays the structure of the tree.

―――――――――――――――― **Figure C–1** ――――――――――――――――

Supertree Menus and Options

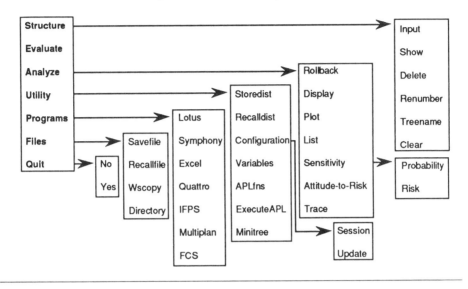

- The Delete option removes nodes. Enter the number of the node to be deleted. Nothing happens if you enter 0 or the number of a non-existent node.

- The Renumber option renumbers nodes.

- The Treename option enters or changes the name used to label results.

- The Clear option clears out any tree structure and results.

Because the Input option is the most complex, input parameters for decision or chance nodes and for endpoint nodes are specified below. For all types of nodes, Input requests the number of the node to be input or modified. Node numbers must be integers between 1 and 99. It is good practice to number the nodes sequentially from left to right in the tree, although this is not mandatory.

Decision or Chance Node Input. Decision or chance nodes have the following input parameters:

- **Type**—This discussion applies to decision or chance nodes.

- **Number of Branches**—Two to sixteen branches are allowed. Nodes with one branch are not allowed.

- **Node Name**—Node names must begin with a letter and be composed of letters and numbers. The node name is used as a descriptive title and also as a variable that will be assigned a value equal to the outcome of the branch being evaluated.

- **Outcomes Depend on Nodes**. These are the numbers of the nodes on which the outcomes depend. Outcomes can depend on any node except endpoint nodes.

- **Probabilities Depend on Nodes** (chance nodes only)—These are the numbers of the nodes on which the probabilities depend. Probabilities can depend on any node except endpoint nodes.

- **Probability** (chance nodes only)—Probabilities are expressed in Supertree as numbers between 0 and 1 and can be entered in the following ways:

  - **Numerical**—Probabilities can be directly entered as a number (e.g., .35) or a fraction (e.g., 2/7). If all the probabilities of a node are numerical, they must add to 1 or 0. (When analyzing, probabilities must add to 1.)

  - **Character**—The name of an APL variable or function can be entered. The variable or function must return a single value.

  - **Dependent probabilities**—Dependent probabilities are entered on a separate screen, as described below.

- **Outcomes**—The outcomes are the values assigned to the node name variable and can be entered in several forms.

  - **Numerical**—Numbers can be entered directly. Expressions and fractions are not allowed; they will be treated as characters.

  - **Character**—Any string of characters can be entered as an outcome. (Blanks will be removed.) Supertree will check whether the string of characters is a number (see above), in which case the outcome will be numerical. If the outcome is not numerical, Supertree will then check whether it is the name of a variable or APL function. In this case, Supertree will use the single value returned by the variable or function as the outcome. If neither of these conditions holds, Supertree will assign the string of characters as the value of the node name variable.

  - **Quoted characters**—Any string of characters between quotes (') can be used as an outcome. (Blanks will be removed.)

  - **Dependent outcomes**—Dependent outcomes are entered on a separate screen, as described below.

- **Rewards**—Rewards must be numerical entries. If there are multiple value measures for the endpoint nodes, the rewards apply only to the first value measure; they are set to zero for the other value measures.

- **Successor Node**—This refers to the number of the node that is to follow each branch.

- **Dependent Probabilities or Outcomes**—If probabilities or outcomes depend on other nodes, you can enter, review, or change these probabilities or outcomes on a separate screen accessible from the main node input screen.

On the dependency input screen, the outcomes for the nodes on which the probabilities or outcomes depend are shown at the left. The highlighted combination of outcomes corresponds to the currently displayed dependent probabilities or outcomes. Advance to the next combination by pressing the `Tab` key (`Shft Tab` returns to the previous combination). Enter dependent probabilities or outcomes (displayed on the right of the screen) and move up or down by pressing the `Enter` key or the cursor/arrow keys.

Dependent probabilities must be numerical. Although they may be entered as a fraction (e.g., 2/7), they will be converted to a decimal in the display. Probabilities must sum to 1 or 0. At the analysis stage, probabilities must sum to 1.

Dependent outcomes must be numerical.

Endpoint Node Input. Supertree can deal with several different endpoint value measures that are calculated during one evaluation. For instance, a Lotus 1-2-3 spreadsheet might calculate three measures during a Supertree evaluation: NPV, sales in 1997, and earnings per share in 2020. Supertree can store and analyze the results for all these measures.

To calculate the results for more than one value measure, enter the list of the value measures separated by semicolons. This list is entered in `Value`, `Expression`, or `Result Name`, as indicated below. If a tree has several endpoints, all must have the same number of semicolons (value measures). Note that `Rewards` apply only to the first value measure and are set to zero for the other value measures. For endpoint nodes, the input parameters are as follows:

- **Name of Program**—This entry determines how values are assigned to paths through the tree. The form of the rest of the input screen will vary depending on the choice of program used to assign these values.

  - **Value**—Numerical values can be entered directly for an endpoint.

  - **Treevalue**—A set of numerical values can be entered for all the combinations of nodes the endpoint depends on.

  - **Excel, Lotus 1-2-3, Multiplan, Quattro, Symphony**—Endpoints can be evaluated through the use of these spreadsheet programs.

  - **Basic**—Basic syntax expressions can be used to evaluate the endpoints.

  - **APL**—APL expressions and APL variables or value-returning functions can be used to evaluate the endpoints. Use the `Value` entry but enter the APL expression, variable name, or function name in the entry box labeled "Value."

- **Value** (Value only)—Enter the numerical value for the endpoint. If multiple value measures are used, enter the list of values separated by semicolons.

- **Descriptive Name** (Treevalue only)—Enter a name to describe the endpoint. Supertree makes no further use of this name.

- **Expression** (Basic only)—Enter a Basic syntax expression. The expression can use the node names as variables in the calculation. If multiple value measures are used, enter the values separated by semicolons.

- **Call from Inside or Outside Supertree** (Lotus 1-2-3, Multiplan, or Symphony only)—These spreadsheet programs are small enough that they can, under certain conditions, be opened from inside Supertree so that the evaluation is performed automatically. However, memory constraints sometimes require evaluation outside Supertree—i.e., temporarily quitting Supertree to run the spreadsheet program.

- **Spreadsheet Name** (Excel, Lotus 1-2-3, Multiplan, or Symphony)—Enter the name of the spreadsheet or worksheet. This spreadsheet must be in the current directory of the drive specified by the `Con-figuration` option of the `Utility` menu.

- **Result Name** (Excel, Lotus 1-2-3, Multiplan, or Symphony)—Enter the cell address or the range name of the cell containing the value to be placed at the endpoint. If multiple value measures are used, enter the list of cells (separated by semicolons) from which these values can be obtained.

- **Nodes Upon Which Endpoint Depends** (all programs except Value with numerical entries)—Enter the numbers of the nodes required to evaluate the endpoints. The endpoint will be evaluated for all combinations of the nodes on which it depends, which shortens the evaluation time. Only the values of the node names (variables) on which the endpoint depends will be transmitted to the external spreadsheet programs.

- **Select to Enter/Review Endpoint Value** (Treevalue only)—Pressing `Enter` in this field will bring up the dependency input screen, which shows (at the left) the outcomes for the nodes on which the endpoint depends. The highlighted combination of outcomes corresponds to the currently displayed dependent endpoint value. Advance to the next combination by pressing the `Tab` key (`Shft Tab` returns to the previous combination). Dependent endpoint values must be numerical.

- **Resulting Endpoint Expression**—This is a display of the information entered on the screen in the form it is recorded by Supertree and shown by the Show option of the Structure menu. The letter before the first $ separator is the first letter in the name of the program given in Name of Program. (A Value entry for Name of Program has no special first letter or $ separators.)

Evaluate

The Evaluate command uses the endpoint program or value to assign a value to each path through the tree. As the evaluation proceeds, Supertree periodically displays a count of completed model runs, e.g., 25 Models Run. (The count interval is set in Configuration.) If a link to another program is being used, Supertree also periodically displays a count of the number of model runs being prepared for the program (e.g., 25 Lotus Runs).

If a program is being used "outside" Supertree (indicated by $ $ as the first separator in the endpoint name), you will need to leave Supertree, call the program, and then return to Supertree. Upon returning and continuing the evaluation, you will be informed: You are now about to pick up the results of a LOTUS, SYMPHONY, FCS, MULTIPLAN, IFPS, EXCEL, or QUATTRO run. Do you wish to continue? If you have had to cancel a run and want to re-Evaluate, answer No and then Evaluate again. Respond Yes if the program runs were successfully completed. If for some reason (e.g., there is an error) you do not wish to pick up these results, respond No. Responding No resets Supertree so that the evaluation can be restarted.

Sometimes knowing the order in which Supertree evaluates endpoints is useful. For symmetric trees (or subtrees), Supertree evaluates endpoints starting with the top branch. It counts branches incrementally, starting with the rightmost node and working to the left—just like the odometer on a car. For asymmetric trees, the process is much more complicated. In general, Supertree determines the largest possible symmetric subtrees. Then it evaluates them for each branch of the asymmetrical nodes (nodes that do not have all successor nodes identical), beginning with the bottom branches of the asymmetrical nodes.

Analyze

The Analyze menu is used to examine and analyze the decision tree. Most of the Analyze options start by displaying a list of the tree node numbers (except for the endpoint nodes) in the order they were evaluated. You then may change the order.

If there are rewards in the tree, some options will ask whether to add them at the nodes where they occur or to add them at the end of the tree as part of the endpoint values. This choice does not affect the optimal decisions or the overall value of the tree. The choice makes a difference in what you see when examining probability distributions at a node other than the first node in the tree (because the rewards either will or will not be added in at that point). This question is also important when the tree is reordered. With reordering, it is unclear whether the event represented by the node (and its reward) has been moved or whether you are seeking the value of information, in which case the reward should stay in its original position. [If you are confused, enter a simple tree with rewards and display the tree (see notes below) in several different node orders.]

In some of the Analyze options, you can select the node at which to perform the option. If this is not the first node in the tree, you must indicate the branches through the nodes that lead to it. Supertree refers to these as the "indices of the preceding node branches." These indices are the numbers of the branches (where 1 = first = top and so on). You need to specify a set of branch numbers that leads to the desired node.

If several value measures are used, you will be asked which measures to use. Two different uses of the measures are specified: the measure to be displayed (shown as the expected value, certain equivalent, probability distribution, etc.) and the measure to be used as the decision criterion at any decision node in the tree.

Rollback. Rollback calculates the value of the decision tree. If you have selected the utility function (through the Attitude-to-Risk option), the certain equivalent of the tree will be given. Otherwise, the expected value will be given.

Display. The Display option is used to draw a selected portion of the tree. The preferred alternative is indicated by an "arrow" symbol (>) at each decision node. Probabilities and values are displayed with field width and decimal places as selected in the Configuration option. Occasionally, it will be necessary to truncate the display of an outcome that is too long. In this case, an asterisk will be the last character printed. The outcome of a node drawn prior to the node on which it depends will be displayed as asterisks, since its value will not be determined until later in the tree.

Displays wider than the 80-column screen are shown in a special format. First, the upper left-hand corner of the display is shown on the screen. You can use the cursor/arrow keys to move the window and see other portions of the tree. Using the Shift cursor/arrow keys moves the window more rapidly. Upon pressing the Escape key, you will be returned to the menu, unless you have requested a printout by pressing Ctrl Prtsc. In this case, the display will be printed in strips, the width of which are set using the printer column width setting in the Configuration option.

Displaying a large tree can take a long time. For this reason, it is usually preferable to draw the specific part of the tree that contains the information desired. Attempting to display large trees or tree parts may exhaust the available memory of the PC or size limits in Supertree. If that happens, you must draw the tree in sections.

Plot. The Plot option lets you display the probability distribution at a given node in cumulative or histogram form. Single or multiple distributions can be plotted.

- **Cumulative plot**—In the cumulative plot, Supertree plots the probability that the value is less than or equal to the value on the horizontal axis. Single or multiple distributions can be plotted.

  A single distribution is the distribution at the chosen node. If the node is a decision node, the distribution is plotted for the preferred alternative. The distributions for other alternatives can be obtained by plotting the distribution at the next node and specifying which branch of the decision node to go through.

A multiple distribution shows the distributions associated with each branch of the chosen node. If the node is a chance node, the distributions displayed are conditional to being on each branch.

In the character plot mode (the only mode available in the student version), small and large graph formats are available. The small format fits on a PC screen. The large graph, intended for printing on wide paper (or with compressed print), is 110 columns wide. If the printer column width is set to fewer than 100 columns by the Configuration option in the Utility menu, the graph will be printed in strips that can be pasted together. When reduced to 70 percent of its original size on a copying machine, the large graph can be used with 8.5″ × 11″ presentation materials.

For multiple distributions in character plots, the branch number (1 = top = first branch, and so on) is used as the plot symbol for each distribution. If two distributions have values that fall on the same point, the lower branch number is shown.

- **Histogram plot**—This histogram plot displays the probabilities that the value falls within given ranges or bins. If the chosen node is a decision node, the distribution for the preferred alternative is displayed.

  A value falls within a bin if it is greater than or equal to the lower bound of the bin and less than the upper bound of the bin. For the rightmost (highest value) bin, however, values equal to the upper bound of the bin are included.

List. This command lets you choose and list several forms of information about the distribution.

Sensitivity. The Sensitivity submenu enables you to perform two types of sensitivity analysis: probability and risk attitude. (Note that these sensitivity analyses are different from the analysis performed by the Sensitivity program. See Appendix D for details.)

- **Probability**—The probability sensitivity analysis option generates a plot showing the sensitivity of the expected value (certain equivalent) of the tree to changes in the probability at a selected node. If the node has three or more branches, the middle branches are set to zero probability. If the selected node has probabilities that depend on another node, this dependence is deleted.

- **Risk attitude**—The risk attitude analysis option generates a plot showing the sensitivity of the certain equivalent of the tree to the value of the risk attitude. This plot uses the built–in exponential utility function in Supertree.

Attitude–to–Risk. By exercising this option, you choose to use the built–in exponential utility function and to set the value of the risk tolerance. The utility function is then used in all analyses until reset by this option.

The function used to calculate the utility is normally $-exp(-$value/risk tolerance). However, if the decision criterion is set (using the Configuration option of the Utility menu) to minimize the expected value or certain equivalent, the function used to calculate the utility is $-exp($value/risk tolerance). This change compensates for the implicit negative signs in costs, thus maintaining a risk-averse utility function.

Trace. This command finds the path through the tree with the value closest to the value specified.

Utility

The Utility menu enables the user to perform a variety of housekeeping tasks. Many of the options deal with file locations and manipulations. If no drive is specified for a file operation, the default drive given in the Configuration option (see below) will be used. Current implementations of Supertree do not permit use of directory names; hence, all files must be in the current directory of a drive.

Storedist. The Storedist option stores a probability distribution in a DOS file. This distribution can then be recalled for plotting by the Recalldist option or by Excel, Lotus 1-2-3, or another software package.

Recalldist. The Recalldist option plots distributions that have been saved by the Storedist option above.

Configuration. With the Configuration option, you set a number of parameters (listed below) for Supertree use. After data entry is complete, a submenu appears giving the following two options:

- **Session.** If you select the Session option, the parameters will be used only until the Configuration command is rerun or until you quit Supertree.

- **Update.** If you select the Update option, the parameters will be saved in a DOS file called SUPERT.CNF on the drive specified when Supertree is loaded.

The parameters specified in the Configuration option depend on the system on which Supertree is run. The following parameters are specific to PC-DOS/MS-DOS:

- **Decision criterion**—With this option, you set whether the decision rule is to maximize or minimize expected value (or certain equivalent) at decision nodes. Because of the implicit negative sign in costs, the utility function is adjusted when you select minimization. (See Attitude-to-Risk in the Analyze menu description for additional details.)

- **Numerical format** (field width, decimal places)—This sets the format for value and result displays. The format consists of two numbers: the total field width (including a place for any negative signs and decimal points) and the number of decimal places to show. (Note that changing the number of decimal places displayed does not change the accuracy of the number that Supertree stores.)

- **Interval at which running total of models run is shown**—The Evaluate option can take a long time to run if you have a large model or many variables, so you may wish to know where Supertree is in the process. If the chosen interval is 25, Supertree will show on the screen when 25, 50, 75, ... models have been run. When one of the links to external programs is used, Supertree will also show when 25, 50, 75, ... runs have been prepared for the external program before it actually proceeds to make the model runs.

- **Use line graphics**—The PC contains line graphics characters for better quality. Many printers, however, cannot print these characters. If your printer does not have the line graphics characters, answer No to this option and Supertree will use plain text characters that print on any printer.

- **Default drive for Supertree (files, models, worksheets, etc.)**—Supertree must know on which drive to find or save files. The default drive is the drive Supertree will address if no other drive is specified. If external programs are used, Supertree will search for models or spreadsheets on the default drive. Supertree will also write the instructions to and read the results from this drive. Because current implementations of Supertree do not permit use of path names, all files must be in the current directory of the drive.

- **Drive for Lotus, Symphony, Multiplan, Excel, or Quattro**—This is the drive on which Supertree will expect to find the modeling program. Specifying this drive is not important if the program is being called from outside Supertree because then you need to start the program yourself. Because current implementations of Supertree do not permit use of path names, all files must be callable from the current directory of the drive.

- **Drive for configuration file, SUPERT.CNF**—This is the drive on which the SUPERT.CNF file will be saved when Update is selected. This file should be in the same directory as the Supertree program file, SUPERT.AWS.

- **Color combination used on screen**—For monochrome or black-and-white monitors, this parameter should be set to 7. This setting will also work for color monitors, but it will give a black-and-white screen.

For color monitors, specify foreground and background colors as follows:

0	black	4	red
1	blue	5	magenta
2	green	6	yellow
3	cyan	7	white

Multiply the background color by 16 and add the foreground color to it; then enter the result. For instance, to obtain white letters on a black background, use $(16 \times 0) + 7 = 7$.

- **Printer port**—Use the DOS port name for the printer port. Dot matrix printers are normally parallel printers and are thus connected to port LPT1. Daisy wheel printers are usually serial printers and thus connected to port COM1.

- **Column width of printer**—This width is normally 80 for 8.5" wide paper and 132 for 14" wide paper. However, when using compressed print, you can fit 110 characters on 8.5" wide paper. This will allow you to print wide output from the Analyze menu without splitting it into pieces.

- **Printer setup message**—If the printer is activated (Ctrl PrtSc), the printer setup message is sent to the printer whenever Supertree returns to the main menu. The message consists of the decimal numbers of the ASCII characters you want to send, with spaces between them.

  Common messages are 15 for compressed print (66 lines per page with 132 columns on narrow paper and 233 columns on wide paper) and 18 for regular print (66 lines per page with 80 columns on narrow paper and 136 columns on wide paper). Tiny print can be produced on some printers by using superscripts, condensed mode, and reduced line spacing; a string that works on some Epson printers is 15 27 83 0 27 51 18 (132 lines per page with 132 columns on narrow paper and 233 columns on wide paper). Consult your printer manual for the specific control codes for your printer.

Variables. When the Variables option is selected, the names of APL variables present in the workspace are shown. The names of variables that are part of Supertree are not shown.

APLfns. When the APLfns option is selected, the names of APL functions present in the workspace are shown. The names of Supertree functions are not shown.

ExecuteAPL. An APL expression can be entered here and executed. The result of the expression (if any) will be displayed.

Minitree. The Minitree option removes 120 kilobytes of Supertree code from memory, leaving only the Files, Evaluate, Programs, and Quit menus. You can thus Evaluate large spreadsheet models more conveniently.

Programs

The `Programs` menu enables you to interrupt the Supertree session and start a modeling program, which, in turn, enables you to inspect or modify models or spreadsheets. Supertree and APL (its underlying language) remain resident in memory, using about 370 kilobytes of memory (or about 250 kilobytes if Minitree has been invoked). If the `Expanded Memory` option is used, these numbers are reduced by 55 kilobytes.

The options under the `Programs` menu and their functions are as follows:

Lotus—Calls Lotus 1-2-3, version 2, 2.2, or 3.

Symphony—Calls Symphony. On most personal computers, you must use the Minitree command first to call Symphony.

Excel—Calls Excel. Current technology does not make enough memory available to call Excel directly from Supertree.

Quattro—Calls Quattro. Current technology does not make enough memory available to call Quattro directly from Supertree.

IFPS—Calls IFPS Personal. Current technology does not make enough memory available to call IFPS directly from Supertree.

Multiplan—Calls Multiplan.

FCS—Calls the FCS modeling program. Note that if memory available is insufficient, calling this program may lock the computer, necessitating a reboot.

Files

The `Files` menu lets you save and recall previous work. Four options are under the `Files` menu.

- **Savefile**—The `Savefile` option saves the tree data, evaluation, and any APL functions and variables in the workspace. Enter the name under which to save the file (e.g., `c:MYFILE`). If the drive name is omitted, the default drive will be used. File names can be no longer than eight characters. Supertree will supply an extension of .ASF to the file name.

- **Recallfile**—When `Recallfile` is selected and the name of a drive is entered, Supertree will list the files saved on that drive. To recall a file, enter the file name.

- **Wscopy**—APL users can copy workspaces developed using STSC's APL*PLUS/PC.

- **Directory**—This command lists the names of all files in the current directory of the drive specified by the user.

Quit

The Quit option is used to exit Supertree and return to DOS. A reminder to save your work is displayed; then you are given the following two options:

- **No**—Do not leave Supertree but return to the main menu.
- **Yes**—Leave Supertree.

D

Sensitivity

The student version of Sensitivity packaged with this text is for teachers' and students' use only. It is not suitable for use in business because it has been restricted in its ability to run problems of the size generally found in the corporate world. Furthermore, the software license that covers this student version legally restricts its use to schools, colleges, universities, and other academic institutions.

This Appendix describes the implementation of Sensitivity on PC-DOS/MS-DOS personal computers. Implementations of Sensitivity on the Macintosh and other systems are similar.

Computer Setup

Sensitivity is best run from the computer's hard disk. The program is not copy protected, so it can be copied to the hard disk from the floppy disks provided with this book. The exact procedure will vary slightly depending on the size and capacity of the floppy disks provided and on the type of computer being used. Instructions for installation and start-up are included with the floppy disks.

The 640K RAM limit on PC-DOS/MS-DOS personal computers occasionally imposes memory limitations on Sensitivity. If your computer has expanded memory, Sensitivity can use 64K of this expanded memory, thus freeing a surprisingly important amount of RAM. To use expanded memory, use Edlin or a text editor to change the batch file `sens.bat` from `rts8 k=u w=sens` to `rts8 k=u w=sens e=8192`. Note, however, that this option is not compatible with Lotus 1-2-3, version 2.2, called from inside Sensitivity.

To check the amount of available RAM, type `chkdsk` after booting the PC. The total bytes of memory and the bytes free will be listed. The first number (total bytes) should be around 655,000 for a 640K machine and the second number (bytes free) should be 570,000 to 590,000. If the second number is much less than this, check the files `\autoexec.bat` and `\config.sys`; there may be memory-resident programs such as mail, menus, and networks using valuable RAM space. To use Sensitivity efficiently, these memory-resident programs should be temporarily disabled.

Color monitors will occasionally have a noisy ("snowy") display. You can minimize the noise by modifying the option that calls the program. Use Edlin or a text editor to change the batch file sens.bat from rts8 k=u w=sens to rts8 k=u w=sens e=64. To combine this option with the use of expanded memory (explained above), change the number at the end of the batch file from e=8192 to e=8256.

Running Sensitivity

Supertree is run from a main option menu that leads to submenus (Figure D–1). The options in the main menu and their functions are as follows:

- Structure inputs, modifies, and displays sensitivity input data.
- Evaluate calculates values for the sensitivities.
- Analyze displays sensitivity results.
- Utility enables you to do "housekeeping" tasks.
- Programs suspends Sensitivity and calls a modeling program.
- Files stores and retrieves previous work.
- Quit permits you to leave Sensitivity.

Menu selections can be made by pressing the Enter key when the entry is highlighted; move the highlight by using the cursor (arrow) keys. Selections can also be made by typing the first letter of the desired option. The ESC (escape) key can be used to move from a submenu to the next higher menu level.

Once you have selected a menu option, Sensitivity displays a screen showing the information it needs to complete the action, with default actions displayed. Use the arrow/cursor keys to move around the screen. The F1 key enters the data. Pressing the Escape key aborts the option and cancels the data input. If you are uncertain about what to enter, type ? and press the Enter key for messages or instructions. Error messages or instructions will be displayed just below the main menu line.

Use the up and down arrow/cursor keys or the PgUp (page up) and PgDn (page down) keys to review screens above and below the current screen.

Press Shft PrtSc to print the current screen of information, or press Ctrl PrtSc to print a copy of everything that appears on the screen; press Ctrl PrtSc again to turn printing off. Some printers print the lines in Sensitivity displays as a capital D. If this happens, go to the Configuration option in the Utility menu and answer No where asked about the use of line graphics.

Structure

The eight Structure menu options enable you to input, modify, or display the sensitivity input data.

Add. Add is the basic option for input of sensitivity data. When you choose the Add option, you will be asked for a name for the sensitivity if you have not yet entered the name. (See the Name option below.)

Figure D–1

Sensitivity Menus and Options

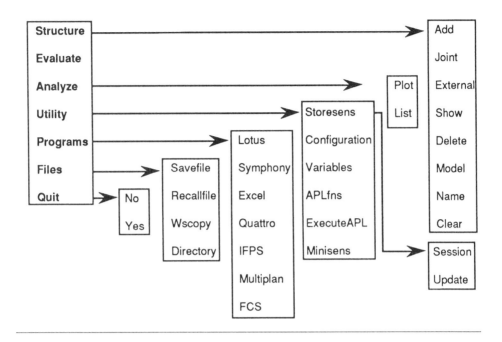

- **Variable Name**—The name of the variable to be varied must begin with a letter, but it can be composed of letters and numbers. Names should correspond to a variable in the model.

- **Variable Description**—This short description of the variable or the nature of its variation is intended to make the results easier to read.

- **Base Value**—The user specifies the value of the variable to use in running the model to obtain a base result. The base value represents the median value of an entire range of possibilities for the data input; there is a 50/50 chance that the value could be higher or lower. Nonnumeric values should be entered between single quotes (').

- **Type of Variation**—The types of variation are value, additive, and multiplicative. A value variation replaces the base value with its low and then high modifier when the model is run; an additive variation adds the low or high modifier to the base value; and the multiplicative variation multiplies the base value by the low or high modifier. (Note that if the base value is nonnumeric, only the value variation makes sense.)

- **Low and High Modifiers**—Numbers are used to modify the base value of the variable to obtain the low and high results. The high value should be such a value that there is only a 10 percent chance of exceeding it. Similarly, the low value should be such a value that there is only a 10 percent chance the actual data input would turn out to be lower.

Joint. The `Joint` command is used for entering joint sensitivity data. A joint sensitivity is one in which two or more variables are changed to their low values simultaneously and the result of the model is calculated. The values of these variables are then changed to their high values and the result of the model is again calculated. Model results for cross-terms (some variables at their low values, some at their high values) are not calculated.

If the name of the joint sensitivity does not already begin with J> (for easy identification), Sensitivity will add the prefix.

External. The `External` option lets you enter sensitivity variations obtained outside the Sensitivity program—e.g., by direct estimate or by some change in the code of the model. If the name of the external sensitivity does not already begin with E> (for easy identification), Sensitivity will automatically add the prefix.

Show. The `Show` option displays the input data for the sensitivity. The final column contains the entry `New` if the variation has been entered or changed or if the model name changed since the last call of the `Evaluate` option; the column contains the entry `Old` if the variation has already been evaluated.

Delete. The `Delete` option enables you to remove variations.

Model. Sensitivity can deal with several different value measures that are calculated during one evaluation. For instance, a Lotus 1-2-3 spreadsheet might calculate three measures during a Sensitivity evaluation: NPV, sales in 1996, and earnings per share in 2020. Sensitivity can store and analyze the results for all these measures.

To calculate the results for more than one value measure, give the list of the value measures, separated by semicolons.

For the model, the input parameters are as follows:

- **Name of Program**—This entry determines how values are calculated for the sensitivity. The form of the rest of the input screen will vary depending on the program chosen to assign these values.

  - **Value**—An APL expression or function name can be used to calculate values. (The title Value is used to maintain parallel terminology with Supertree.)

  - **Excel, Lotus 1-2-3, Multiplan, Quattro, Symphony**—Values can be calculated through the use of these spreadsheet programs.

  - **Basic**—Basic syntax expressions can be used to calculate values.

- **Expression** (Basic only)—Enter a Basic syntax expression here. The expression can use the node names as variables in the calculation. If multiple value measures are used, enter the list of values separated by semicolons.

- **Call from Inside or Outside Sensitivity** (Lotus 1-2-3, Multiplan, or Symphony only)—These spreadsheet programs are small enough that they can, under certain conditions, be opened from inside Sensitivity so that the evaluation is performed automatically. However, memory constraints sometimes require evaluation outside Sensitivity—i.e., temporarily quitting Sensitivity to run the spreadsheet program.

- **Spreadsheet Name** (Excel, Lotus 1-2-3, Multiplan, or Symphony)—Enter the name of the spreadsheet or worksheet. This spreadsheet must be in the current directory of the drive determined by the Configuration option of the Utility menu.

- **Result Name** (Excel, Lotus 1-2-3, Multiplan, or Symphony)—Enter the cell address or the range name of the cell containing the value for the sensitivity. If multiple value measures are used, enter the list of cells (separated by semicolons) from which these values can be obtained.

- **Resulting Endpoint Expression**—This is a display of the information entered on the screen in the form it is recorded by Sensitivity and shown by the Show option of the Structure menu. The letter before the first $ separator is the first letter in the name you entered in Name of Program. (A Value entry for Name of Program has no special first letter or $ separators.)

Name. With the Name option, you can enter or change the descriptive name used to label results.

Clear. The Clear option clears any input data or results.

Evaluate

The Evaluate option uses the model to calculate the base, low, and high values implied by the sensitivity data. As the run proceeds, Sensitivity displays the number of models that have been run; e.g., 25 Models Run. (The count interval is set in Configuration.)

Sensitivity sets all variables to their base levels (including those already evaluated and those occurring only in joint sensitivities) and calculates the base value of the model. The low and high modifiers for each variable are then used to run the model. The value of the variable is reset to the base value between each variable run.

If a spreadsheet or other model is used, Sensitivity displays the number of model runs being prepared for the interface; e.g., 25 Lotus Runs.

If a program is being used outside Sensitivity (indicated as $$ separator in the model name), you will need to leave Sensitivity, call the program, and then return to Sensitivity. Upon returning and continuing the evaluation, you will be informed: You are now about to pick up the results of a LOTUS, SYMPHONY, MULTIPLAN,

FCS, IFPS, EXCEL, or QUATTRO run. Do you wish to continue? If you have had to cancel a run and want to reevaluate, answer No below and then Evaluate again. Respond Yes if the program runs were successfully completed. If you do not wish to pick up the results, respond No, resetting Sensitivity so the evaluation can be started over.

If some sensitivities have been previously evaluated, Sensitivity gives you the choice of evaluating only the new or changed variations or of reevaluating all the variations. Sensitivity also keeps track of the base value and, if only the new variations are evaluated and a base value is not equal to the one previously indicated, will give you the choice of retaining only the new or only the old evaluation. (You cannot retain both because the evaluations are inconsistent.)

Analyze

The Analyze menu contains two options for showing the results obtained from the model evaluation. If only a subset of the variations has been evaluated, you will be informed, and results will be displayed for the variations that were evaluated (labeled as Old in the Show option display).

If several value measures are used, you will be asked which measure to display.

Plot. The Plot option displays sensitivity results in graph form. The swings in the variables are shown in order of their effect on the result measure.

Occasionally, the low and high results are *both* either less than or greater than the base value. Sensitivity defines the swing as the largest absolute value difference between the base, high, and low values.

In the character plot mode (the only mode available in the student version), the display is often too wide for the screen. If the display is too wide to be shown on the 80-column screen, it will be split into several pieces displayed one above the other. Use the arrow/cursor keys or PgUp and PgDn keys to see pieces that have scrolled offscreen. If you have requested printing (by pressing Ctrl PrtSc) and if the printer column width is greater than 80 (as set in the Configuration option of the Utility menu), the display will be shown for the printer width. In this case, output on the screen may wrap around and appear garbled.

List. The List option lists the sensitivity results and input data in tabular form.

Utility

The Utility menu enables you to perform a variety of housekeeping tasks. Many of the options deal with file locations and manipulations. If no drive is specified for a file operation, the default drive given in the Configuration option (see below) will be used. Current implementations of Sensitivity do not permit use of path names; hence, all files must be in the current directory of a drive.

Storesens. Use the Storesens option to write the sensitivity results to a text file on disk. This file can be used as an input to graphics programs or text editors.

The option requests the name to be given to the DOS file that will store the distribution (e.g., C : SENSRES). If the file already exists, you will be asked whether or not to replace it. The name of a DOS file is limited to eight characters. Sensitivity supplies the extension . PRN to the file name. If the drive is not specified, the default drive will be used. The data for each variation are separated by tabs and stored in a line of the file. The first line of the file gives the base-case value.

Configuration. With the Configuration option, you can set a number of parameters for Sensitivity by responding to a series of questions. After data entry is complete, a submenu will appear giving two options.

- **Session**—If you select the Session option, the parameters will be used only until the Configuration option is rerun or until you quit Sensitivity.

- **Update**—If you select the Update option, the parameters will be saved in a DOS file called SENS . CNF on the drive specified. These parameters will be used each time Sensitivity is loaded.

  The parameters specified in the Configuration option depend on the system on which Supertree is run. The following parameters are specific to PC-DOS/MS-DOS:

- **Numerical Format (field width, decimal places)**—This sets the format for value and result displays. The format consists of two numbers: the total field width (including a place for any negative signs and decimal points) and the number of decimal places to show.

  Note that changing the number of decimal places displayed does not change the accuracy of the number that Sensitivity stores.

- **Interval at Which Running Total of Models Run Is Shown**—The Evaluate option can take a long time to run if you have a large model or many variables, so you may wish to know where Sensitivity is in the process. If the chosen interval is 25, Sensitivity will show on the screen when 25, 50, 75, ... models have been run. When one of the links to external programs is used, Sensitivity will also show when 25, 50, 75, ... runs have been prepared for the external program before it actually proceeds to make the model runs.

- **Use Line Graphics**—The PC contains line graphics characters for better quality. Many printers, however, cannot print these characters. If your printer does not have the line graphics characters, answer No to this option and Sensitivity will use plain text characters that print on any printer.

- **Default Drive for Sensitivity (files, models, worksheets, etc.)**—Sensitivity must know on which drive to find or save files. The default drive is the drive Sensitivity will address if no other drive is specified. If external programs are used, Sensitivity will search for models or spreadsheets on the default drive. Sensitivity will also write the instructions to and read the results from this drive. Because current implementations of Sensitivity do not permit use of path names, all files must be in the current directory of the drive.

- **Drive for Lotus, Symphony, Multiplan, Excel, or Quattro**—This is the drive on which Sensitivity will expect to find the modeling program. Specifying this drive is not important if the program is being called from outside Sensitivity because then you need to start the program yourself. Because current implementations of Sensitivity do not permit use of path names, all files must be callable from the current directory of the drive.

- **Drive for Configuration File, SENS.CNF**—This is the drive on which the SENS.CNF file will be saved when Update is selected. This file should be in the same directory as the Sensitivity program file, SENS.AWS.

- **Color Combination Used on Screen.** For monochrome or black and white monitors, this parameter should be set to 7. This setting will also work for color monitors, but it will give a black-and-white screen.

  For color monitors, you can specify foreground and background colors as follows:

0	black	4	red
1	blue	5	magenta
2	green	6	yellow
3	cyan	7	white

  Multiply the background color by 16 and add the foreground color to it; then enter the result. For instance, to obtain white letters on a black background, use $(16 \times 0) + 7 = 7$.

- **Printer Port**—Use the DOS port name for this parameter. Dot matrix printers are usually parallel printers and are thus connected to port LPT1. Daisy wheel printers are usually serial printers and thus connected to port COM1.

- **Column Width of Printer**—This width is normally 80 for 8.5" wide paper and 132 for 14" wide paper. However, when using compressed print, you can fit 110 characters on 8.5" wide paper. This will allow you to print wide output from the Analyze menu without splitting it into pieces.

- **Printer Setup Message**—If the printer is activated (Ctrl PrtSc), this message is sent to the printer whenever Sensitivity returns to the main menu. The message consists of the decimal numbers of the ASCII characters you want to send, with spaces between them.

Common messages are 15 for compressed print (66 lines per page with 132 columns on narrow paper and 233 columns on wide paper) and 18 for regular print (66 lines per page with 80 columns on narrow paper and 136 columns on wide paper). Tiny print can be produced on some printers by using superscripts, condensed mode, and reduced line spacing; a string that works on some Epson printers is 15 27 83 0 27 51 18 (132 lines per page with 132 columns on narrow paper and 233 columns on wide paper). Consult your printer manual for the specific control codes for your printer.

Variables. When the Variables option is selected, the names of APL variables present in the workspace are shown. The names of variables that are part of Sensitivity are not shown.

APLfns. When the APLfns option is selected, the names of APL functions present in the workspace are shown. The names of Sensitivity functions are not shown.

ExecuteAPL. An APL expression can be entered here and executed. The result of the expression (if any) will be displayed.

Minisens. Minisens removes 47 kilobytes of Sensitivity code from memory, leaving only the Files, Evaluate, Programs, and Quit menus. This permits you to Evaluate large spreadsheet models more conveniently than would otherwise be possible.

Programs

The Programs menu enables you to interrupt the Sensitivity session and start a modeling program, which, in turn, enables you to inspect or modify models or spreadsheets. Sensitivity and APL (its underlying language) remain resident in memory, using about 280 kilobytes of memory (or about 230 kilobytes if Minisens has been invoked). If the expanded memory option is used, these numbers are reduced by 55 kilobytes.

The options under Programs are as follows:

- **Lotus**—Calls Lotus 1-2-3, version 2, 2.2, or 3.

- **Symphony**—Calls Symphony. On most personal computers, you must use the Minisens command first to call Symphony.

- **Excel**—Calls Excel. Current technology does not make enough memory available to call Excel directly from Sensitivity.

- **Quattro**—Calls Quattro. Current technology does not make enough memory available to call Quattro directly from Sensitivity.

- **IFPS**—Calls IFPS Personal. Current technology does not make enough memory available to call IFPS directly from Sensitivity.

- **Multiplan**—Calls Multiplan.

- **FCS**—Calls the FCS modeling program. Note that if available memory is insufficient, calling this program may lock the computer and necessitate a reboot.

Files

The Files menu lets you save and recall previous work through the following options:

- **Savefile**—The Savefile option saves the data, evaluation, and any APL functions and variables in the workspace. Enter the name under which to save the file (e.g., c:MYFILE). If the drive name is omitted, the default drive will be used. File names can be no longer than eight characters. Sensitivity will supply an extension of .ASF to the file name.

- **Recallfile**—When Recallfile is selected and the name of a drive is entered, Sensitivity will list the files saved on that drive. To recall a file, enter the file name.

- **Wscopy**—APL users can copy workspaces developed using STSC's APL*PLUS/PC.

- **Directory**—This command lists the names of all files in the current directory of the drive specified by the user.

Quit

The Quit option is used to exit Sensitivity and return to DOS. A reminder to save your work is displayed; then you are given the following two options:

No—Do not leave Sensitivity but return to the main menu.

Yes—Leave Sensitivity.

E

Modeling Programs

Basic Syntax Statements

Supertree and Sensitivity allow you to create one-line statements with Basic syntax and symbols in endpoint nodes and models. The names of the nodes in the tree (variables in the sensitivity analysis) can be used as variables in the statement. In Supertree, these node name variables will assume the values of the outcomes for each particular scenario or path through the tree. In Sensitivity, these variables will assume the values obtained by using the base value and the low and high modifiers. In addition to these variable names, you can use numbers in the statement and any of the following operators:

+	addition	<=,=<	less than or equal to
–	subtraction	>	greater than
*	multiplication	>=,=>	greater than or equal to
/	division	><,<>	not equal to
A^B	A to the power B	NOT	logical negation
ABS	absolute value	AND	logical and
INT	integer	OR	logical or
LOG	logarithm	(	left parenthesis
=	equal to	)	right parenthesis
<	less than		

The order of execution follows usual Basic precedence: functions and logical operations are calculated first, then powers and roots, then multiplication and division, and then addition and subtraction. One exception to standard Basic is that a true logical condition will produce a +1, not the usual –1.

Lotus 1–2–3

Preparing the Spreadsheet

Parameterize the spreadsheet input data as much as possible. Supertree passes single-number node outcomes to the spreadsheet, so you need to have prepared the cells to enter these single numbers. You cannot pass a whole string of numbers to the spreadsheet at once.

If you need to have the outcome of a node change more than one input number in the spreadsheet, a number of useful functions are available. The most convenient technique is to send the Supertree or Sensitivity value to a cell in the spreadsheet that will serve as an index. Set up a lookup table using the Lotus Hlookup or Vlookup functions to use this index and set values of other cells. The Choose function is another convenient way of using this index to set values of other cells.

Entering the Macro

A sequence of four commands creates a macro and names it \0, which makes it an autoexecute macro enabling Supertree to run Lotus.

1. Go to an empty column in the spreadsheet (make sure it is empty) and type the following commands without moving the cursor (enter no spaces—they can cause trouble):

   {goto}\0~{down}/fitlottr~   Return

   /Range Name Create \0   Return Return

   The word "Return" above indicates pressing the Return or Enter key.

3. Save the spreadsheet.

4. Check the /Worksheet Global Default Directory and make sure it matches the one set in the Supertree Configuration file. Correct the directory if necessary and Update.

Setting Up and Running the Tree

To set up a tree to run with the spreadsheet, execute the following procedures:

1. Use cell names (such as C12) or range names as node names. If you use a range name, it must refer to a single cell. Node outcomes can be numbers, range names in the form +rangename, or formulas in the form +formula. Any other type of node outcome will be entered into the spreadsheet as a label.

2. Name the endpoint L$model$resultcell, where model is the name of the Lotus spreadsheet (without any file name extension) and resultcell is the cell (such as B7 or a range name) in the spread-

sheet that contains the desired result (such as a net present value). The endpoint node input screen in Supertree and the model input screen in Sensitivity will construct this expression for you. The endpoint should "depend on" those nodes whose values you want to substitute into the spreadsheet.

3. Select Evaluate to run the tree.

    If the spreadsheet or the tree (or both) are large enough, you may get a MEMORY FULL message when Lotus is trying to load the spreadsheet. If so, use the Minitree option (in Supertree) or the Minisens option (in Sensitivity) and follow the procedure outlined below. The procedure for Sensitivity is identical to that for Supertree.

    1. Select Minitree or Minisens from the Utility menu. This option will erase all the code not required for the Files, Evaluate, Programs, and Quit options, thus freeing memory.

    2. Select Evaluate to evaluate the tree.

    3. After the evaluation is complete, select Files and then Savefile to save the evaluated tree.

    4. Select Quit to leave Supertree.

    5. Restart Supertree to reload a complete copy of the software.

    6. Select Files and then Recallfile to bring in the evaluated tree. You can now use the full copy of the software to analyze the tree.

    If this procedure does not free sufficient memory for the evaluation, call Lotus 1-2-3 from outside Supertree. The input screen will rename the endpoint node with two dollar signs after the L:L$$model$resultcell. This will lead you through the following procedure (in which Supertree and Lotus are not loaded at the same time) when you Evaluate:

    1. Select Evaluate. Instructions will appear to perform the following steps.

    2. Select Files and then Savefile to save the partially evaluated tree.

    3. Quit Supertree to return to DOS.

    4. Type 123 to start Lotus. Lotus will retrieve the spreadsheet, calculate the necessary numbers, turn itself off, and return to DOS.

    5. Start Supertree again and Recall the tree file.

    6. Select Evaluate again to finish evaluating the tree.

    7. Respond Yes when Supertree says that it is about to pick up the results of a Lotus run and asks whether you want to continue. If

there are any problems with the results (such as a division by zero error), Supertree will display the offending result. Correct the spreadsheet and try again.

If you still get a MEMORY FULL message, break up the endpoint into two or three endpoints and try the Minitree procedure again. Alternatively, use extended memory to address memory above 640K and use the first procedure for evaluating the tree or the second procedure without having to break up the endpoint.

The following are common reasons for errors while evaluating the tree:

- Lotus cannot be called by typing 123 in the current directory.

- The spreadsheet is not in the current directory.

- The Worksheet Global Default Directory in Lotus 1-2-3 is not set to be the current directory.

- The Supertree configuration is set to the incorrect disk.

- The macro was not entered into the spreadsheet or was incorrectly typed in.

- The macro was not created with the name \0 (backslash zero).

- A node name in Supertree does not correspond to a range name in the spreadsheet.

- A name used for the result cell does not correspond to a range name in the spreadsheet

Symphony

The procedure for using Symphony with Supertree and Sensitivity is practically the same as that for Lotus 1-2-3. The principal difference is that the macro for Symphony is the following:

```
{goto}\a~{down}{s}fitlottr~   Return
/Range Name Create \a   Return Return
```

The word "Return" above indicates pressing the Return or Enter key.

These commands create a macro and name it \a rather than the \0 for Lotus. Each time Symphony is called, you will need to press Alt a (hold down the Alt key and press the a key) to start the macro running.

Quattro

The procedure for using Quattro with Supertree and Sensitivity is practically the same as that for Lotus 1-2-3. The principal difference is that the macro for Quattro is the following:

```
{goto}SUPERMACRO~{down}{/ File,ImportText}lottr~  Return
/Macro Name SUPERMACRO   Return Return
```

The word "Return" above indicates pressing the Return or Enter key. These commands create a macro and name it SUPERMACRO. Note that there is a space before the word "File" in the macro but no other spaces.

Because of its size, Quattro is run outside Supertree. When Evaluate is chosen, instructions are given that are very similar to those for running Lotus outside Supertree. The only difference is that, instead of typing 123 at the DOS prompt, you type Q model SUPERMACRO, where model is the name of the spreadsheet.

Multiplan

The procedure for using Multiplan with Supertree and Sensitivity is practically the same as that for Lotus 1-2-3. The principal difference is that the macro for Multiplan is the following:

```
AGNAUTOEXEC'RT'DKTINSTRUCT'RT Return
NAUTOEXEC  Tab Tab Y  Return
```

The word "Return" above indicates pressing the Return or Enter key, and the word "Tab" indicates pressing the Tab key. There are no spaces in the above expressions. Note that the first "A" in the first line above tells Multiplan that you are doing alpha input, so the "A" will not appear in the cell.

These commands create a macro called autoexec that enables Supertree to run the spreadsheet. If you load the spreadsheet other than as part of a Supertree run, the macro will cause the machine to beep and control will be returned to the keyboard.

Multiplan can be run from inside Supertree. If it is run from outside Supertree, instructions are given when Evaluate is chosen. The instructions are very similar to those for running Lotus outside Supertree. The only difference is that, instead of typing 123 at the DOS prompt, you type MP model, where model is the name of the spreadsheet.

Excel

Preparing the Spreadsheet

Parameterize the spreadsheet input data as much as possible. Supertree passes single-number node outcomes to the spreadsheet, so you need to have prepared the cells to enter these single numbers. You cannot pass a whole string of numbers to the spreadsheet at once.

If you need to have the outcome of a node change more than one input number in the spreadsheet, a number of useful functions are available. The most convenient technique is to send the Supertree or Sensitivity value to a cell in the spreadsheet that will serve as an index. Set up a lookup table using the Excel Hlookup or Vlookup functions to use this index and set values of other cells. The Choose function is another convenient way of using this index to set values of other cells.

Setting Up the Tree

To set up Supertree to run with the spreadsheet, execute the procedure outlined below. The same procedure is to be followed for Sensitivity with an Excel spreadsheet as the model.

1. Use cell names (such as C12) or range names as node names. If you use a range name, it must refer to a single cell. Node outcomes can be numbers, range names in the form =rangename, or formulas in the form =formula. Any other type of node outcome will be entered into the spreadsheet as a label.

2. Name the endpoint E$$model$resultcell$answercolumn. "model" is the name of the Excel spreadsheet. It can be in any of the following forms: model, c:model, or c:\directory\model.

When Supertree's macro is run by Excel, in the first form it will open model from the current disk and directory; in the second form, it will open model from the current directory of the c: drive; in the third form, it will open model from the \directory directory of the c: drive.

resultcell is the cell in the spreadsheet that contains the desired result, such as a net present value.

answercolumn is the letter of an empty column (e.g., E for the fifth column or AA for the 27th column) that Supertree can use for the list of results from the spreadsheet calculations.

The endpoint node input screen in Supertree and the model input screen in Sensitivity will construct this expression for you. The endpoint should depend on those nodes whose values you want to substitute into the spreadsheet.

Running the Tree

To run the tree, perform the following steps:

1. Make sure the Excel spreadsheet is on the disk and in the directory specified in the tree.

2. Select Evaluate to have Supertree make the instruction file for the Excel runs.

3. Select Files and then Savefile to save the partially evaluated tree.

4. Quit Supertree to return to DOS.

5. Start Excel.

6. From Excel, open the file called SUPERMAC.XLM.

7. Go to the Macro menu in Excel and choose Run. A dialog box will appear; in the Reference box, type A1 (if it is not already there) and then choose OK. Excel will then make the data substitutions and calculations specified by Supertree and save the results.

8. Quit Excel.

9. Start Supertree again and Recall the tree file.

10. Select Evaluate again to finish evaluating the tree.

11. Respond Yes when Supertree says that it is about to pick up the results of an Excel run and asks whether you want to continue. If there are any problems with the results, Supertree will display the offending result. You should recheck the spreadsheet and try again.

Bibliography

The literature on decision analysis is extensive, and there are several quite different areas of investigation discussed in this literature. The following books should help the interested reader delve more deeply into these areas.

Behn, Robert D., and James W. Vaupel, *Quick Analysis for Busy Decision Makers*, New York: Basic Books, Inc., 1982.

Bodily, S., *Modern Decision Making: A Guide to Modeling with Decision Support Systems*, New York: McGraw-Hill Book Co., 1984.

Brown, Rex V., A. S. Kahn, and C. R. Peterson, *Decision Analysis: An Overview*, New York: Holt, Rinehart, and Winston, 1974.

Bunn, D. W., *Applied Decision & Analysis*, New York: McGraw-Hill, 1984.

Holloway, Charles A., *Decision Making Under Uncertainty: Models and Choices*, Englewood Cliffs, NJ: Prentice-Hall Inc., 1979.

Howard, Ronald A., and James E. Matheson, eds., *Readings on the Principles and Applications of Decision Analysis*, 2 volumes, Menlo Park, California: Strategic Decisions Group, 1984.

Keeney, Ralph L., and Howard Raiffa, *Decisions with Multiple Objectives: Preferences and Value Tradeoffs*, New York: John Wiley & Sons, Inc., 1976.

Merkhofer, M. W., *Decision Science and Social Risk Management*, Boston: Reidel, 1987.

Newendorp, Paul D., *Decision Analysis for Petroleum Exploration*, PennWell Books, 1976.

Raiffa, Howard, *Decision Analysis: Introductory Lectures on Choices Under Uncertainty*, New York: Random House, Inc., 1986.

Samson, Danny, *Managerial Decision Analysis*, Homewood, IL: Richard D. Irwin, Inc., 1988.

Schlaifer, Robert, *Analysis of Decisions under Uncertainty*, Melbourne, FL: Robert E. Krieger Publishing Co., Inc., 1969.

Spurr, William A., and Charles P. Bonini, *Statistical Analysis for Business Decisions*, Homewood, IL: Richard D. Irwin, Inc., 1973.

Thompson, Mark S., *Decision Analysis for Program Evaluation*, Cambridge, MA: Ballinger Publishing Co., 1982.

Tummala, V. M., and Richard C. Henshaw, eds., *Concepts and Applications of Modern Decision Models*, Michigan State University Press, 1976.

von Winterfeldt, Detlov, and Ward Edwards, *Decision Analysis and Behavioral Research*, New York, NY: Cambridge University Press, 1988.

Index

Authors

Peter McNamee

Peter McNamee obtained a Ph.D. in theoretical physics from Stanford University. After ten years of university teaching and physics research, he decided to leave the realm of academia for the practical world of decision analysis. He feels, however, that both vocations have similar purposes: to find the order in seeming chaos and to communicate the insights obtained in the process.

First with SRI International (formerly Stanford Research Institute) and now with Strategic Decisions Group, Peter has worked for companies in many areas, including energy, consumer goods, oil, telecommunications, chemicals, and insurance. Peter has lectured on decision analysis both in the United States and abroad. One of his ongoing interests is education, which led to his co-authoring of this book. He feels computer software is essential to making decision analysis more practical. For this reason, he has played a principal role in developing several generations of Supertree software.

In addition to working on decision problems, teaching decision analysis, and keeping software and hardware working harmoniously together, Peter somehow manages to to keep up with his three small children and the demands of house and garden—in California, the grass always needs mowing.

John Celona

John Celona has pursued his long-time interest in decision problems through a number of disciplines and vocations; first with a degree in industrial engineering and engineering management, then as a consultant for Strategic Decisions Group for four years, and now as a lawyer specializing in litigation risk analysis. He is currently a law clerk with the Supreme Court of Hawaii and plans to return to consulting at the end of his clerkship.

John's other professional interests run to the relations between ethical and legal systems and to the principles of constitutional jurisprudence. Playtime goes to things like cooking, triathlons, and writing science fiction. John's wife, Karen Schwartz, works as a molecular biologist and at making John take a vacation once in a while.

Software License

END USER LICENSE AGREEMENT
SUPERTREE® and SENSITIVITY®
Student Version

NOTICE TO END USER: BY OPENING THE SOFTWARE PACKAGE YOU ACCEPT ALL THE TERMS AND CONDITIONS OF THIS AGREEMENT. If you do not agree with the terms and conditions of this Agreement, return the package UNOPENED to SDG Decision Systems ("SDGDS") at the address listed below, or to the location where you obtained it, for a full refund.

In return for acquiring a license to use SDGDS' Student Version of Supertree or Sensitivity decision support software (the "SDGDS Student Software"), and for acquiring the accompanying documentation, you ("End User") agree as follows:

1. **License Grant.** SDG Decision Systems ("SDGDS") grants End User a nonexclusive, non-transferable license: (a) to use the SDGDS Student Software on any single personal computer system located at End User's site, provided that such use is not in conjunction with any multi-user, network, shared file or shared disk multi-computer system unless such right has been specifically granted by SDGDS in writing; and (b) to copy the SDGDS Student Software solely for the purposes of installing it on End User's computer and for backup and archival storage. End User agrees to reproduce the same copyright and other proprietary notices appearing on the original SDGDS Student Software on any copies. End User may not transfer, sell or distribute copies of the SDGDS Student Software to others. End User may assign its rights under this Agreement to a third party provided the third party agrees in writing to be bound by the terms of this Agreement and End User transfers all copies of the SDGDS Student Software and associated documentation to the third party or destroys any copies not transferred.

2. **Student or Teacher Use.** User agrees that this software will be used for teaching purposes, or by a student in either a classroom or personal study environment. SDGDS Student Software is not licensed for use in commercial or business applications.

2. **No Other Rights.** The SDGDS Student Software is copyrighted by SDGDS and its suppliers and is proprietary to SDGDS and its suppliers, which retain ownership of the SDGDS Student Software. The license granted above is not a sale of the SDGDS Student Software, and except as stated above, this Agreement does not give End User any rights to patents, copyrights, trade secrets, trademarks or any other rights or licenses with respect to the SDGDS Student Software and documentation. End User agrees to hold the SDGDS Student Software and documentation in confidence and to take reasonable steps to prevent unauthorized copying or disclosure.

3. **No Modifications or Reverse Compilation.** END USER MAY NOT MODIFY, TRANSLATE, DISASSEMBLE OR DECOMPILE THE SDGDS SOFTWARE OR DOCUMENTATION OR ANY COPY, IN WHOLE OR IN PART.

4. **Limited Warranty.** SDGDS warrants only to End User (and not to any transferee) that the disk on which the SDGDS Student Software is recorded is free of defects in materials and workmanship under normal use, and the SDGDS Student Software will perform substantially in accordance with the accompanying documentation, for a period of ninety (90) days from the date of delivery to End User. If the disk is defective or the SDGDS Student Software does not perform substantially in accordance with the accompanying documentation, SDGDS' entire liability and End User's exclusive remedy shall be, at SDGDS' option, either (a) to return to End User the price paid for the SDGDS Student Software or (b) to repair or replace the SDGDS Student Software at no charge, if it is returned to SDGDS at the address below along with proof of payment within ninety (90) days after End User acquired it. If the defect or nonconformance has resulted from accident, misuse, or misapplication of the SDGDS Student Software, SDGDS shall have no obligation to refund End User's license fee or repair or replace the SDGDS Student Software.

SDGDS does not warrant that the SDGDS Student Software is error-free or will operate without interruption. THE ABOVE WARRANTY IS THE ONLY WARRANTY OR REPRESENTATION OF ANY KIND WITH RESPECT TO THE SDGDS SOFTWARE AND ANY ASSOCIATED DOCUMENTATION MADE BY SDGDS OR ANYONE ELSE INVOLVED IN THE CREATION, PRODUCTION, DELIVERY OR LICENSING OF THE SDGDS SOFTWARE AND DOCUMENTATION. SDGDS DISCLAIMS ALL OTHER WARRANTIES, WHETHER EXPRESS OR IMPLIED, INCLUDING BUT NOT LIMITED TO IMPLIED WARRANTIES OF NONINFRINGEMENT, FITNESS FOR A PARTICULAR PURPOSE AND MERCHANTABILITY WITH RESPECT TO THE SDGDS SOFTWARE AND ANY ASSOCIATED DOCUMENTATION.

5. **Limit of Liability.** IN NO EVENT SHALL SDGDS OR ANYONE ELSE INVOLVED IN THE CREATION, PRODUCTION, DELIVERY OR LICENSING OF THE SDGDS SOFTWARE BE LIABLE TO END USER FOR ANY CONSEQUENTIAL, SPECIAL, INCIDENTAL, DIRECT OR INDIRECT DAMAGES OF ANY KIND ARISING OUT OF THE USE OF THE SDGDS SOFTWARE, EVEN IF SDGDS OR ANYONE ELSE INVOLVED IN THE CREATION, PRODUCTION, DELIVERY OR LICENSING OF THE SDGDS SOFTWARE HAS BEEN ADVISED OF THE POSSIBILITY OF SUCH DAMAGES. IN NO EVENT WILL SDGDS' LIABILITY FOR ANY CLAIM, WHETHER IN CONTRACT, TORT OR ANY OTHER THEORY OF LIABILITY, EXCEED THE LICENSE FEE PAID BY END USER.

6. **Government End Users.** If the SDGDS Student Software is acquired directly or indirectly on behalf of a unit or agency of the United States Government, this provision applies.

(a) For civilian agencies: The SDGDS Student Software (1) was developed at private expense; is existing computer software and no part of it was developed with government funds; (2) is a trade secret of SDGDS for all purposes of the Freedom of Information Act; (3) is "restricted computer software" submitted with restricted rights in accordance with subparagraphs (a) through (d) of the Commercial Computer Software—Restricted Rights clause at 52.227-19 of the Federal Acquisition Regulations ("FAR") and its successors and as expressly stated in SDGDS' standard commercial agreement incorporated into the contract or purchase order between SDGDS and the government entity; (4) in all respects is proprietary data of SDGDS; and (5) is unpublished and all rights are reserved under the copyright laws of the United States.

(b) For units of the Department of Defense "(DoD)": The SDGDS Student Software is licensed only with "Restricted Rights" as that term is defined in the DoD Supplement to the FAR, clause 52.227-7013(c)(1)(ii), Rights in Technical Data and Computer Software and its successors, and use, duplication or disclosure is subject to the restrictions set forth therein. SDG Decision Systems, 2440 Sand Hill Road, Menlo Park, CA 94025.

7. **Effect of State Laws.** Some states do not allow the exclusion of implied warranties or limitations on how long an implied warranty may last, or the exclusion or limitation of incidental or consequential damages, so the above limitations or exclusions may not apply to you. The warranty in Section 4 gives you specific legal rights and you may also have other rights which vary from state to state.

8. **Choice of Law.** This Agreement will be governed by the laws of the state of California as applied to transactions taking place wholly within California between California residents.

9. **Term.** This Agreement is effective until the year 2038. End User may terminate this Agreement and the license it grants at any time by destroying the SDGDS Student Software and documentation and all copies or by returning them to SDGDS. SDGDS has the right to terminate this Agreement and the license it grants immediately if End User fails to comply with any term or condition of this Agreement. End User agrees that upon any such termination by SDGDS, End User will destroy the SDGDS Student Software and documentation and all copies.

10. **Integration.** END USER ACKNOWLEDGES AND AGREES THAT END USER HAS READ THIS AGREEMENT, UNDERSTANDS IT, AND THAT IT IS THE ENTIRE AGREEMENT BETWEEN SDGDS AND END USER WHICH SUPERSEDES ANY PRIOR AGREEMENT, WHETHER WRITTEN OR ORAL, AND ANY OTHER COMMUNICATIONS BETWEEN SDGDS AND END USER RELATING TO THE SUBJECT MATTER OF THIS AGREEMENT, AND THAT YOUR OBLIGATIONS UNDER THIS AGREEMENT SHALL INURE TO THE BENEFIT OF SDGDS' SUPPLIERS WHOSE RIGHTS ARE LICENSED UNDER THIS AGREEMENT. NO VARIATION OF THE TERMS OF THIS AGREEMENT OR ANY DIFFERENT TERMS WILL BE ENFORCEABLE AGAINST SDGDS UNLESS SDGDS GIVE ITS EXPRESS CONSENT, INCLUDING AN EXPRESS WAIVER OF THE TERMS OF THIS AGREEMENT, IN A WRITING SIGNED BY SDGDS.

12. **Communications.** If you have any questions about this Agreement, or if you desire to contact SDGDS for any reason, please write or fax: SDG Decision Systems, 2440 Sand Hill Road, Menlo Park, California 94025-6900. Telephone: 800-852-1236 or 415-854-9000. Fax: 415-854-6718.

Software Installation

Overview

The computer software supplied with this text is for operation on MS-DOS or PC-DOS personal computers. Depending on the version ordered, the software will be supplied on either two 360K 5.25-inch low density floppy disks or on a single 720K 3.50-inch floppy disk. Your computer should be equipped with 640K RAM and a hard disk.

Hard Disk Operation

1. Prepare a directory named \super on the hard disk c: by typing

   ```
   md c:\super
   ```

2. Copy the files to the hard disk, insert the Supertree/Sensitivity disk(s) into drive a: and type

   ```
   copy a:*.* c:\super
   ```

   or, if the disk is in drive b:, type

   ```
   copy b:*.* c:\super
   ```

3. To run Supertree, make sure you are using the hard disk by typing c:

   Then change to the \super directory by typing

   ```
   cd \super
   ```

   To run Supertree, type

   ```
   supertree
   ```

   To run Sensitivity, type

   ```
   sens
   ```

Floppy Disk Operation _____

Supertree and Sensitivity can also be run from floppy disks.

3.5-inch Floppy Disk

Insert the disk in drive `a:` and change to drive `a:` by typing

```
a:
```

To run Supertree, type

```
supertree
```

To run Sensitivity, type

```
sens
```

Two 360K, 5.25-inch Floppy Disks

Insert disk 1 in drive `a:` and disk 2 in drive `b:`.

To run Supertree, type

```
b:rts8 k=u w=0 supert
```

To run Sensitivity, type

```
b:rts8 k=u w=1 sens
```

High Density 1.4 Meg, 5.25-inch Floppy Disk

If you have a 1.4 Meg 5.25-inch floppy disk drive and would like to operate from this drive, you can copy all the files supplied with this text onto a single high density disk and follow the instructions for running the 3.5-inch floppy disk version.

Important Notice to All Floppy Disk Users

If you run Supertree or Sensitivity from floppy disks, you must change the default drives by using the `Configuration` option in the `Utility` menu of each program and saving the new configuration.

Macintosh Computers _____

Examples in this text feature operation of Supertree and Sensitivity on PC computers. Macintosh student software is available for use on Macintosh SE, SE/30, and Macintosh II machines. The programs are sufficiently similar that, despite some differences in the names of menu commands and changes to reflect "Mac-like" operation, the reader should experience little difficulty in using Macintosh software with this text.

Hard Disk Installation

Insert the Supertree/Sensitivity disk into the disk drive. Drag the icon of the disk onto the hard disk. This procedure will create a folder named Supertree on the hard disk.

Operation

To run Supertree, double click on the Supertree icon. To run Sensitivity, double click on the Sensitivity icon. (You can not double click on saved Supertree or Sensitivity files. To open them, first open Supertree or Sensitivity and then `Open` the saved files from the `File` menu.)

To use Excel with Supertree or Sensitivity, place a copy of Excel in the Supertree folder; it must be named `Excel` (not, for instance, "Excel 2.2.") To use Wingz with Supertree or Sensitivity, place a copy of Wingz, WZScript and DG in the Supertree folder; the Wingz program must be named `Wingz`.